Dear Reader:

The book you are about to read is the latest bestseller from the St. Martin's True Crime Library, the imprint the *New York Times* calls "the leader in true crime!" Each month, we offer you a fascinating account of the latest, most sensational crime that has captured the national attention. St. Martin's is the publisher of perennial bestselling true crime author Jack Olsen (SON and DOC) whose SALT OF THE EARTH is the true story of how one woman fought and triumphed over life-shattering violence; Joseph Wambaugh called it "powerful and absorbing." DEATH OF A LITTLE PRINCESS recounts the investigation into the horrifying murder of child beauty queen JonBenét Ramsey. FALLEN HERO is the *New York Times* bestselling account of the O.J. Simpson case. Peter Meyer tells how a teenage love pact turned deadly in BLIND LOVE: *The True Story of the Texas Cadet Murders*. Fannie Weinstein and Melinda Wilson tell the story of a beautiful honors student who was lured into the dark world of sex for hire in THE COED CALL GIRL MURDER.

St. Martin's True Crime Library gives you the stories *behind* the headlines. Our authors take you right to the scene of the crime and into the minds of the most notorious murderers to show you what really makes them tick. St. Martin's True Crime Library paperbacks are better than the most terrifying thriller, because it's all true! The next time you want a crackling good read, make sure it's got the St. Martin's True Crime Library logo on the spine—you'll be up all night!

Charles E. Spicer, Jr.
Senior Editor, St. Martin's

D1522844

BENEATH THE GROUNDS OF A SPRAWLING ESTATE LAY ONE OF THE MOST HIDEOUS CRIMES OF THE CENTURY

THE VICTIMS

In May 1993, gay men began disappearing from the streets of Indianapolis—among them, friendly, childlike Roger Goodlet; children's home worker Manuel Resendez; Steven Hale, who had a record for burglary and prostitution; Richard Hamilton, a tough-talking young street hustler; and others . . .

THE SURVIVOR

But one man did escape. Wiry, six-foot seven-inch-tall Tony met a good-looking tanned man at a gay bar and agreed to a tryst at a nearby mansion . . . and lived through a night of terror he would never forget . . .

THE KILLER

Herb Baumeister, like Ted Bundy, seemed normal. But he got away with horrific mass murder. Get the inside story on why he wasn't caught sooner . . . what led to his own violent end . . . and how his wife and children dealt with the devastating news of Herb's deadly secret life.

WHERE THE BODIES ARE BURIED

St. Martin's Paperbacks Titles by
Fannie Weinstein and Melinda Wilson

THE COED CALL GIRL MURDER

WHERE THE BODIES ARE BURIED

WHERE THE BODIES ARE BURIED

FANNIE WEINSTEIN AND MELINDA WILSON

St. Martin's Paperbacks

WHERE THE BODIES ARE BURIED

Copyright © 1998 by Fannie Weinstein and Melinda Wilson.

Cover photograph of landscape by John Zich. Cover photograph of Herbert Baumeister courtesy of Indiana State Police. Cover photograph of Julie Baumeister courtesy of Thomas D. Coughlin/Root Studios Inc.

ISBN: 0-312-96653-9

Printed in the United States of America

St. Martin's Paperbacks edition / September 1998

10 9 8 7 6 5 4 3 2 1

ACKNOWLEDGMENTS

I owe many people my deepest gratitude.

First, thanks to my agent, Jane Dystel, and my editor, Charles Spicer, for their continuing encouragement and guidance;

To the following for their contributions to the article on Herbert Baumeister which I reported for *People* and which provided the background and the inspiration for this book: Joe Treen, Giovanna Breu, Susan Hornik, Richard Jerome, Lisa Morris, John Zich, and Greg Adkins;

To Catherine Araujo, for sharing her beloved Roger;

To Jim Brown, Bruce Ceyburt, Ted Fleischaker, and Josh Thomas for their insightful thoughts and comments;

To Garry Donna, John Egloff, Alpha Kerl, Ivy Phelps, Kenneth Phelps, and others who shared their recollections of Herbert Baumeister, for the time and assistance they so generously provided;

To sources who asked not to be named, for their invaluable help;

To Ruth Coughlin, for her keen editorial advice and unending patience;

To Meg Grant, for her around-the-clock support;

Lastly, special thanks to Demetrios Argyropoulos, Maureen Linker, and Maria Slowiaczek, without whom this book would not have been completed.

F.W.

Without the gracious gift of time from *Detroit News* publisher Mark Silverman, this would not have been possible, and I thank him.

I also owe a world of gratitude to private investigators Virgil Vandagriff and Connie Pierce and to all of the generous men and women at the Hamilton County, Indiana Sheriff's Department, particularly Detective Kenneth Whisman.

Indianapolis Police Detective Mary Wilson was most helpful, as was Preble County, Ohio investigator David Lindloff.

Special thanks for the encouragements of Joe Rokiscak, Michael Green, and Kevin Lynch. And to my everythings, Amelia and Lily: I thank God every day for both of you.

M.G.W.

AUTHORS' NOTE

The material in this book derives from personal interviews, public records, and news reports.

The dialogue was reconstructed from documents, courtroom testimony, and personal recollections by participants.

Pseudonyms were used for five individuals, solely at the author's discretion, to protect their privacy. The pseudonyms are: Douglas Anderson, Albert Davis, Kevin Dennison, Bill Donovan, and Tony Harris.

Finally, neither were monetary inducements offered, nor editorial promises made, to sources in exchange for information.

"They're like wolves and the others are like deer. That's as near as I can say. They watch for the sick ones, the weak ones. They tear 'em down, so to speak. They sense it like blood. And those are the ones they go for. They never go for the stronger ones."

—*Psychic discussing the disappearance of Roger*
Alan Goodlet with a private investigator
AUGUST 1994

ONE

His arms and chest were completely hairless, as if every last strand had been shaved or burnt off.

And he didn't like being alone.

Tony Harris never wavered about those two details, at least, in his varying accounts of the night he spent with the tanned "Indiana Republican" he met in an Indianapolis gay bar in August 1994.

Indy was in a celebratory mood that week. The Indianapolis Speedway had just launched a new event, the Brickyard 400, and the city's radio and newspapers were full of ads hyping the new stock car race.

Harris, an outgoing twenty-six-year-old chatterbox with an imposing six-foot seven-inch frame and a thick mop of light brown hair, had just finished a late-night shift cleaning offices and had stopped at the 501 Tavern, one of Indy's gay nightclubs, for last call.

It had been raining all night, a warm summer downpour that would relent for a few minutes, only to open up again in a torrent that seemed determined to wash clean the sticky remains of the day.

Tony was sitting at the bar when he noticed him.

He'd seen him around before, in other gay bars in downtown Indianapolis. But he'd never really captured Harris's attention, until that moment.

He was staring at a poster of Roger Alan Goodlet, a casual friend of Harris's who had been missing for several weeks. Harris wasn't sure, but he thought he had seen the same man with Goodlet several weeks earlier.

Goodlet's mother had gotten some of her son's friends to put up posters in the bars he frequented. Tony Harris was helping with the search.

"Have you seen him?" Harris asked, stepping up close behind the stranger and startling him. The stranger spun around, frightened. His face quickly relaxed, though, as he looked up at Harris.

"Hi," he said, shyly smiling and ignoring Harris's opening remark as if he hadn't heard it.

His name was Brian, he told Tony. He was a landscaper from Ohio. He was in town for a couple of weeks, working at a mansion just north of Indy. A couple from Atlanta had just bought the house and was moving there next week.

Brian wasn't handsome in any conventional kind of way, Tony noted. He had full, pouty lips and large, round eyes that gave him a delicate, almost vulnerable appearance. And his skin was leathery from too much tanning. He told Tony he was twenty-eight, but Tony thought he looked much older.

His conservative clothes—a long-sleeved business shirt buttoned to the second button and dark pants—were wrinkled, "like he'd dressed out of a duffel bag," Tony later recalled. And his voice was tiny and timid, like that of a child's.

"I bet you've got a wife and kids stashed somewhere," Tony had teased, testing Brian's reaction. Brian simply smiled and shrugged.

No anger. No denial. Just an embarrassed, almost imperceptible shrug of his shoulders, as if to say he had no idea what Tony was talking about, and even if he did it was of no consequence to him.

He had other things on his mind.

"Let's go back to the place I'm staying at and have a cocktail and a swim," Brian suggested with a shy smile.

Tony didn't have to be asked twice. He wasn't the least

bit frightened to be alone with Brian. Brian was so soft and honest-looking, Tony would say later, it was difficult, if not impossible, to be intimidated by him.

In the parking lot, Brian tried to coax Tony into driving his own car.

"Follow me," Brian told him, his soft voice turning insistent for the first time. "That way, if you want to leave, you'll have your car."

If Brian's words were designed to put Tony at ease, they had the opposite effect.

Tony felt decidedly safer leaving his car parked at the bar, a visible reminder to all that he had left there and planned to return. He slipped into the passenger seat of Brian's gray Buick.

Brian steered them onto Meridian Street, heading north until it turned into U.S. I-31, a state highway that bisects the city. He offered a flask of something he was drinking to Tony, who waved it off.

Brian colored at Tony's refusal to drink, a small, visible bubble of anger rising up in him, the same way it had when Tony had refused to drive his own car.

Tony, it seemed, wasn't following the script.

Brian was quiet as they traveled north, the concrete expanses of downtown disappearing behind them as the city's greener suburbs emerged. There was no more talk of Alan, as Roger was known to his friends. It was as if Brian had never heard Tony's words about the missing man in the bar, or if he had, they simply hadn't registered.

Tony didn't often venture this far north of Indianapolis, but he knew they were heading into "rich people" territory.

Brian confirmed his hunch by pulling off the highway somewhere past 121st Street, an east-west thoroughfare north of downtown. After several turns, he found himself on a quiet street dotted with expensive new homes and horse farms, set off by split-rail fences.

At an asphalt driveway marked by a sign atop a landscaped stone embankment, Brian slowed. Something "Farm" was all Tony could make out on the sign.

He wasn't lying about the mansion part, at least, Tony thought as they pulled to the end of a long circular drive and the outlines of a sprawling, stone Tudor home appeared before him.

Several dogs and cats came bounding up to them when they got out of the car, begging for food or shelter from the rain.

"Don't pet them," Brian instructed, his voice sharp as he pushed the animals aside with his leg. "The owners don't want them hanging around here."

Brian led Tony through an unlocked side door and into a garage, where the mess the home's elegant exterior had hidden immediately struck Tony. An antique black car took up half the garage. The rest of the space was jammed with odd furniture and boxes stacked haphazardly, their contents spilling onto the floor. The inside of the house was even messier.

There were cobwebs everywhere. Tony felt them brushing against his face and hands. It was difficult to make out much of the clutter because it was dark, but again it appeared to Tony that there was little furniture and still more boxes and junk piled willy-nilly in each room.

"I can't turn on the lights up here," Brian explained. "The owners haven't had the power turned on here yet. But there's electricity in the basement," he said, disappearing down a dark staircase. Tony followed him.

Brian flicked on the basement light, illuminating a recreation room with the indoor pool he had told Tony about. There was also a wet bar. Again, the room looked messy, unlived in. A large-screen television stood out from one wall, unplugged. Behind it stood an older console television. Cushions from a foldout bed were strewn all over the floor.

There were, however, several carefully placed items in the room. Mannequins. At least three of them, the sight of which sent chills up Tony's spine. Two of the three were nude male figures, both perched beside the pool. One, a dark brown color, was propped up in a thinking pose, its chin resting in one hand, a la Rodin. The other, a sparkly silver figure, lay stomach-down, stretched out, its fingers reaching up to touch a large, decorative plastic shell.

The third mannequin stood behind the bar, wearing a shirt and a woman's wig.

"What's with the mannequins?" Tony asked, gesturing to the lifeless figures.

"I get lonely out here," Brian said with a smirk. "I don't like to be alone."

Brian had just contradicted himself, Tony noted. He was supposed to be looking after the house for just a week. Yet he'd had enough time to get lonely and buy mannequins? That was crazy. He didn't say anything. Brian quickly changed the subject.

He wanted to know if Tony did cocaine.

"Nope, I stay away from that. I just like pot," Tony informed him. With that, Tony took out a joint, lit it, and passed it to Brian.

After the two men finished the joint, Brian began fussing behind the bar, fixing drinks. Brian offered Tony a clear liquid in a festive, plastic glass.

"You can take a shower in there if you want," Brian brought up brightly, pointing out a bathroom off the pool area.

Tony took the drink from him and excused himself to use the bathroom. Away from Brian, he dumped out the glass, rinsed it, and filled it with water.

When Tony finished his water, Brian offered him another. He hoisted up a bottle of liquor from behind the bar to show he had plenty and he was willing to share. Tony shook his head no.

C'mon, Brian coaxed. Let's party. Have something to drink, he kept insisting. When Tony wouldn't budge, Brian got angry. Not screaming or yelling angry. But his voice was constricted in a tight little knot and his face was flushed. He was quietly enraged, Tony could tell.

But Brian's dark mood didn't last long. He left the room for several minutes and came back all cheerful and bubbly, considerably more animated than he had been in the bar and in the car. It was as if his shyness had simply melted away.

Tony thought for certain that Brian must have done some kind of drug in his absence—cocaine, he speculated. He'd seen the same buoyancy in other people who were coked up. And Brian was beyond buoyant. He wouldn't shut up. All of a sudden, he wanted to talk about everything. His mom and dad. About being gay.

"It would kill them if they knew," he confided to Tony. "What about your family? Do they know?"

"My people know everything I do. I don't keep any secrets," Tony told him.

Not like you, he thought to himself.

Brian wanted Tony to get in the pool. Take a swim, he urged. He didn't say anything about his own swimming plans. But he kept insisting that Tony get in. The water's great, he told him. It's nice and warm.

It was hot in the room, Tony noticed. Even with the cool rain outside, the water in the pool was so warm, steam was rising off it. Tony finally complied, taking off his clothes and jumping in. It was a lap pool, he discovered, whose depth was the same at both ends.

Brian stayed on the side, watching. And talking. As Tony swam around, Brian turned off the lights and opened the sliding glass doors to let the air in from outside.

The hot indoor air mixed with the cool outside breeze, making for even thicker clouds of steam. The darkness and the steam now obscured much of the room, making the mannequins look more than ever like silent human observers.

"I just learned this really neat trick," Brian said, picking up a pool hose and coming closer to Tony on the edge of the pool.

If you choke someone while you're having sex, it feels really great, he told Tony. You really get a great rush.

Brian then sat down on the pool's edge, and wrapped the hose around Tony's neck, gently caressing his throat with the rubber tube.

"You want to try?" he asked in a seductive whisper.

Tony had heard enough. He pulled Brian into the pool and began punching him in the face.

"You fucking pervert," he screamed at him, pushing and hitting the smaller man. "You sicko psychopath. You killed Alan, didn't you? You strangled him. You son of a bitch."

"How do you like it, you sick motherfucker?" Tony said, tightening his hands around Brian's neck, who began to cough and turn blue. After several seconds he went limp in Tony's arms. When Tony let go of him, he slipped under the water, seemingly unconscious.

After what seemed like an interminable amount of time to Tony, Brian came up coughing and spitting. Weakly, Brian pulled himself out of the pool and lay down on the edge.

Tony stared at him, disbelieving.

The bastard was smiling. An enormous grin had broken across Brian's face, as if he'd just experienced the thrill of a lifetime.

"Wow," he said, now propped up on his side, chin in hand, beaming at Tony. "You could have killed me, but that was so cool. It was such a rush. But you're supposed to hold me above water when I lose consciousness."

Brian was ebullient about the possibility that he'd found a kindred soul, Tony could tell. Someone with whom he could share his little dance with death.

Brian went upstairs and came back down holding a tie in one hand, a wide leather belt draped around his neck.

"See, you really don't want to strangle somebody," Brian began, his voice far more practiced and authoritative than that of someone who had just learned a really neat trick, Tony thought.

"You just want to pinch these two veins, right here," Brian continued, touching his own carotid arteries—the arteries that carry blood to the brain—on both sides of his neck and pushing them with his thumbs. He demonstrated on Tony.

Brian, in fact, was full of "neat tricks," all of which he was eager to share with Tony, his words pouring forth in a jumbled rush. A belt or tie around someone's neck can also produce the same effect, he told Tony. So could a plastic bag. And if you were alone, he confided, you could put your head in a noose hanging from the ceiling and bend your knees.

The whole scene was safe, Brian assured him. The partner being strangled merely had to throw up a hand signal to let the other person know he needed to loosen his grip.

"And it's such a great buzz," Brian was saying, his voice excited, his eyes shining. "You should see how someone looks when you're doing it to them. It's beautiful. Their lips change color. That's how you can tell it's working. And their eyes." Brian was really flying high now, Tony noticed. His words were slurred, a by-product of whatever he was drinking or taking, but he almost sang as he talked about the way people's faces changed while being strangled, what they looked like, how it felt.

This is what really unlocks this guy: watching the life drain out of somebody else's body. And feeling himself tee-tering on the edge.

At that moment, Tony knew with certainty that Brian knew about Alan. And if he got out of there alive, he sure as hell planned to tell somebody.

Brian pulled out the sofa bed and lay down. He'd taken off his wet clothes. Tony noticed Brian's entire body was covered with light stubble, as if he'd either shaved or burned off hair on his body. He asked him about it. He'd singed himself burning leaves, he explained, again quickly chang-ing the subject.

"Do it to me," Brian begged, handing the necktie to Tony. Tony lay down next to him on the foldout couch and complied, pulling the tie tight around Brian's neck while Brian masturbated.

By then, Tony was so horrified, so numb, he felt com-pelled to do whatever Brian wanted. Too, it was clear that despite what Brian said about his strangling tricks being new, he had obviously been through this routine many times. The only way to find out how these particular sex games ended, Tony reasoned, was to take it all the way with this guy.

Tony put Brian's hands on his own neck, and then touched himself. But instead of giving Brian a hand signal indicating that he had had enough, Tony went limp on the bed, feigning unconsciousness.

I wonder what the hell he's going to do now, Tony thought.

Brian called his name, his voice choked with genuine fright. Tony finally opened his eyes.

"You scared the shit out of me," Brian said testily. "Don't do that again. You know, you can die doing this. There have been accidents. You could drown in the pool. You could lose consciousness," Brian's voice trailed off.

"Is that what happened to Alan? Was he one of your accidents, Brian?" Tony taunted the other man. "There were others besides Alan, weren't there?"

The whole scene with Brian was so macabre, so bizarre, Tony didn't see any reason for hiding his suspicions. And Brian looked so out of it. He was babbling, his words running together. Nothing Tony said seemed to make the slightest impression on Brian.

"You've been here before, haven't you?" Brian told him, wagging his finger at him as he would at a badly behaving child. "I knew it. You must have been here some other time. When? When were you here?"

"I've never set foot in this house before. Why?"

"You know too much. I know you've been here before."

The two went back and forth like that for a while, Brian insisting Tony had known him and had been to the house in the past, and Tony denying it.

Still, Brian neither admitted he'd ever met Alan, nor did he elaborate about the "accidents."

In all, Brian acted as if the whole thing—strangulation, Tony's presence there that evening, his accusations about Alan—were an amusing little game that he controlled completely. It was, however, an exercise of which he seemed to be tiring, at least for the evening. Incoherent from whatever he had been drinking or ingesting, he finally passed out on the foldout couch. Tony pretended to drift off, too.

When Brian's breathing became even and Tony was certain he'd fallen asleep, he got out of bed and fished around in Brian's pants pocket. He wanted a peek at his wallet. There isn't a chance in hell his real name is Brian, Tony thought. Just as his hands touched the billfold, Brian stirred, making a small noise in his sleep. Tony dropped the wallet and the pants as if they'd caught fire.

Tony then snuck upstairs, wandering from room to room, his heart pounding in fear that Brian would wake up. He called his sister, Tammy, sketching out as quickly and quietly as he could the jam he'd gotten himself into.

"I'm up around Carmel with this guy who's into strangulation. Someone's gotta know that I'm here. It's off 31, it's a mansion," he told her. "This guy is not right. He scares the shit out of me."

He knew his directions had been laughably vague and the chances of Tammy's being able to rescue him at that point were dim. But he couldn't think of what else to do. It was something, anyway. Unable to see much in the dark, he finally padded softly downstairs and lay down next to Brian.

Just after the sun came up, Brian awoke. He had to run some errands to "pick up some papers," he announced. He put on the clothes he had been wearing the night before and went upstairs, grabbing an accordion-style portfolio full of paperwork before heading out the door.

He'd be back in a bit, he informed Tony. Feel free to go back to sleep or whatever, he told him.

Tony let out a sigh of relief at Brian's departure. He had survived the night. And he would be able to explore the house for real to look for something of Alan Goodlet's. Nothing would be hidden by darkness. No one would be stirring in the basement. This guy knew something about Alan, Tony felt it in his gut. He wanted to find something, anything, to confirm his hunch.

He started with the first floor, noticing first a fake Christmas tree, fully decorated and standing in what must have been a family room. With so little furniture in the house, it was difficult to tell what the rooms were used for.

Mostly, he was struck by how disheveled the place was, as if it hadn't been lived in in a long while. Yet there were strange exceptions to that emptiness, he noticed. A woman's purse lay on the kitchen counter, as if it had been casually left there only hours before. And although the carpeting looked new, there was a thin layer of dust on it as though someone was remodeling and had not yet moved in.

Upstairs, the cleanest bedroom had two twin beds. Tony thought it looked as if it might be a child's bedroom. He peeked in the closet. But instead of children's clothing, it was full of expensive camera equipment. Tripods. Video cameras. Videotapes. Tony was no camera expert, but some of it appeared to be sophisticated stuff. Christ, he thought, staring at all the equipment, maybe this guy is some kind of strange filmmaker.

In another room, there were women's clothes. More purses. Was Brian a cross-dresser? I wouldn't put it past him, Tony thought. The previous night's rain had stopped, and Tony noticed that a large piece of construction equipment was parked behind the house. After about a half hour of aimless wandering he was anxious for Brian to return. He was exhausted. And he wanted more than anything to get the hell out of that place.

When Brian finally did come back more than an hour later, he was all business. Yes, he told Tony, I'll take you back to your car right away. But he acted put out about it. As the two men prepared to leave, Brian kept looking around, as if expecting something, or somebody, to intervene to keep Tony there.

When it became clear that nothing would forestall their car ride back to the bar, Brian finally picked up his keys and led Tony out. The two men said little during the half-hour drive.

Although Brian's ire seemed to deepen as they got closer to the bar, his mood lightened just as they pulled into the parking lot, a smile breaking over his face like a sunrise.

"Hey, you're a good sport," he told Tony, giving him a little pat on the leg.

"We should go out sometime," Tony blurted out. The last thing Tony wanted to do was to be alone with Brian again, but he didn't want him walking away either.

Brian, or whoever he was, knew something about Alan. Tony was certain of it. He didn't have a shred of evidence to prove it. Other than some wild, cockamamie story about strangulation and mannequins and a mansion that no one was ever going to buy. Especially coming from him, in conservative, Republican, white-bread Indianapolis.

Brian scribbled two phone numbers on a piece of paper— one was his cellular phone, the other was his Ohio number, he told Tony—and Tony stuffed it in his pocket, promising he'd try to make it back to the 501 the following Wednesday for more "fun and games."

"I really had a good time. You really know how to play, Sport," Brian said, smiling broadly before wheeling out of the parking lot.

When Tony tried to put the key in the ignition of his car, he realized his hands were shaking. He kept hearing Brian's parting words and his chilling admission from the night before: "You know, you can die doing this. There have been accidents."

A sick fear washed over him. That bastard is dangerous as hell, he thought. And no one is going to believe a single word I say.

TWO

Indianapolis has always been something of an Everytown. Outsiders translate this to mean dull. "Naptown," they call it. Or "India-no-place." But to those who make their home in the nation's twelfth-largest city, this averageness is a source of pride. Residents of the self-proclaimed "Crossroads of America"—seven interstates crisscross Indiana, more than in any other state—feel no need to apologize for being centrists. In Indianapolis, conservative is not a dirty word, at least not to the white, middle-class, Protestant Republicans who make up the majority of the metropolitan area's population of roughly one million people.

Indianapolis, too, has long promoted itself as a place that offers the best of both worlds: the advantages of a major metropolitan area, and, thanks to its neighborhoods filled with tree-lined streets and well-maintained homes, small-town charm. It also enjoys a reputation as a friendly city, a town where locals will gladly point you in the right direction or give you change for a quarter.

But in the early '90s, something scary happened in Indianapolis. Gay men began disappearing. Ten would be reported missing between April 1993 and August 1995 alone. The youngest was twenty; the oldest, forty-six. Some had loved ones who searched in vain for clues to their whereabouts. Others vanished and were gone for months before anyone noticed. The missing men shared something in common, though. All, like Roger Alan Goodlet, were known to frequent the trendy gay bars and nightclubs that dot the northeastern corner of downtown Indianapolis. They were not, in the words of longtime gay activist and journalist Josh Thomas, "happily-partnered, thirty-five-year-old junior vice-presidents who go to the opera and perform in a gay men's choir." To the contrary, most of them held marginal jobs—if they held jobs at all. Some had serious substance abuse problems or, at the very least, a tendency to drink to excess. Several were estranged from their families and had few close friends. Some were transients with no permanent address. A few had multiple arrests for prostitution. They were, as Thomas puts it, "the lowest people on society's totem pole."

Still, each was somebody's son. Somebody's brother. Somebody's friend. Yet according to many members of Indianapolis's gay community, no one in a position to do something about the disappearances seemed to care that a serial killer was operating unchecked in the city's midst. The police, in the absence of an enraged public clamoring for answers—these were gay men and not pretty coeds, after all—dragged their feet from the start, it was said. The media, too, critics insisted, turned a deaf ear. "This town is sewn up tighter than a drum by Dan Quayle's family," proffered Thomas, referring to the fact that Eugene Pulliam, publisher of the politically conservative *Indianapolis Star* and *Indianapolis News*, also happens to be the uncle of the former Republican vice president and "family values" torchbearer. "The last thing those newspapers want to report on is the gay community."

But it wasn't just the police and the media, some observers say, who chose to ignore what was happening. Even in some corners of the gay community, there was little sympathy for the missing men, particularly those known to have engaged in prostitution. "A good chunk of the gay community felt they were getting what they deserved," says Ted Fleischaker, publisher of the *Indiana Word*, an Indianapolis-based gay and lesbian monthly newspaper that boasts a circulation of 14,000 in Indiana, Ohio, and Kentucky. "They were doing pay-for-play even though they'd been told for years that somebody was going to kill them."

Not that there wasn't any concern within the gay community. "People would say, 'Gee, I haven't seen so-and-so for a while,'" recalls Fleischaker. Confirms Jim Brown, owner of the Metropolitan Restaurant and Nightclub, a popular gay nightspot, "People were talking about it and did suspect there was something else going on besides all these people just leaving town. There were too many people disappearing for that to be happening." The talk, however, essentially amounted to no more than bar gossip. "I guess people thought the police department would handle it," Brown says with a sigh.

A migratory phenomenon unique to Indiana also may have contributed to the slow response, Thomas and others suggest. Gay men and women who grow up in small towns and rural areas across the country often feel uncomfortable about being open about their sexuality. So they leave these locales behind to start anew in larger cities; urban oases where diversity is not only tolerated, but appreciated. But native Hoosiers, unlike the gay men and women from other states who flock to gay meccas like New York, San Francisco, and Boston, have a tendency to relocate to Indianapolis, where they settle for good. "Family ties are very strong in Indiana, maybe even more so than in other Midwestern states," notes Thomas, a native of Indiana himself. But what this also means, he adds, is that the many members of Indianapolis's gay population live half in and half out of the closet. In other words, while they may lead open or semiopen everyday lives, they hide their sexual orientation when they return to their hometowns. " 'Mama would die if she found out I was queer,' " Thomas says, voicing what he perceives as the major worry of many of Indianapolis's gay transplants. "That's what it always comes down to."

It's this very fear, and fears such as facing discrimination on the job, observers say, that over the years has kept Indianapolis's gay community from becoming the kind of well-oiled political machine found in other large American cities. "If one gay man after another had started to disappear in New York, the head of the local gay and lesbian political organization would have marched over to city hall and demanded action," Thomas insists. "Here, there was nobody to march anywhere.

"The bottom line," he says unapologetically, "is that Indianapolis, by any standard, is a socially backward city."

The Indianapolis Police Department eventually did seek the gay community's cooperation with its investigation into the missing men's fates. They asked Fleischaker, for instance, to publicize the disappearance of one of the victims, a thirty-one-year-old man who was reported missing in September 1993, more than two months after he was last spotted outside an east side Salvation Army shelter and detoxification center. Fleischaker ran an article about the man, and later, items about other missing men. He hoped they would provide answers. He had another goal in mind, too: saving lives. "I wanted to do the same thing that milk cartons do for missing kids," Fleischaker explains. "I wanted to let people know that men were disappearing and that nobody knew what was happening to them."

Word did spread, and lives may have been spared as a result. But in the end, it was the killer himself who provided police with the clues that ultimately brought his spree to an end. Experts say that even the wiliest serial killers slip up eventually. Either they get arrogant or sloppy, or their own world, for one reason or another, starts to unravel. And then there are those times when they simply miscalculate. They choose a victim they think no one cares about, someone who wouldn't be missed. But it turns out they're wrong.

Dead wrong.

THREE

In the years immediately following World War II, Indian-apolis, like virtually every other major American city, ex-perienced tremendous growth, mostly thanks to the GIs who came marching back from overseas, anxious to resume their civilian lives. Buoyed by the nation's robust economy, they enrolled in college, found jobs, and started families. They also either bought or built homes in record numbers, not downtown but in previously low-populated outlying areas.

Herbert E. Baumeister was no exception. Though born in Columbus, Ohio, he spent most of his youth in Indianapolis. After a wartime stint in the army, Baumeister returned to Indiana and in 1950 graduated from Indiana University School of Medicine. Around this time, Herbert, an anesthe-siologist, and his wife, Elizabeth Ann, or E. A., as she is called, purchased a home in a neighborhood on the city's north side known as Butler-Tarkington.

Once lush farmland, the area was named for nearby Butler University and onetime resident, author Booth Tarkington, best known for his 1918 novel, *The Magnificent Ambersons*. By the time the Baumeisters settled there, Butler-Tarkington was a middle-class neighborhood popular with upwardly mobile professionals: professors from Butler, Eli Lilly sci-entists, and young doctors like Herbert himself.

Herbert was still in medical school when E. A. gave birth, on April 7, 1947, to the couple's first child, a boy they named Herbert Richard. Within a decade, "Herbie," as the younger Baumeister was known during his youth, had a sister and two brothers: Barbara, born in 1949; Brad, born in 1954; and Richard, born in 1956.

Life for the Baumeister clan was very much like that depicted on '50s television programs like *Leave It to Beaver* and *The Donna Reed Show*. Each day, Herb would trundle off to work—he joined the staff of Methodist Hospital, Indianapolis's largest, not long after Richard was born—while E. A. remained at home, caring for Herbie and his siblings and busying herself intermittently with various community and charitable projects. The children attended neighborhood schools and whiled away their afternoons playing tag and whiffle ball. Though not especially athletic, Herbie joined in. But the truth was he was more interested in games that exercised his mind, not his muscles. His idea of a fun activity, childhood playmate Bill Donovan remembered years later, was gathering together all the kids who lived on the Baumeisters' block for what he called his "weather club." Each member of the club would select a geographic area and then report on the weather there. Herbie, his onetime friend recalls, moderated the discussions.

By the time Herbie—now Herb—reached high school, he had moved with his family to a new home even farther north of downtown, in a fast-growing area known as Washington Township. The move to the 3,200-square-foot brick house, situated on 3.3 acres of prime residential real estate, was a step up the socioeconomic ladder for the Baumeisters, one of thousands of young Indianapolis families who were flocking to new subdivisions, planned communities that offered both the advantages of suburban living and, for breadwinners who commuted by car, easy access to downtown jobs.

Bright but quiet, the teenaged Herb remained more interested in academics than athletics during his four years at North Central High School. Although sports ruled at the 2,550-student school—nearly a third of the students participated in either a varsity sport or an intramural program—Herb was involved with more intellectual pursuits. At North

Central, his extracurricular activities included stints in the Biology, Geology, Government, and International Relations Clubs. By the end of his senior year, he could also claim four years in the school's Beginning Chess Club, where, according to his senior yearbook, "members learned that being able to concentrate intensely is a skill that can be transferred to other activities."

Like the majority of his peers in North Central's Class of '65, Herb enrolled in college the fall after graduation. In his case, his grades were good enough to earn him admission to his father's alma mater, Indiana University in Bloomington. Eventually, Herb would declare anatomy as his major. For a time, at least, he appeared determined to follow in his father's large footsteps.

During the middle and late 1960s, the counterculture was as alive at IU as it was at every major university in the United States. But for less progressive members of the student body, life outside the classroom, on weekends at least, still revolved around the school's popular athletic teams. In 1967, thanks to the Hoosier football team's Big 10 championship season, IU students had much to cheer about. So did Herb. Just prior to the gridders' appearance in the 1968 Rose Bowl, he met a pretty brunette named Juliana Saiter, a fellow Indianapolis native who, in November 1971, would become Mrs. Herb Baumeister.

Juliana, or Julie, as she preferred to be called, was the daughter of a superintendent at the Naval Air Warfare Center, a research and development facility on Indianapolis's east side. She and her older brother, Daniel, grew up in a middle-class neighborhood filled with one-story ranch homes, well-kept lawns, and driveway basketball hoops. In terms of location, it was not all that far from where Herb spent his early childhood years. Smart and ambitious, Julie attended Lawrence Central High School and was as busy most afternoons as she was during the day. She participated in more than a dozen extracurricular activities, from the Science and Spanish Clubs to the Booster and Drama Clubs.

She also sang with a vocal group called the Jubilaires and reported stories for the student newspaper. Moreover, with an obvious eye toward her eventual profession, she was a member of the school's chapter of Future Teachers of America.

A little more than a year younger than Herb, Julie entered IU in the fall of 1966. Eighteen months later, just before New Year's 1968, she and Herb were introduced by a mutual friend.

"He was nice, fun to be with and good-looking," she once told *People* magazine, recalling her initial impression of Herb.

She also appreciated Herb's unique decorating skills. Unlike most college students, Herb didn't hang posters on his apartment walls. Instead, he'd do things like staple old hubcaps onto pieces of burlap and display them as art.

Herb and Julie had common interests, too.

"We both liked cars," she said in *People*, "and we were both Young Republicans."

Yet at the time they met, Herb wasn't actually in school. He had taken the fall 1967 semester off to work as a copy boy for the advertising department at the *Indianapolis Star*. It wasn't an especially lucrative endeavor, paying about two dollars an hour. Still, a coworker at the newspaper says Herb was conscientious and eager to please.

"It wasn't a very glamorous job, but he took it pretty seriously," said Garry Donna, who worked in the newspaper's classified advertising department. "He made it important by going out of his way to be helpful to me and the other ad reps."

One day, for instance, Donna had gone on foot to run an errand downtown. But by the time he had completed his business, it was raining heavily.

"I hadn't walked but maybe a half block when I saw my car pulling up," he said. Herb, who knew where Donna kept his keys, was behind the wheel.

"What are you doing here?" a grateful Donna asked as he opened the passenger door.

"I didn't think you wanted to get soaked," said Herb.

Because Herb was living in Indianapolis as opposed to Bloomington, his and Julie's romance initially was a long-distance one. But the ninety miles between the two cities did little to prevent them from growing closer, and in May 1971, three-and-a-half years after they met and a month before Julie graduated with a bachelor of science degree in education, they became engaged.

Herb, who'd always had a flair for the dramatic, didn't disappoint when it came to popping the question. One night, out of the blue, he arrived at Julie's Bloomington apartment, *sans* ring, and asked her to marry him. She said yes. A mere two hours later, Herb turned around and drove back to Indianapolis.

Herb and Julie were married on November 21, 1971 at Irvington United Methodist Church, a brick, English gothic architectural gem located on Indianapolis's east side. The newlyweds lived briefly in an apartment in the northern Indianapolis suburb of Carmel. Then, in 1972, they bought a half-stone, half-wood, 1,623-square-foot house on 72nd Street, only minutes away from the home where Herb's parents still lived. Julie was teaching English and journalism at the time at Indianapolis's Broad Ripple High School. Herb, meanwhile, had taken a job as a clerical worker with the state Bureau of Motor Vehicles.

Like most young newlyweds, the pair enthusiastically threw themselves into making their new house a home.

"We loved doing it," Julie would later say of her and Herb's home improvement campaign. "And we did everything together. He would push the mower, and I would trim the bushes. We had the most beautiful yard in the neighborhood."

Few who lived on the same block would argue that point, especially when it came to Herb's outdoor Christmas decorations.

"He was famous for his light displays," one longtime neighbor said. "He'd cover their bushes with thousands of lights."

Nearly every year, according to the neighbor, Herb's creations earned high marks from the judges of the neighborhood's annual holiday decoration contest.

"I'm not even sure they ever won it," the woman said. "But you always thought they should."

Julie's years at Broad Ripple were busy ones. Besides her teaching schedule, she also worked with students involved in extracurricular activities. In the acknowledgments section of the school's 1975 yearbook, the student staff she'd advised during the year praised her for being a "never-dry source of fresh ideas." But by the end of that very same school year, Julie had decided to give up her job. Her reason was not a complicated one. As she explained it, she was simply "burned out on teaching."

Herb remained at the BMV through 1985, working his way up the ladder until he reached the position of program director for the department now known as financial operations. Julie always believed he would have left the bureau "if a better offer had come along." Maybe. Maybe not. According to one former coworker, Herb was an excellent, people-oriented boss. Susan Pierce, who reported to him for twelve years, told the *Indianapolis Star* that Herb was a caring man, too. She explained how he once used one of his own vacation days to drive her one hundred and forty miles to a bank in South Bend when she was going through a divorce.

Julie, after leaving Broad Ripple, began working as what she called a "professional volunteer." As her mother-in-law did, she donated her time and skills to a number of charitable and community organizations, most notably the Indianapolis Junior League. It was also during this time that Julie gave birth to the couple's three children: Marne, born in November 1979; Erich, born in January 1981; and Emily, born in August 1984.

According to Julie, Herb was "very supportive" of her desire to be a stay-at-home mom. As she put it one day, "He wanted his kids to be raised the same way he was: with their mother at home."

From the day each of the infants arrived home from the hospital, Herb was extremely involved in their upbringing. Whether it was a matter of deciding where they attended preschool, choosing their Christmas presents, or helping plan meals, Herb was an eager contributor.

Living on one rather than two incomes, though, required some sacrifice. It meant clipping coupons, shopping for bargains, and becoming home do-it-yourselfers. With Julie not working, repairmen, for example, became a luxury that she and Herb could not afford.

In this sense, they were very much like other young Indianapolis families just getting started. As Julie later wrote in an article for *Indianapolis Monthly* magazine, on weekdays, she would hold dinner until Herb came home from work. Weekends, meanwhile, were reserved for family activities, from yard work to building a play center behind the house.

Then, in 1985, Herb left his job at the Bureau of Motor Vehicles. According to Julie, there was no single reason behind his departure. Instead, as she remembered it, he simply felt ready to move on. Despite the financial impact it would have on the family's day-to-day life, Julie supported Herb wholeheartedly, as he had her. He deserved to be happy, she told herself at the time.

Herb ended up between jobs for about a year. During this time he and Julie lived on their savings. To help cut corners, Herb helped out around the house. Among other chores, he assumed cooking duties. He made a mean peanut butter sandwich. Another of Herb's budget specialties was a creation he called "pizza crackers": saltines dabbed with tomato sauce and topped with a piece of hot dog or bologna.

Julie, at this point, was still devoting her days to volunteering for charities like the Indianapolis chapter of the Junior League. But she was getting restless. Nearing forty, she felt ready to return to the work world. Herb, meanwhile, had taken a job at an Indianapolis thrift store. But he quickly grew frustrated. The position, he complained, wasn't enough of a challenge.

Herb and Julie brainstormed and before long, they came up with a solution to both their dilemmas. The answer, they concluded, was to pursue what Julie would later call their joint "vision": owning and running a chain of upscale thrift stores.

"We really wanted to own our own business," Julie said. "And we really wanted to do something together."

Running a thrift store was the perfect job for Herb. A rabid collector with eclectic tastes, he routinely attended garage and estate sales and shopped secondhand stores. Moreover, he was not above searching through Dumpsters for treasures other people had simply deemed useless and tossed away.

He was, in fact, anything but discerning. From discarded car parts to old tools to light fixtures, his standard was an uncomplicated one. Simply put, Julie said, it was "anything he liked . . . If he had run across an old Nixon bumper sticker in someone's trash, he would have pulled it out and saved it."

Julie's interests would be served, too. The thrift shops, she and the socially conscious Herb agreed, would provide income not only for them but for a local child advocacy organization as well.

It would end up taking roughly three years for Herb and Julie's dream to become reality. In the meantime, they lived, again, mostly on their savings and on the money Herb earned at various part-time jobs. It wasn't easy, but it wasn't an unendurable struggle either.

"It's amazing how little you can get by on if you don't have credit card debt," noted Julie.

Finally, in 1988, Herb and Julie founded Thrift Management, Inc., the corporate arm of their operation. That same year, they opened their first Sav-A-Lot thrift store, on 46th Street, on the east side of Indianapolis. And, after considering several organizations, they settled on the Children's Bureau of Indianapolis as the shop's charitable beneficiary.

Founded in 1851 and generally regarded as the charity of choice of Indianapolis's old money, the Children's Bureau was originally known as the Widows' and Orphans' Friends Society. Initially, it sought out donations and provided housing and jobs for poor widows, with the goal of keeping fatherless families together. Later, it began catering to orphans only. Today, the bureau provides adoption, foster care, emergency shelter, and expectant parent and counseling services. It also facilitates group home care and independent living programs, and operates a child abuse hotline.

For the always-in-need organization, the arrangement would mean a continuing source of funding over an indefinite period of time. Needless to say, bureau officials eagerly embraced Herb and Julie's plan.

"They came to us and said they wanted their thrift stores to be fund-raisers for the Children's Bureau and we, of course, were interested," recalled executive director Kenneth Phelps.

"The idea was they would collect used clothing, furniture—whatever might sell in a thrift store. Everything they collected, the inventory, so to speak, would then technically belong to the Children's Bureau. Then, based on our contract, they would sell the goods at their stores and we would get a percentage of the profits."

Phelps remembered being struck by both Julie and Herb's dedication to the enterprise. Julie would later say that Herb's sincerity was one thing about him that couldn't be doubted. Herb envisioned the 46th Street store and those that would follow as assets to each of the communities where they were located. The clean and tidy establishments, he said, would be "a pleasure to shop at."

Indianapolis lawyer John Egloff, who helped Herb and Julie get Thrift Management off the ground, said Herb expressed a similar sentiment to him from the outset.

When Herb first approached him in the spring of 1988, Egloff would later recall, he explained his and Julie's conception of the stores. "He thought it was an idea that nobody had explored," said Egloff.

Yet it was also clear from the start that Thrift Management was more than just a business operation to Herb. According to Egloff, Herb seemed convinced it was "his ticket to the American dream."

Herb was certain, Egloff said, that if the thrift store he had worked at briefly had been run differently and had served a more upscale market, that it would have had "infinite potential."

"When he looked at other thrift stores, he was amazed by the goods people would donate," said Egloff. "He said if you went to the right neighborhood in search of donations, that you could get designer dresses with the tags still on them, dresses that didn't fit the owner anymore or didn't match a pair of shoes, dresses that the owners just didn't feel like taking back to the stores where they had purchased them."

And if the stores stocked this kind of inventory, Herb told Egloff, they would attract upscale customers, "a better clientele that would pay more than ten cents for a suit if it was a nice suit."

For the "seed" money needed to start the business, Herb and Julie borrowed $350,000 from Herb's mother. (His father had died two years earlier.) And to stretch that loan as far as possible, they rolled up their sleeves and did much of the required repair work at the 46th Street store themselves. For a time, they spent nearly all their waking hours drywalling, painting and plastering.

The pair's hard work paid off and in the first year alone, their efforts generated roughly $50,000 in proceeds for the Children's Bureau. The store was so profitable, in fact, that before long, Herb and Julie started to think about expansion.

In 1990, they opened their second Sav-A-Lot. Located on West Washington Street on Indianapolis's southwest side, it, too, was a success, eventually earning the distinction of being named the best place in the city to buy used jeans in an *Indianapolis Monthly* "Best Of" roundup.

Going into business, though, wasn't the only dramatic change Herb and Julie's lives underwent at this time. In November 1991, they moved from the only home they'd known as a married couple into a magnificent estate just outside Westfield, a still-countrified but about-ready-to-boom suburb seventeen miles north of Indianapolis.

Located at the intersection of U.S. 31 and State Road 32, the town of Westfield was founded in 1834. Home for many years to a large Quaker population, during the nineteenth century it was a key stop on the Underground Railroad used by slaves from the South to escape to the North. The people of Westfield also have long emphasized education. Though no longer in existence, the town's Union High School was one of the first schools to open in the surrounding area.

It is a well-to-do neighborhood, too. According to 1996 Westfield–Washington Township Chamber of Commerce figures, nearly 14 percent of the households, which were close to 99 percent white, claim annual incomes of $100,000 or more. Roughly two thirds of the households owned two or more vehicles. Professionals, executives, and managers made up more than a quarter of the working population.

"Utopia." That's how Julie described the family's new Tudor-style home to *People* magazine. Also known as Fox Hollow Farm, it was surrounded by a multi-million-dollar horse farm on three sides and a subdivision with quarter-million-dollar homes on the fourth. It was spacious, boasting fifteen finished rooms, including four bedrooms, five full bathrooms, and a family room. It even had an indoor swimming pool, and should the owners happen to be equestrians, there was a barn and a stable on the grounds.

But it wasn't just the house and the other amenities that appealed to Herb and Julie. For years, they'd longed to live somewhere tranquil, somewhere, as Julie would say in *People*, the kids "could Rollerblade without having to worry about cars coming around the corner."

Already financially strapped because of their commitment to Thrift Management, scraping together the money required to move into Fox Hollow was no easy task. Valued by some at as much as one million dollars, primarily because it sits on eighteen-and-a-half acres of desirable Hamilton County real estate, the property, on face value, was out of Herb and Julie's price range. But as luck would have it, the then-owner was anxious to sell. As a result, they were able to purchase the house "on contract." Under this kind of agreement, the seller acts, in effect, as the mortgage lender. The seller and the buyer then settle on mutually agreeable sales terms, including an atypically small down payment. Buying a house on contract is an option sometimes exercised when a seller has had difficulty selling a property, or when a buyer has had difficulty obtaining a mortgage through a bank or conventional lender.

Thus, to move into Fox Hollow, Herb and Julie needed to come up with what Julie has described as only a "nominal" down payment, money they were able to pool from their savings, a small bank loan, and a cash settlement they received after winning a business-related lawsuit. The contract they signed with the seller then called for them to pay the balance of the purchase price over a period of sixty months, beginning March 1, 1992 and continuing through February 1, 1997.

Yet as their first move as newlyweds had required, this one, too, called for Herb and Julie to scrimp and save in order to get by.

"We had to make sacrifices," Julie would later concede. Dining out, for example, became a luxury they simply couldn't afford.

"So we cooked at home," Julie said matter-of-factly. "And we ate at home."

Herb and Julie also saved money, as they had when they purchased the 72nd Street house, by doing all repairs and upkeep themselves.

"We were the maintenance crew," Julie said. "If a room in the house needed to be painted, we painted it. If a fence needed to be built, we built it. We did everything ourselves—and we enjoyed it."

That Julie and Herb found time to maintain the home is all the more impressive in light of the hours they were keeping at work.

"Ours were seven-days-a-week jobs," Julie said.

She and Herb were always on call, too. Even on days

when they managed to slip away, leaving employees to lock up at closing time, they had to be available at all hours, ready to handle any unforeseen problems or emergencies that might arise.

The family's tight budget and the fact that Herb and Julie were running a business together also meant pricey family vacations were out of the question.

"We couldn't both just leave town," Julie explained. So instead, during the summer, she and the children would spend whatever time they could at a condominium Herb's mother owned on Lake Wawasee, a resort area about a hundred miles north of Indianapolis. Whenever Julie could arrange the time off, she and the children would head for the lake in the early or middle part of the week. Herb would join them on weekends, then return to Indianapolis in time to work on Monday, while Julie and the kids stayed on for another couple of days.

It was, to say the least, a draining existence. But, as Julie would later say, it was also a fulfilling one. Together, she and Herb had slowly but surely built a life for themselves. They'd started out as a struggling young couple with little in the bank but their hopes for the future. But through hard work and unyielding determination, they arrived at a place that not all that many years before seemed so far away. They'd moved from a modest apartment to one dream house, and then to another. They were raising three children they were proud to say were the center of their universe. And they'd started a business that had grown into a success faster than most.

They couldn't have dreamed of more.

But before long, Herb and Julie's near fairy-tale existence would prove to be just that. Not only was their life together nothing like it appeared from a distance, but the real Herb bore little resemblance to the Herb the outside world saw.

Nobody, it would turn out, knew Herb Baumeister at all.

FOUR

As much as Herb's childhood exuded normalcy, by the time he reached adolescence, it became apparent that something about him wasn't quite right.

"He started to have a hard time fitting in," childhood playmate Bill Donovan would recall as an adult. "It wasn't like he ever did anything to hurt anybody. He just didn't blend in.

"There was something about him that just didn't click."

There were also things about Herb, according to his one-time friend, that were downright strange.

"He once asked me, 'What do think it would be like to drink human urine?'" Donovan remembered. "I told him that wasn't something I wanted to find out. Nobody else I knew back then would have asked something like that."

The young Herb demonstrated a morbid streak, too.

"He'd build these little figures out of clay and then leave them out in the street in the middle of the night so cars would run over them," Donovan said. "I know a lot of kids do things like that, but there was something about the way Herb did it."

Then there was the time Herb came across a dead crow while walking to school one day.

"That bird had blood all over it," Donovan said. "But Herb picked it right up and put it inside his coat. Then when we got to class, he took it out and put it on the teacher's desk.''

"We'll scare her," Herb had said.

"You've got to be kidding," his friend told him. "That thing's a mess."

Herb simply shrugged, and in the end, got his wish.

"Our teacher almost had a heart attack," Donovan recalled.

The woman, as one might expect, was furious.

"She wouldn't let it drop until someone confessed," said Donovan. "So Herb finally confessed and was sent to the principal's office."

School, however, wasn't the only place where Herb was disciplined. According to Donovan, the elder Herbert Baumeister was, for the most part, a mild-mannered gentleman. But there was something about his firstborn son that tore at him.

"I think he had a real difficult relationship with his father," his friend said. "It always seemed to be strained.

"Herb always got in trouble with him, much more so than either Barbara or his brothers did. It wasn't so much that he got out of line the most. But maybe because he was the oldest, his father expected more of him.

"Herb had these great electric trains and his dad, from time to time, would ask him to clean up the room where he kept them. Herb was pretty good about that. But when he didn't do it, which seems pretty harmless, his dad would really blow up at him. I think that made him feel pretty inadequate, like he could never please his dad."

Moreover, said Donovan, the elder Baumeister's outbursts weren't only verbal.

"He'd spank him or kind of whack him across the head and say things like, 'Herbie, how could you be so stupid?' "

These incidents sometimes occurred in front of other people, too. Herb, though, never seemed fazed, even when his father became physical.

"He never showed any emotion," said Donovan, who

recalled witnessing several such displays. "He just sat there quietly. He just took it."

Around the same time, Herb also became something of the neighborhood punching bag.

"I can remember some of the kids saying things like, 'Boy, he's really goofy,' " Donovan would later recall.

One reason Herb was ostracized may have been his lack of athletic ability. Eventually, most of the neighborhood boys who had been his friends started playing organized sports like baseball and basketball. Herb didn't. Making matters worse, his younger sister evidenced more physical prowess than he did.

"Barbara used to play baseball and football with us," said Donovan. "She was a lot more athletic than he was."

A slight weight problem also made Herb the target of ridicule.

"It wasn't like he was fat," Donovan said. "But he had a large frame, so he always looked a little bit overweight."

No longer part of the crowd, Herb withdrew. More and more, he began spending time alone. His behavior bordered on ritualistic.

"Every day, at five o'clock, he'd sit down in front of the TV and watch cartoons," Donovan recalled. "And every time, he'd sit there and eat a peanut butter sandwich and a bag of carrots. Every single day. No other kid did stuff like that."

In high school, too, Herb faded into the background. Although he participated in several extracurricular activities, more than a few former classmates who were in the same clubs have said they don't remember him.

"It was almost like he was invisible," Donovan explained. "You just never saw him."

Herb's friend cannot recall his demonstrating any interest in girls, either.

"Not at all," he said. "Zero. I never saw him date."

College also proved to be a difficult time for Herb.

According to Indiana University records, Herb left school after completing just the first semester of his freshman year.

He returned sporadically over the next four-and-a-half years. He'd enroll one semester, then drop out the next. Needless to say, he never graduated.

"I never questioned it," Julie would later say, when asked about Herb's college career. "I don't think he knew what he wanted to do, so school wasn't his focus at that time."

Exactly how Herb secured his copy boy job at the *Indianapolis Star* is unclear. But it was no secret at the newspaper that such positions were handed to the children of prominent Indianapolis citizens who knew how to pull the right strings.

Garry Donna, the classified advertising account executive who befriended Herb when he worked at the *Star*, would remember him years later as eager and helpful, but also as a driven perfectionist who was overly preoccupied with how he was perceived by higher-ups.

"He bent over backwards to try to be accommodating," said Donna. "He was also so concerned about how people in the department viewed him and whether they liked him, more than you think a nineteen- or twenty-year-old kid would have. The other copy people in the building weren't like that. They didn't really care. But Herb was always kind of sensitive about that. He wanted to fit in somewhere, somehow, some way."

Donna believed this is why even a simple invitation to lunch seemed to mean much more to Herb than it would to the average person.

"Lunch isn't a big deal-type thing," said Donna. "But you could tell by the inflection in his voice if you asked him to go, that to him, it was a big deal. I think he was more used to being excluded than to being included, so when he was included, it meant a lot to him."

According to Donna, Herb's style of dress also set him apart from the other copy clerks.

"He was a meticulous dresser," Donna said. "The other copy boys wore blue jeans. Herb was always well dressed. He was very neat and very conscious of how he looked."

But knowing the neighborhood where Herb had grown up and the high school he attended, this came as little surprise to Donna.

"It was the affluent part of town," he explained, noting how many of Herb's fellow students at North Central chauffeured themselves to school in expensive cars. "That's the world he lived in."

Yet despite this moneyed upbringing, Donna said Herb always came across as more eccentric than privileged.

"At the time, you might have used the word fuddy-duddy," he said. "He was just kind of different, kind of in his own world a little bit."

For a time, Donna said, this extended to Herb's taste in automobiles.

Once, for instance, after learning that Donna and several friends had tickets to an IU football game, Herb offered to drive the group and their dates to Bloomington.

"I don't think you have a car that big," Donna said.

He was wrong.

"I could ride you guys down in my hearse," he told Donna.

"And I said, 'Your hearse?' "

Thinking his friends would probably get a kick out of it, Donna accepted Herb's offer.

"Hey, do you mind if my girlfriend comes along?" Herb then asked.

The question caught Donna off guard. Herb had never mentioned any friends before, let alone a girlfriend.

"Sure," Donna said. After all, he and all of his friends were bringing dates.

The day of the excursion, Herb did have a girl with him. But as Donna would remember it, "she didn't say three words the whole time."

Donna, in fact, ended up doubting that she really was Herb's girlfriend, as he had described her.

Otherwise, though, Herb played his role that day to the hilt, doing whatever he could to please Donna and his friends. When he realized they were running late, for instance, he turned on the hearse's siren and the flashing red light that sat atop its roof.

"People started pulling off the road," Donna remembered. "He even wore a chauffeur's cap. He thought it was kind of funny."

Donna's friends, on the other hand, found it more bizarre than amusing.

"I remember them saying, 'What's the deal with this guy?' " he said. "And I just said, like we always did, 'Well, Herb's just Herb.' "

Herb, though, was totally oblivious to the fact that his passengers perceived him in this manner.

"These weren't the kind of people Herb normally went out with," Donna said. "But that's why it meant so much to him. It was the kind of thing he longed for. That day, he was one of the guys."

Herb didn't fare much better in the years following his stints at IU and the *Star*. He was clearly troubled. But whatever his problem was, his family tried to keep it a secret, even from Julie.

It wasn't long after he started working at the Bureau of Motor Vehicles—another job his father is rumored to have secured for him—that Herb began behaving strangely, ranting and raving at fellow employees for no apparent reason.

It became obvious to Julie, too, that something was terribly wrong.

"He'd just sit in the living room and cry and cry and cry," a friend would later recall.

Strangely, Julie maintained for years that it was Herb's despair over a car that had not been properly repaired that led to his breakdown. But the fact that Herbert, Sr., took the action that he did suggests he knew Herb's problems had little to do with a bad mechanic.

Herb and Julie were still newlyweds when Herb's father had him committed to Larue D. Carter Memorial Hospital. Named for Larue Depew Carter, a prominent IU School of Medicine neuropsychiatrist and neurology professor and the first president of the Indiana Council for Mental Health, the state-run psychiatric institution opened its doors in 1952. Its purpose was to serve as a research and teaching facility for IU faculty and students.

Why the elder Baumeister chose to have Herb sent to Carter when he easily could have afforded a private hospital is unclear. His decision, though, said a great deal about the degree of help he felt Herb needed.

"If you were a doctor in this town back then and you put your child in LaRue Carter," said one lifelong resident of Indianapolis, "you were essentially admitting you knew he or she had a long-term problem."

Said another longtime resident of the city, "That's not where somebody who was just a little disoriented went. That's where somebody went if they had serious psychological problems."

Julie visited Herb often during what ended up being his roughly two-month stay at Carter. Almost unbelievably—she would say it was because he began to seem like his old self once he returned home—she would later claim to have never broached the subject of Herb's hospitalization with either him or his father.

Herb eventually returned to his job at the Bureau of Motor Vehicles. But his tenure over the years there was marked by odd behavior, according to former coworkers and others who dealt with him in varying capacities.

He raised eyebrows one year with a photo Christmas card he sent out to fellow employees. The photo showed Herb and another man dressed in drag. Herb had on a curly, brunette wig. His friend wore blond tresses and a high-necked blouse. Both looked rather matronly.

Coworkers also recalled Herb displaying an insistence on exactness that bordered on the neurotic. BMV employee Susan Pierce told the *Indianapolis Star* that when she went shopping with Herb and Julie for a Christmas tree one holiday season, Herb had very specific height requirements. "It had to be exactly forty feet tall," she said. It couldn't be thirty-nine feet and nine inches. It had to be forty feet."

As had been the case at the *Star*, Herb, while working

for the BMV, had a habit of flaunting his wealth. Ever the impeccable dresser, he always wore a suit as opposed to a sportcoat. Herb also had no qualms about letting people know exactly what his wardrobe cost. Pierce recalled in the *Star*, for instance, how after she accidentally stepped on his foot one day, he made a point of noting that his shoes cost three hundred dollars.

Herb boasted about his upbringing, too.

"He always bragged about his father being a physician," said retired Indiana State Police Commander Fred Hays who, during Herb's years at the BMV, served as a liaison between the bureau and the state police.

Hays had frequent dealings with Herb, especially after Herb became head of the financial operations department. According to Hays, Herb often displayed an air of self-importance.

"He always wanted to be the star, the key person in any group," Hays would later recall.

Hays, though, wasn't impressed. "He was articulate and he could carry on a conversation," he said. "But he wasn't a wizard or a genius. Once you got beneath the skin, I didn't see much there."

Herb also had a habit of disappearing from the office during the workday.

"It wasn't unusual when I went up to speak to him about a matter, that I couldn't find him," Hays said. "It was kind of a come-and-go-as-you-want place with Herb in charge."

Hays said it also quickly became obvious that Herb played favorites. As a result, employees that he liked knew that however they behaved, they didn't have to worry about being disciplined.

"There was a lot of dirty laundry Herb didn't want me to know about, a lot of sexual harassment-type stuff—'grab ass' we called it then," said Hays. "Everyone who was in on it thought it was cute, and if you were in good with Herb, you didn't get in trouble for it."

As Hays remembered it, the near-forty Herb, who was

often described as baby-faced, was especially tight with his department's younger employees.

"He was running around with coworkers quite a bit younger than him," he said. "They went out partying a lot after work and Herb was always the oldest guy in the group."

According to Hays, Herb had an especially close relationship with a BMV coworker named Gregory Moe.

"He was mesmerized by Herb," Hays said of the blond-haired, blue-eyed Moe who at the time stood six-foot-one and weighed 170 pounds. "He was always at Herb's side."

It was as a result of an incident that took place not long before he left his BMV job that Herb had his first run-in with the law.

On September 3, 1985, Herb and a group of his employees, including Moe, who was then twenty-three, decided to play hooky and ended up having a party at a rural property to which one of the workers had access.

"They were drinking and having a big time, which was problematic for two reasons," Hays said. "One, some of the employees were underage. Two, they had just abandoned the office in the middle of the day."

At some point during the day, Herb ended up behind the wheel of Moe's 1978 Chevy Camaro. Drunk, he hit the back end of another vehicle. Not wanting to face drunken driving charges, Herb told Moe that they weren't going to contact the police, and instead of reporting the accident, he simply drove away from the scene.

Later, Herb asked Moe for the keys to the car. Moe assumed Herb was taking the car to be repaired. But three days later, Herb told him the car had disappeared. Worried about the consequences of questioning his boss, Moe reported the car stolen. In October, he received a $2,200 settlement from his insurer. He also had received a payment of $546 to cover the cost of a rental car.

Herb likely believed he'd gotten away with the crime. But what he didn't realize was that some of the employees in his department who knew what had happened were becoming fed up with his behavior.

"Now he was into criminal acts," said Hays. "They said, 'Enough is enough.' "

A group of these workers approached Hays and gave him statements about what had transpired the day of Herb's fender-bender. Hays began investigating the incident and eventually even Moe turned on Herb.

In the end, everyone who had left the office that day admitted their involvement. Everybody, that is, except Herb.

"He lied through his teeth," said Hays. But as a result of the other workers' statements and Moe's agreement to testify in exchange for a plea bargain, Hays had enough evidence to bring charges against Herb.

Warrants for Herb and Moe's arrest were issued on March 27, 1986. Both were charged with theft, a Class A misdemeanor, and conspiracy to commit theft, a Class D felony. On April 3, Herb was taken into custody. That same day, he was released on his own recognizance after his brother, Richard, paid $350 in bond money, or ten percent of Herb's total bail of $3,500.

After Moe agreed to testify against Herb, Hays was convinced the case against Herb would stick. Although the evidence he had gathered was circumstantial, he believed Moe's testimony and that of the other BMV employees was strong enough to stand alone. Herb, though, didn't seem worried. He was, Hays recalled, as cocky after his arrest as he was before it.

"Herb was always a smart-ass," the retired commander noted recently. "He always had a 'big me-little you,' arrogant kind of attitude."

Herb had opted to have his case heard before a judge rather than a jury. In the end, he lucked out. Once in court, the other BMV workers, as Hays remembered, "went all wishy-washy on the stand." Moe, meanwhile, changed his mind at the last minute and refused to testify at all. Herb was found not guilty on both counts.

As a result of one delay after another, Herb's trial didn't

take place for nearly a year after his arrest. By this time, he had been fired from the BMV.

For years, Herb had displayed what those who knew him characterized as a bizarre sense of humor. While at the BMV, it took the form of his urinating on his boss's desk. He would wait until his boss had left for the day, then commit the deed. It was no secret around the office who the culprit was. Still, Herb somehow managed to avoid being fired. His good fortune came to an end, though, after he urinated on a letter addressed to the governor of Indiana. Shortly thereafter, Herb was terminated.

FIVE

Little about Herb and Julie's marriage was what it seemed either. Julie, in particular, wanted the outside world to believe that she and Herb had achieved domestic bliss. And from a distance, for a time at least, it did look that way. The solid marriage. The kids. The house. She and Herb seemed to have everything. But in the end, it all proved to be a façade.

For starters, there was no happy union. Over a quarter century of marriage, Julie would eventually concede, she and Herb had sexual relations no more than a half dozen times. She said that because she didn't have any close women friends, there was no one with whom she could broach the subject. As a result, she never realized how atypical their sex life was.

Julie, in fact, would eventually disclose that she never saw her husband nude over the course of their marriage either. Herb dressed in the bathroom, with the door closed, she said. And when it came time to go to bed, he would always put on pajamas and then after the lights had been turned out, slip between the sheets.

Herb, in fact, was so self-conscious about his lanky, six-foot three-inch body that he usually begged off at family swims.

Family acquaintances, once they learned the truth, suggested Julie was willing to accept this fate as long as her children, essentially the sole focus of her universe, didn't suffer, and Herb appears to have gone to great lengths to ensure that didn't happen. Even when they couldn't afford it, Herb showered the children with expensive gifts. He bought jet-skis for each, which they kept at his mother's condo in Lake Wawasee. They also each had go-carts of their own, at least one of which came with a cellular phone. And the backyard playhouse Herb built at the 72nd Street home, after he wired it for electricity and covered the roof with cedar shingles, ended up costing thousands of dollars.

Both Herb and Julie had a tendency to splurge around the holidays, too. In a video shot by Herb one Christmas morning, the family Christmas tree is obscured by a mountain of expensive gifts that Julie and the children spent literally hours opening. Among the pricey toys the children were given that year: CD players and stereo systems. And Emily, who was around nine at the time, received a video camera of her own.

Someone familiar with how the family lived once remarked that, with his extravagance, Herb may have been trying, at least when it came to the children, to make up for an everyday life that was often less than ideal.

"Herb," he said, with little hesitation, "was trying to buy those kids' love."

One thing Herb and Julie didn't open their wallets for, however, was any kind of housecleaning service.

Behind Fox Hollow Farm's well-maintained exterior was a home consumed by clutter. But it wasn't just Herb's off-beat collectibles that contributed to the chaos, or Julie's insistence that a fully decorated fake Christmas tree be kept up in the family room year-round. According to observers who entered the house just before the family cleared out for good, trash bags were piled to the ceiling in some rooms. "And you could hardly move in the garage," said one. "There were tools, clothes, furniture . . . box after box of stuff."

There were sanitary problems, too. The house's roof was so under siege by the area's vast raccoon population that raccoon feces and urine had begun to seep through the ceilings in some of the upstairs bedrooms. The smell, said someone who toured the residence, was horrendous.

To the few family intimates who had glimpsed the sad reality of Herb and Julie's life together, there was little question as to why they came close to splitting up more than once.

But for many years, they managed to keep the truth hidden.

John Egloff, Herb and Julie's onetime lawyer, said Herb and Julie struck him from the start as your average, upscale, suburban Indianapolis couple.

"They appeared to me to be typical, upper-middle-class people who were concerned about their kids' activities and friends and schooling," he said. "That fit right in with that whole kind of Carmel environment." (Carmel is a wealthy suburb slightly southeast of Westfield.)

Julie, in particular, he said, impressed him as "dedicated, hardworking and conscientious." Yet he felt that she, to a great extent, lived in Herb's shadow.

"Herb was kind of timid, but he called the shots and Julie went along for the ride," Egloff said, recalling Thrift Management's early days.

"Whenever they disagreed about what should be done with respect to a particular matter, Herb would basically take over the conversation. He'd say, 'Julie, that's not what we're going to do. Here's what we're going to do.'

"So my perception was that Julie deferred to Herb, but that she wasn't very happy about it. She was brighter than Herb gave her credit for. I remember one matter that ended up in court. Herb wanted to do all the talking. But Julie ended up being a far better witness than Herb was, as far as being articulate and being able to communicate a point. Herb tended to ramble, particularly if he was nervous or upset. Julie came across as very convincing."

*   *   *

On one level, Thrift Management was a success from the start. Inventory moved; Julie and Herb were able to pay themselves more-than-respectable salaries; and the Children's Bureau reaped tens of thousands of dollars.

Yet there were problems all along, too, due in part to what Egloff called some poor business decisions. The locations Herb and Julie chose for the stores—sites that had been vacant for some time and were not necessarily in areas that would draw the ideal clientele—were among them. According to Egloff, they also "made bad business deals with some of their landlords."

Then there was the matter of Herb's perfectionist tendencies.

"When I first met Herb, he was totally exuberant about the whole idea," said Egloff. "But from there, I watched him go downhill as his dreams got crushed by all these problems associated with the business.

"And the problems became all the more overwhelming because of Herb's perfectionism. He never managed to get the stores opened on time because every 'i' had to be dotted and every 't' had to be crossed.

"I remember him, at the beginning, telling me how Thrift Management was a total win-win proposition. He and Julie were going to make a comfortable living running a successful chain of stores and the Children's Bureau was going to become the most well-endowed charity in Indiana. But in the end he was totally despondent."

Julie would later call Thrift Management's difficulties in the early years "normal business problems." Normal, they might have been. But they placed a great deal of strain on the Baumeisters' marriage. So much so that in February 1991, Herb moved out of the 72nd Street house—they didn't purchase Fox Hollow until November of that year—and filed for divorce.

In his petition for the dissolution of his and Julie's marriage, Herb declared there had been "an irretrievable breakdown" in the union. He filed for joint custody of Marne, then eleven; Erich, then ten; and Emily, then just six; and a "reasonable property settlement." He claimed that Julie was in possession of all of their papers, bank books, and business records. He said that as a result, he was "without sufficient money, means, income, or property with which to pay attorney's fees," and asked that those be covered as well.

Finally, saying he was fearful that Julie might attempt to hide property, he requested the court issue a temporary restraining order enjoining her from "transferring, selling, or secreting any property."

But several weeks later, Herb had a change of heart. He moved back home and he and Julie reconciled. Herb's divorce lawyer, Indianapolis attorney Franklin Miroff, would later recall that when Herb first came to him, it was clear he was extremely concerned about both the business and his family. And with good reason, Miroff thought at the time.

"The business was not being run in a very businesslike fashion," he said, "and it was a very chaotic, disorganized family. Everything was sort of at odds and ends."

Herb, he added, was "very emotional about the whole process.

"But frankly," said Miroff, who saw Herb as a weak and ineffectual type, "neither I nor anybody else was able to get to the bottom of what was really going on."

That, of course, would change.

SIX

Despite the personal and professional problems Herb and Julie battled after Thrift Management's 1988 start-up, life at the seemingly idyllic Fox Hollow was relatively uneventful.

Relatively.

One day in the fall of 1994, Erich Baumeister, then thirteen, made a gruesome discovery in a densely wooded area roughly twenty yards behind the house: a human skull.

The youth, who was playing with a friend, placed it atop a stick and the two boys galloped home to scare young Emily. When Julie saw them, she naturally was startled.

"Show me where you found that, Erich," she asked her son, compelled to check the site herself.

Julie followed him back to the area where he had been playing. There, she came across a second disturbing discovery. Scattered on the ground were even more bones.

Puzzled and somewhat concerned, she left the skull and the bones behind and returned inside.

"I wonder if Herb knows anything about them," she thought to herself.

When Herb came home that night, she asked him about the bones. He told her they belonged to a skeleton his father had used while attending medical school. He was cool, almost casual.

Julie would later concede Herb's explanation really wasn't all that plausible. She'd never seen a skeleton belonging to her late father-in-law among the couple's possessions before. Back then, though, she took Herb at his word.

"They seemed insignificant," she explained once when asked about the bones. Also, she said, she had more pressing matters to attend to. Besides running the household, she and Herb were well into plans they had made to close the Sav-A-Lot on 46th Street and to open another in its place in Castleton, a major retail center on the north side of Indianapolis.

As Julie would put it, somewhat defensively, "It wasn't like I was just sitting at home with nothing else to think about."

But in truth, she didn't forget about the bones altogether. She didn't bring them up to Herb again, but something about them nagged at her.

Several days after Erich had discovered the skull, Julie, mainly out of curiosity, returned to the site. She wanted to take another look. But when she reached the spot where she had seen the bones several days earlier, they weren't there. She was in the right place. She was certain. Yet there were no bones to be found.

Some of the small forest animals that regularly patrolled the area must have carried them off, she thought to herself. She turned to go back to the house.

It would be just over a year later before the bones would cross Julie's mind again.

SEVEN

Catherine Araujo and Julie Baumeister's lives bear some resemblance. Both are Indianapolis natives who never strayed far from their hometown. Both married young, and both went on to have three children.

But that's essentially where the similarities end.

Julie's life was always a relatively comfortable one, thanks to her middle-class upbringing and subsequent two-decades-plus marriage to the son of a prominent physician.

Catherine, on the other hand, came to know struggle. She and the father of her children divorced when the youngest was just three months old. Later, she moved her family to a house out of which she also operated a beauty salon. This way, she could support herself and her children and be there when they came home after school. Yet in a cruel twist of fate, the two women's lives ultimately became intertwined in a way neither ever dreamed possible.

Roger Alan Goodlet, Catherine Araujo's youngest child, liked his friends to call him by his middle name: Alan. But to his mother and the rest of his family, he was always Roger.

As an infant and toddler, he lived with his mother and his older siblings, brother J. R. and sister Cynthia, in a modest home on Indianapolis's south side. When Roger was three, the family moved to a middle-class neighborhood on the city's west side, into the house where Catherine owned her beauty shop.

Roger was always small for his age, and although he began walking at about the same time most children do, talking didn't come quite as easily.

"He never spoke a word and noises didn't bother him, so we wondered if maybe he couldn't hear," Catherine remembered thinking at the time.

It turned out Roger's hearing was fine. Doctors determined instead that he had suffered brain damage when his brain was bruised during a difficult birth. He finally began speaking at the age of four. It was clear, though, that learning would always be a challenge.

Worried that Roger wouldn't be given the special attention he needed in Indianapolis's public school system, Catherine enrolled her son in a local parochial school.

"The nuns were crazy about him," she said, beaming. "Everybody there loved him, and he loved them back. He never missed a day of school."

The young Roger, who loved cats, amusement parks, and toy planes, also proved to have some special talents.

"He could draw," his mother said. "And he loved maps. He used to ask me to drive him to all the new subdivisions in town. Then he'd come back to the house and draw a map of all the streets. He remembered them all just by going by them once."

Roger eventually graduated from Indianapolis's Cardinal Ritter High School. "Of course, he didn't make the grades," Catherine conceded. "But they let him finish anyway."

As an adult, with the exception of a single year in his early twenties, Roger continued to live with Catherine and her second husband, Henry, a retired structural engineer, whom Catherine had married when Roger was eight.

"We put him in an apartment once, a condo that I rented, to see if he could manage on his own," his mother explained. "He did OK. He lived there for maybe a year. Then he moved back home."

Over the years, Roger held a variety of part-time jobs,

from car jockey to restaurant dishwasher. He also, for a while, worked part-time for his brother's Indianapolis tele-marketing firm.

"He liked helping his brother," Catherine said. "But he didn't like being on the phone all the time."

When he was working for his brother, and to get around town in general, Roger relied on the city's bus system.

According to his mother, "He didn't want to be driven around. He wanted to be independent."

To this day, Catherine still isn't sure what made her do it.

But on the morning of July 21, 1994, she decided she would give Roger the birthday present she had purchased for him, even though his thirty-fourth birthday was still nine days away.

"I had bought him a whole new outfit," she would later explain, tears welling in her eyes. "Jeans shorts that went below his knees, a green-, gold-, and white-striped shirt with a hood, and a pair of black boots, the kind that go to just above your ankle.

"Something just told me," she said, "to give it to him early."

Catherine's premonition proved tragically on target.

Later that day, Roger left the three-bedroom ranch house that had been his home for so many years to help a friend move a washer and dryer.

He never came home again.

The afternoon of July 21, the phone at the Araujo home rang several times.

"Tell him I'm not home," Roger instructed his mother each time she told him it was his friend, Jeff, on the other end.

At the time, Catherine didn't know very much about Jeff, the friend who had asked Roger to help him move some appliances. She had met him just once, in February, when he had come by to take Roger for a haircut. This wasn't all that unusual. For the most part, Roger never brought his friends around to the house.

Catherine was at a loss as to why Roger was trying to dodge his friend. But after Jeff's third or fourth call, she managed to convince her son to come to the phone.

It was approximately 3 P.M.

"Why don't you just go help him?" she urged Roger as she handed him the receiver.

To this day, Catherine doesn't know to whom the washer and dryer belonged or where the appliances needed to be moved. All she knows is that after Roger and Jeff finished the chore, they stopped in at Our Place, a leather bar at 16th and Alabama and long a popular mainstay in the gay community.

Exactly when Roger began frequenting gay bars—and drinking—is unclear. But Catherine has long suspected he was introduced to the scene by someone he met while riding the bus or simply hanging out downtown, something he was known to do. He never drank as a teenager or at home as an adult. But his drinking eventually did become problematic. More often than not, he'd return home in the early morning hours, still inebriated from the prior evening's revelry.

Catherine believed alcohol made it easier for Roger to socialize and make friends when he was out at the bars.

"It made him feel more like one of them," she surmised, referring to the bars' other patrons.

"He felt comfortable with those people. He considered them his friends. He always talked about 'my friends.'"

The bars' regulars, Catherine would learn after Roger disappeared, liked him, too.

"All the bartenders said how nice he was," said Catherine, who got to know several of them fairly well while searching for her son. "One even said he was the kind of person who would give you the shirt off his back."

Roger, though, may have been generous to a fault.

"If he had ten dollars," Catherine said, "he'd spend it on anybody."

Whether Roger was gay, at least in his mother's eyes, is another question entirely.

"It's hard for me to say he was gay because he never told me he was," said Catherine.

She was aware, though, that Roger was no stranger to the Indianapolis police, who arrested him a total of eighteen times for charges ranging from prostitution to public indecency to public intoxication.

"He didn't realize he was doing anything wrong," Catherine would argue in her son's defense. This was especially true, she said, when it came to the solicitation charges. As she put it, "He didn't know you don't do that."

The judges who encountered Roger in their courtrooms over the years appear to have felt similarly. According to police records, despite his lengthy record, he served less than a week in jail for all of his offenses combined.

"I think the judges let him loose because they knew who he was," said Catherine. "He'd get picked up, then he'd call me from the station and say, 'Mommy, come and get me,' just like a little child."

But Roger, always came home. So when Catherine woke up the morning of July 22 and realized that he had never returned, she sensed something might be wrong.

She picked up the phone and called Jeff, whose number she had from having taken his messages the day before.

"What happened to Roger?" she asked him. "He didn't come home."

Jeff explained that they had gone by OP's, as Our Place is commonly known. They'd driven there in Jeff's car. But he left Roger behind, he conceded, after promising to give someone else a ride home. Roger was still at the bar when he left, Jeff told Catherine. No, he said, he didn't know how much Roger had had to drink that night.

That was all a somewhat perturbed Catherine was able to extract from Jeff.

"I'll call Rick," she thought to herself after hanging up the phone.

One of Roger's oldest friends—they met around the time

Roger graduated from high school—Rick was the person Catherine relied on to keep an eye on her son when he was out partying.

"If Roger was drinking, Rick would see that he got home OK," she said. "He'd take him somewhere where he could sober up, and then he'd take him to the bus. I knew I could trust him."

Unfortunately, Rick had stayed in the night before. He hadn't seen Roger and he hadn't heard from him either.

"Roger didn't come home," Catherine told him. "And nobody's seen him. I think something's happened."

Rick promised to see what he could find out. Catherine, in the meantime, decided to pick up her son's trail where it had left off. She pulled out the phone book and found the telephone number for Our Place.

"Probably not," the man who answered at OP's told Catherine when she asked whether one of the bartenders who'd worked the night before had seen Roger leave with anyone. "When we're busy, they don't have time to pay attention to who leaves with who."

But the man did offer Catherine some advice. He suggested she contact Indianapolis Police Detective Mary Wilson, who handled missing persons cases. Wilson, he happened to know, already was investigating the disappearance of several other young men, all of whom were also known to frequent the city's gay bars.

Later that day, Wilson knocked on Catherine's door.

"The minute she walked in, she put her arms around me," she would later recall. "I knew right then that she cared."

"We'll find out what happened to Roger," Wilson assured Catherine.

It turned out, though, that because of Indianapolis Police Department policy, Wilson herself couldn't begin working on the case for another thirty days. Catherine was both gracious and appreciative. But somehow, it didn't seem like enough. Roger was out there somewhere, maybe hurt. There had to be someone else who could help.

EIGHT

Catherine Araujo wasn't the first mother to consult a private detective about a son who went missing.

At least two men had disappeared that summer, and both cases ended up in the lap of Virgil Vandagriff, a retired Marion County sheriff with a small investigations firm on Indianapolis's north side.

Mary Beasley got Vandagriff's name out of the Yellow Pages, she informed the detective when she called him in late June, looking for help finding her twenty-eight-year-old son, Alan Broussard.

Alan was a nurse's assistant at an AIDS hospital. He'd last been seen June 6, 1994, coming out of Brothers, a gay bar on Illinois Street. Although Alan's lifestyle was erratic—he drank too much, he kept late hours—he talked to his mother or they visited each other once a week. She was frantic. She didn't have a clue where he might be.

Vandagriff wasn't the first person she'd called, admitted Beasley, who lived in North Vernon, a small town south of Indianapolis. She'd talked to the Indianapolis police, of course. She'd also hired a psychic. And another private investigator.

One of the reasons Alan's disappearance was so upsetting, she explained, was that another of her three sons had been killed earlier that year in a car accident. She didn't know if she could bear any more heartbreak. She didn't see how it could hurt to have as many people looking for Alan as possible.

Actually, having two detectives looking for the same man could slow the search, thought Vandagriff, a stocky fifty-three-year-old with a thatch of chalky white hair and a bushy mustache to match.

But he forgave Beasley her anxiety. Missing persons cases, he knew from experience, were among the most tragic. Many people decided for whatever reason that they didn't want to talk to their families anymore. It was often a simple enough matter just to disappear, leaving their old lives behind.

Nor were the police all that helpful, especially when a missing adult was concerned. By law, police in most states couldn't even act on a missing persons case involving an adult until someone had been gone for twenty-four hours.

Indianapolis went a step further, keeping its missing persons cases in district offices for thirty days before turning them over to the missing persons department at headquarters. It made for hit-or-miss early investigations involving missing people. Sometimes the district detectives did an excellent job. Other times the cases were handed over a month later with little or no work done on them.

Inevitably, cases of this sort, in Indianapolis and other large cities, wound up in an understaffed, overworked missing persons office at police headquarters, law enforcement's equivalent of the dead letter file in a post office.

A number of shady operators capitalized on law enforcement's disinterest, from phony psychics to con artists posing as detectives, all of whom were perfectly happy to bilk money from families desperate to track down a loved one.

Vandagriff, who specialized in polygraph exams and employment investigations, was not fond of missing persons cases.

But he invited Mary Beasley to come see him at his office, a converted, one-story brick house on a main street near the Indianapolis airport.

Mary didn't have any problems giving Virgil the basics

about her son: his height and weight—five-foot-eight, about 145 pounds—his last address, the names and telephone numbers of his friends.

But she was less comfortable talking about Alan's life-style, Virgil noticed. She admitted he had a drinking problem. In fact, after a second drunk driving arrest, she'd taken away a car she'd bought for him that year, a 1985 Ford LTD which he adored. He'd been angry with her.

Despite his legal problems, Alan seemed to be in good spirits when she'd last spoken to him. He was his usual, outgoing, upbeat self. No hint of distress. No sign that he might run away or want to harm himself.

Vandagriff had a hunch there was a darker side to her son that she wasn't willing to talk about. But he didn't press. Whatever it was, it might be too painful or embarrassing for a mother to talk about, he reasoned. He'd get it from one of Alan's friends. They agreed that Virgil's office would make up MISSING posters and distribute them throughout the city, concentrating on the gay nightclubs that Alan frequented.

Mary Beasley left a copy of a photograph of her son with Virgil for the poster, one that showed off Alan's classic, dark-haired good looks: clad in a striped rugby shirt and dark pants, he was leaning against a tree, his deep dimples and broad white smile those of a young man who—at least by all outward appearances—seemed to have the world on a string.

Within days, that sunny visage was staring out from posters tacked up in stores and bars all over the city. Virgil and his associates had also questioned bartenders at a lot of the clubs and bathhouses Alan frequented, connecting with the gay community as closely as they could.

They didn't get much. Alan had been a fixture in the clubs, even working at a private gay club, the Unicorn, as a stripper for a few months. But the owner said he had to fire him because he drank too much on the job.

In a gay magazine one of Virgil's detectives picked up at a club, the *Indiana Word*, Virgil noticed an article about another missing gay man, one Jeff Jones, a thirty-one-year-old who'd last been seen outside the Salvation Army's alcohol detox center in downtown Indianapolis in July of 1993.

The photo of Jones showed a smiling, dark-haired, handsome man in a rugby shirt. The two men looked so similar, if Virgil hadn't known better, he'd have sworn he was looking at Broussard's brother, or maybe a cousin. Both had brown eyes and brown hair. Both were of medium height and on the slim side.

The eerie similarities between the two didn't end with outward appearance. Like Broussard, Jeff Jones was gay. He'd gone missing during the previous summer. Jones's parents had described their son as "likable, outgoing"—almost word for word the description Alan Broussard's mother had given of her son.

Perhaps more significantly, like Broussard, Jones abused alcohol.

"If a man said, 'I live on this estate, I have an indoor swimming pool and let's have some alcohol,' Jeff would have said, 'Why didn't we leave yesterday?' " Jones's aunt, Debbie Alamo, told the *Indianapolis Star*.

The *Indiana Word* article on Jones said his parents had dropped him off at the detox center so that he could sign up for an alcohol rehabilitation program, which he hadn't done.

A close friend reported seeing Jones the following morning and then never again. His family hadn't heard from him since.

Anyone with information about Jones was asked to call Mary Wilson at the Indianapolis Police Department's Missing Persons unit.

Virgil couldn't shake thoughts about the similarities between Jones and Broussard. There was no doubt in his mind both of the men had put themselves in harm's way because of alcohol.

The question was: What kind of monster would prey on that vulnerability?

Jones hadn't been heard from in a year. Virgil doubted he would ever surface. In fact, he was coming to the same grim prognosis for Alan Broussard.

The detective's outlook grew even bleaker when he spoke to Frank Furfaro, a nurse and close friend of Alan's who worked with him at the AIDS hospital. Alan had been working as a prostitute for at least six months, Frank told Virgil.

"At the hospital, we tried and tried to tell him that was bad news, you know," Frank said with a heavy sigh. "He just wouldn't listen."

That past November Alan had begun working for a catering company that operated as a front for a prostitution ring. It was a dangerous outfit, run by lowlifes, Frank told Virgil.

He not only went out on dates for them, Alan answered their phones.

He was methodical about checking in with the service to find out about his appointments, which he hadn't done the day he was last seen, Frank said.

"I find it highly unlikely that he didn't at least contact them to see if he had a run before he left," Frank said.

Frank described Alan as a "party boy" who needed to mature. Like a lot of young gay men in Indianapolis, Alan had come from a small Indiana town where there was no support for gays and little in the way of a gay culture.

In Alan's mind, living in Indianapolis meant he'd arrived. He didn't want to go back home. Unfortunately, Alan believed that his ticket to staying in the big city was hooking up with an older, wealthier man, Frank said.

"A lot of young, cute guys like Alan get involved with older guys to support their asses," Frank recalled years later. "Alan thought he could peddle his looks, that these guys were going to take care of his ass."

An escort service owner apparently played on Alan's Cinder-fella fantasy, approaching Alan in a bar and telling him he could earn up to $2,000 a night, simply by dating businessmen in from out of town and "older gentlemen," Frank remembered Alan telling him.

Intrigued, Alan hired on with the service. But the reality of escorting proved less lucrative and a lot more sleazy than his new boss had intimated, Frank said.

Alan didn't often get more than one date a week, and when he did, his typical earnings were anywhere from $150 to $400.

Frank said Alan shared details of most of his appointments with him, the two laughing at the pathetic, sad lengths to which some closeted gay men would go to just to find a warm body. Once he danced for a group of men, in a fraternity-type setting. Another time he went to a hotel downtown and simply undressed for an elderly man.

"Alan thought the more money people showed, the more character they had," Frank said. "He was always short of cash. He lived pillar to post. I felt for the guy. He only made six-fifty an hour at the hospital and they kept cutting his hours. He didn't want to go home, though, and be a gay guy in North Vernon. There was nothing there for him."

Despite his financial and legal problems, Alan was perennially bubbly and sweet, Frank said. And in reality, he faced an even bigger threat: Alan was HIV positive. He'd known about it for a year. He'd gotten sick at the hospital the summer before, running a high fever for an entire week. Frank and the other nurses had insisted that he get checked out; that was when he'd been diagnosed.

Alan didn't hide his HIV-positive status, informing every potential partner that he had the virus. "He wouldn't intentionally infect somebody," Frank said. "He knew too much about the disease.

"He worked with it every day. It wasn't uncommon for us to see a death every day at the hospital. Or for a patient to come in and die the same day. But Alan never thought he was going to get sick. He honestly thought nothing was ever going to happen to him."

Alan wanted to go back to nursing school, Frank said. The escort thing was a low point in his life, yes, Frank conceded. But Alan was looking forward to the future. He was a good caregiver, loving and generous, in a field that desperately needed people like him. Patients loved him. And he enjoyed his work. He wouldn't have done anything to harm himself.

Virgil showed Frank both the article and photograph of Jeff Jones.

Jones didn't look familiar, Frank reported. But he couldn't shed much more light on the escort service Alan worked for. Alan had kept his escorting acquaintances separate from his work friends. The few men Frank had met from the service were "riffraff," he said.

Virgil turned to the tape made by the psychic for further clues about Alan. According to the psychic, he was in Medina, Ohio.

Something violent had happened to him and "there are marks upon that of the forehead, the cheek, and . . . the shoulders, and lacerations, even across that of the buttocks. For the entity [Alan] allowed itself to get into a situation where romance went out of the window and lust entered in."

Unfazed by the arcane language and talk of Alan as an "entity," Virgil tracked down the Medina lead, calling the police there, but came up empty-handed.

Virgil was a man of few words, many of them mispronounced—his Dutch tongue often stumbled over words like "flustrated" and "pecific." At face value, he seemed the least likely person to turn to the mystical when solving a case. But the detective's gruff, simple façade hid an open mind.

His investigative style, in reality, relied on a wide variety of tools and philosophies, from psychics to high-powered computer search tools. Virgil remembered all too well how difficult it had been to convince the Marion County Sheriff's Department to send him to the Los Angeles Police Department for hypnosis training in the mid-1970s, something that wasn't being done then in the Midwest. Vandagriff's father, an electrician, had dabbled in hypnosis, and Virgil knew its potential lay beyond mere parlor tricks.

After the Los Angeles seminar, he not only pioneered

forensic hypnosis in the Midwest, he mastered it. The technique his superiors first called "mumbo-jumbo" went on to become a standard in law enforcement agencies nationwide, most often used to jog the blurry memories of witnesses to crimes. Virgil went on to use it in more than three hundred cases.

In the celebrated Indianapolis case of Brett Kimberlin, the Speedway bomber who set off six bombs in the Speedway neighborhood of the city in 1977, including one that killed an elderly woman, Virgil hypnotized several employees of Radio Shack who had sold Kimberlin an unusual timing device that police determined was used in the bombings.

Under hypnosis, the clerks were able to remember enough about the then-unknown customer to allow police sketch artists to make a composite drawing of Kimberlin. Later convicted, Kimberlin surfaced in the news in 1992 after he claimed to reporters that he had once sold Dan Quayle marijuana. (Quayle denies the claim.)

Equally open-minded was Virgil's assistant and companion, Connie Pierce, a tall, forty-three-year-old curly-headed blonde with a warm personality and a big nurturing streak.

While Virgil could be terse, Connie, a mother of two, was talkative, filling in conversational gaps, drawing people out. Virgil liked to look at the big picture, Connie was rabid for details.

Although Connie did the secretarial work around the office, Virgil often pulled her in on interviews. She wasn't trained in law enforcement, but she was curious and friendly. To her, investigations were fascinating tales with people at their heart. If someone didn't warm to Virgil, they usually took to Connie. She was difficult to dislike, and she had a way of giving everyone the benefit of the doubt, making them feel as if she were on their team, especially if no one else was.

In that way, the duo worked well together, yin and yang partners who had seen so much during the seven years they'd worked together that they took in stride most of the convoluted plot twists and bizarre human behavior exhibited as a case ran its course.

"I can't tell you how many calls to our office start with someone saying, 'This is really weird, so don't think I'm strange or anything,' " Connie said.

Her stock response: "Try me."

Still, when Virgil's involvement in the Broussard case came to an abrupt end after a couple of weeks—Mary Beasley's insistence on hiring two detectives had made for divided resources and duplicated work—Virgil and Connie were relieved. So, too, were some of the agency's other detectives, several of whom had felt less than comfortable combing Indianapolis's gay bathhouses and bars.

Little did they know that another case was about to take them back into that world, in a far more involved and macabre way than Broussard's disappearance ever had.

NINE

Catherine Araujo got Virgil Vandagriff's name from Virgil's sister, Shirley. The two women belonged to a women's sorority that met several times a month to play cards or plan charitable functions. After Catherine relayed her fears to the group's members at a meeting in mid-July, Shirley urged her to call Virgil.

"If he can't find Roger at least he can give you some advice about what to do next," Shirley had told her friend.

Catherine wept as she told Virgil about Roger, his childlike demeanor, his trusting nature, his tendency to drink too much—the whole litany of factors that made Roger vulnerable alone out on the streets.

She told him about Roger's arrests; how he'd been picked up nearly twenty times. But each time, she stressed, he was unaware that he'd done anything wrong.

Listening to Catherine felt like a repeat of Virgil's session with Alan Broussard's mother.

Two mothers distraught about missing sons. Two young men who drank too much and frequented gay bars. Both men were even named Alan, given that Goodlet was known on the street by the name Alan.

Virgil and Catherine agreed that the detective agency would circulate posters and establish a telephone tip line for people who might have information about Roger.

He left Catherine with as upbeat an outlook as he could

muster without being misleading, assuring her they would do everything they could to bring Roger back. Still, the detective's first move was to comb the morgue and the hospitals for someone matching Roger's description.

When he found nothing, he checked Roger's record, which showed his eighteen arrests. Virgil wasn't interested in Roger's troubles with the law because he thought Catherine might be holding out on him. He was hoping the incident reports would list other people involved in his arrests, someone who could lead him to Roger. But they offered little more than a pattern, really. Roger inevitably got arrested outside gay bars or somewhere in the northern downtown neighborhood around the bars.

Despite talking about Roger's return with Catherine, Virgil was becoming more and more certain that it was never going to happen. Goodlet's case was too similar to Jones's and Broussard's, Virgil felt. All three men, he thought, had met the same fate: a serial killer.

A serial killer who preyed on gay hustlers and alcoholics sounded macabre and dramatic, but in fact it was a sickeningly familiar scenario to the gay community in Indianapolis.

Few in the city, including Vandagriff, had forgotten the reign of terror wrought by Larry Eyler, who in the mid-1980s admitted to kidnapping, torturing, and murdering as many as twenty-three young men, many of them from Indianapolis, scattering their remains in embankments off remote sections of highway in Indiana and Illinois.

Eyler's gruesome trademark had been to drug, handcuff, and disembowel his victims—basically field-dressing them as one would an animal. Most were left with their pants pulled down around their ankles.

In 1994, after confessing to having killed seventeen young men on his own and taking part in the murders of another four, Eyler died of AIDS on death row. A statewide police task force in Indiana arrested him in November 1983 but wasn't able to bring him down. He was released by an Illinois judge on $1,000 bail after the 1983 arrest was deemed illegal. The Chicago police caught up with him again in August 1984 after he dismembered a teenager named Danny Bridges and then threw Bridges's body parts into a Dumpster. Like dozens of Indiana law enforcement professionals, Virgil had worked on a small part of the case, having been brought in to interview witnesses and family members of the men in Indiana whom Eyler admitted killing.

Not only Indiana, but the Midwest as a whole, had a decades-long history as the epicenter of homosexual serial killers. Gays numbered among cannibal killer Jeffrey Dahmer's seventeen victims in Ohio and Milwaukee from 1978 to 1991. Before that, John Wayne Gacy had been even more voracious, killing at least thirty-three men, many of whom he lured back to his Chicago-area home, promising money for sex.

But Eyler, Dahmer, and Gacy were gone. And the task force that had been established to nail Eyler, made up of Indiana state and county law enforcement officials, had been disbanded in 1984.

Still, like a warped record album playing over and over again, someone was following in Eyler's footsteps. And so similar were the milieus in which they operated, it seemed as though this new killer could have trained at Eyler's knee.

One of the Indianapolis nightspots Eyler frequented, Our Place, was also a favorite of both Broussard and Goodlet. Both men went missing from the city's north neighborhood, the nearly two-square-mile area of downtown that had also been Eyler's playground. And like Eyler at the time of his killing spree a decade earlier, this newly minted monster was picking up the pace.

Jones had disappeared in 1993. Broussard and Goodlet vanished within a month of each other the following year.

When Bill Hilzley, an investigator who worked for Virgil, began asking about the two at gay bars, however, the response was largely blasé or nonexistent. Members of the gay community, Virgil thought, must know more. The trick was getting them to come forward.

The posters of Goodlet opened some doors. As soon as

the circulars went up with Vandagriff's number on them, calls started to trickle into his office. Many were from Roger's friends, fishing for information. Jeff Wynn, one of Goodlet's good friends, called once or twice a day. Goodlet's lover, Rick "Dog" Rigney, called even more often, eventually becoming an irritant.

"Frankly, Dog," Connie finally told him, "Catherine is our client. You're not. Even if we did find out something new, we couldn't tell you."

A social worker from Chicago called. A street person with amnesia and an alcohol problem had wandered into the rescue mission she ran. Another patient had seen the Indianapolis poster and thought he might be Roger Goodlet. But the man's hair and eye color didn't check out.

Another caller had a tip about an all-male escort service with offices in Dallas and Atlanta. Connie ran it down—they had no employees that fit Roger's description.

A man named John Childers called. He'd talked to the police, too, he told Connie, who was handling most of the tip calls, while Virgil and Hilzley made the rounds of the gay bars and bathhouses.

Childers said he'd seen Goodlet drinking at Our Place the night he'd disappeared. Childers had been playing pool so he hadn't paid much attention when Alan—as Goodlet was known on the street—casually passed him, saying hello and not much else. Roger had been drinking beer and had a "little buzz" on, but he wasn't totally blitzed, Childers told Connie.

Later that night, sometime after three A.M., Childers said, he had driven by "the flags," a park lined with flagpoles near the city's main library where male prostitutes often peddled their wares. Goodlet spent so much time in that area, Childers said, he and Goodlet jokingly referred to it as Goodlet's "office."

That night, Goodlet left "the flags" in a light-blue car with Ohio license plates. He hadn't seen the driver very clearly, but he thought he might have been bald.

Catherine Araujo was convinced that Roger knew whoever was behind the wheel of the car he got in.

"I always told him, 'Never hitch a ride with a stranger. The wrong person will pick you up and you'll get killed,' " she said. "That's why he wouldn't have gotten in a car with someone he didn't know."

Several days after the Childers tip, Jeff called Catherine, breathless with excitement. There'd been a breakthrough in Roger's disappearance, he said.

"This Tony guy I know might have gone home with the guy that picked up Alan," he told Araujo. Tell Tony to call Vandagriff's office, she urged Jeff.

Catherine alerted Connie that a call might be coming from someone named Tony, but when Connie heard the source was Jeff, she was discouraged.

Jeff had seemed like a nice enough person, but he'd done more in the way of looking for information than in offering it. Connie didn't have high hopes that Jeff's friend Tony would be the breakthrough Catherine was praying for.

Tony proved even more of a disappointment when he called the agency the next day. "I think I know what happened to Alan. I called the FBI. I called the police. They all told me to get lost. You guys have got to do something about it."

"Can you come into our office and talk about it?" Connie asked, keeping her warm voice as gentle and nonthreatening as possible.

"I don't know about coming in," he said. "I don't want anybody to know who I am. If this guy finds out, he'd probably kill me. I don't want to talk to the police."

"We're not the police," Connie assured him. "And we're not going to turn you in to the police. We just want information about Roger Alan Goodlet."

Tony considered, hesitating for a moment.

"Let me think about it. I'll call you again tomorrow," he said, hanging up before Connie could get his telephone number or last name.

Virgil welcomed the news about the mysterious Tony as

the break they definitely needed. Hilzley was striking out at the gay bars.

Everyone, it seemed, knew Roger Alan Goodlet. That much was clear. But as sweet and easygoing as he'd been, Goodlet's street habits had made him so vulnerable a target, he might as well have shown up in the woods on the opening day of hunting season dressed as an eight-point buck, Hilzley thought.

Not only that, the gay community was being completely tight-lipped. Getting anyone in the bars to give up even the tiniest bit of information, such as the names of Goodlet's regular customers or "tricks," had been almost impossible.

Hilzley told Virgil the discouraging news when the two men sat down to compare notes.

"Virg, either people don't give a shit about this guy because he's gay or if they're gay themselves they ain't saying nothing."

Virgil told him about the nibble they'd gotten from the posters by the man named Tony. The two agreed it was worth a shot—if Tony came in and talked to them. If Hilzley's reception in the gay community had been any indication of the chances of that, they decided not to hold their collective breath.

A nervous Tony did call back the next day. He might come in, he conceded to Connie. But he didn't want the Indianapolis police involved.

"They accused me of being high on drugs," Tony complained. "Screw them. I'm not dealing with those assholes."

Again, Connie assured him that any information he gave them could be anonymous. They just wanted to find Roger Goodlet, she told him.

"Well, if he went home with the same guy I did—this guy from Dayton—you might never find him," Tony said.

"Yeah, I'll come in," he added, almost as an afterthought. "You need to check this guy out. The police aren't going to."

Tony had dropped another crumb of news. The man Tony had met was from Dayton. That would match Childers's description of Roger getting into a car with an Ohio license plate.

Connie gave Virgil the information with a heavy heart. It was a breakthrough, yes. He sounded like he really had made up his mind to share his story with them. But Connie heard real fear in his voice when he talked about this stranger from Ohio.

Catherine still held tight to the hope that Roger would be returned to her safely. But she knew the chances of that actually happening grew slimmer with each passing day, a realization cemented by a dream she had about a week after Roger disappeared, a dream in which her late mother appeared to her and told her Roger was safe.

"He probably found Grandma or Grandma found him," Catherine's daughter told her. "She's letting us know he's okay."

Nervous and frightened, Tony finally did come in several days later. As soon as he entered the tiny, low-ceilinged office his body language seemed to scream that he'd rather be anywhere else but there. Full of her usual bright chitchat, Connie did everything she could think of to make him comfortable, bringing him coffee and an ashtray as he settled into a chair in Virgil's office, his long legs tucked under Virgil's desk.

"We're going to tape this, I hope you don't mind," Virgil told him, setting up the recorder on the desk in front of him.

Virgil didn't want to spook him even more, but he wanted it clear this wasn't a game. And he wanted to be able to share the interview verbatim with Catherine, if Tony said anything of value.

"I don't care," Tony said, lighting a cigarette. "I don't have nothing to hide. I just don't want this guy to find out what I told you. You don't know this psycho. He'd kill me."

"So this guy that wants to kill you, he's supposedly from Dayton?" Virgil started, pressing down the RECORD button.

"I'd never been alone with the character before," Tony

replied. ''The first time I was alone with him was last Wednesday night.''

Tony told Virgil about meeting Brian at the 501 Tavern. He'd seen him around at other gay bars before that night ''four or five times,'' Tony said. He'd also seen him with Roger Alan Goodlet about the time Goodlet disappeared, which is the reason he spoke to him in the first place.

''Did he approach you to do some things for him? Sexual things?'' Virgil wanted to know.

''No. This is how it all happened,'' Tony said, taking a deep drag on his cigarette. ''I wasn't sure who he was. It was dark. And I don't think he knew exactly who I was until he started talking to me. Then he turns around. We talk light conversation—nothin' in particular.''

Tony looked at Connie. ''I'm not a hustler, by the way,'' he confided to her. ''I am a legitimately employed person. But, you know, this guy didn't know that.

''Anyway, he started talking to me, light conversation. Tells me he has access to a mansion in Carmel with an indoor swimming pool. He seems to be an honest-enough-looking person to go back there with. He told me that the mansion belonged to someone that was moving there from Atlanta, Georgia, and that he was watching the house for a week, doing some work or something. That's what he was in town for. He told me he lived with his parents in Dayton, Ohio.''

''Did you ever get a chance to find out what his name was?'' Virgil asked.

''He told me his name was Brian, Brian Smart. The guy went to sleep. I tried to get into his wallet to get an ID. I was suspicious at this point because of the fact that he was into this strangulation fetish thing.''

Tony was all over the place, Virgil noted. First he was in the bar with this guy, and then the guy's asleep, presumably at the house in Carmel. Now he's talking about a strangulation fetish. What strangulation fetish? Virgil had to bite his tongue not to interrupt, but he could see Tony was comfortable reeling off the events of that night as he remembered them. This wasn't a police interrogation. Tony was doing them a favor—possibly at risk to himself.

Tony never did get a look at Brian's wallet, but Brian told him he was twenty-eight years old, something the twenty-five-year-old Tony found almost laughable.

"He's older than that, I'm sure," Tony said, flicking the ash from his cigarette. "I think he's lying about his name and his age."

Tony said he never got a chance to look at Brian's wallet, "because he started to stir like he was gonna wake up, so I threw it down and just played it off like I wasn't doin' nothin'. But it was a Dayton, Ohio, driver's license that he was carrying."

Brian was about six-feet-one or -two inches tall, slim, with brown hair, Tony remembered. His eyes were blue, he said with certainty.

"And I know for a fact that the guy shaves his body hair. Chest, arms, everything."

Brian had been drinking beer that night, Tony recalled, but he didn't think he was a heavy drinker.

"He did mention cocaine to me, asked if I did the stuff. I told him no."

Tony eyed Virgil warily. "You're not a cop, right?"

No, he wasn't a cop, Virgil told him. Of course, he'd been one for two decades, but now wasn't the time to quibble about his law enforcement background.

"Because I did burn a joint with him," Tony admitted. "But it was my stuff, not his, so I know it wasn't laced. He tried to get me to drink with him. I wouldn't. I was, you know, afraid of being drugged, or whatever. It made him very irritated that I wouldn't take the drink," Tony remembered.

Brian had been driving a gray Buick, Tony recalled. But there were four or five other cars parked at this house, and at least one had an Ohio license plate, he remembered.

He was sketchy about how they'd gotten to the house and precisely where it was. Tony thought they'd driven "twenty-three to twenty-five minutes" once they'd gotten off of 31.

"I know it's due north on 31 just past 146th and before 156th, from the west side of 31," he said. "The place has a title to it. It's a ranch. There's horses there. It's called something 'Farms.'

"If you was to buy a home like that, you would have to have at least two million in your pocket. This is not a slum. Indoor swimming pool, the whole nine yards. But it's all run-down and cobwebbed over. You know, like nobody's cleaned in quite some time."

For all his specificity about the house, however, frustratingly, he didn't think he could make his way back there.

"I tried to find it myself and I can't. The place is a bit overgrown, unkempt. A lot of cobwebs and dust in the house. And this is another really strange thing that scared me. There are mannequins in the house. There's probably all in all, twelve to twenty mannequins in the home. One of them is sitting beside the pool with a lifeguard shirt on. There's even a Christmas tree left decorated in the house.

"These games he was into, I'll explain them to you real quickly," Tony told Virgil, leaning forward and putting his hands around his own neck to illustrate.

"It's not a strangulation. It's more of a pinching of the jugular vein, causing a tremendous head rush. After this he starts bringing out a wide leather belt around his neck. He's wanting me to do these things to him, and then he will return the favor, reciprocate, of course. Then he tries with a silk tie."

That was all Tony wanted to say about their sexual activities that night, and Virgil didn't probe for additional details. Brian's strangulation fetish spoke volumes. Virgil did, however, want more specifics about the house and about Brian's ties to Roger Alan Goodlet.

"Did he ever admit to knowing Alan?" Virgil asked.

"No," Tony admitted. "He seemed indifferent toward Alan. You know, the fact that I would bring it up and talk to him about it. We seen a guy there at the same club we're both in. We were jokin' about it, 'cause the guy looked like Charles Manson. That's what brung up the serial killer thing. So, you know, we started talking about it then. But like I said, you know, I firmly believe that this guy had something to do with Alan's disappearance because I'd seen Alan talking with this individual, ah, I'd say several weeks before.''

Now it was Tony's time for questions. He was afraid, he told them. His grandmother had read about the unsolved murders of several men in Ohio. Were they connected to Alan's disappearance?

Virgil couldn't answer him. He honestly hadn't heard about the Ohio murders. And he had no idea if they were tied to Goodlet's or Broussard's disappearances, although he promised him he would try to find out.

Almost as a way of reassuring himself, however, Tony quickly launched into an explanation of why he didn't think Brian could be responsible for any crime that was ''too gross.''

''He was very delicate, very clean, you know. He wasn't nothing like you would expect a butcher to be, or anything like that,'' Tony said, stubbing out his cigarette.

''Of course, Jeffrey Dahmer wasn't either,'' Tony added with a smile.

Mannequins. Christmas trees. Manson. Dahmer. Shit, thought Virgil. Either this guy has one hell of an imagination or something truly off-the-wall went on in Carmel that night. To top it off, Tony had promised to meet this Brian Smart person again—this Wednesday. In two days.

Tony wasn't going, but he was fairly certain Brian would show. He had pretty much conned him into thinking that he was into sexual strangulation, Tony said. Brian's parting compliment, that he knew ''how to play,'' had convinced Tony of that. Virgil assured him they'd stake out the bar. They would also do what they could to track down a Brian Smart from Ohio.

After the taping was finished, Tony came back to talk to Connie in her office. Unable to restrain her mothering instinct, she gave him a tongue-lashing for having ever left the bar with this Brian guy in the first place. Something about Tony brought out her protective streak.

"Didn't your mother ever tell you not to leave with strangers?" she scolded. Tony just laughed.

After Tony left, Virgil and Connie tried to digest what they'd just heard. Tony was no angel, that was clear. Hard-edged and streetwise, he seemed to be given to hyperbole. Twelve to twenty mannequins? And he'd glossed over the extent of his actual sexual activity with Brian. They were certain they hadn't heard all of the details about that part of the evening. It didn't help, either, that he'd been smoking pot the night he'd been with Brian.

Still, Connie and Virgil agreed that the core of what Tony had told them had been the truth. He may have talked fast, his thoughts zigzagging all over the place, but his words seemed unrehearsed. He sounded sincere.

In the end, they decided that at the very least he had gone to a house north of Indianapolis with another man and the two had engaged in sexual strangulation. That meant a lot of things.

It meant that Tony had somehow, miraculously, escaped the clutches of someone who could very well have been a monster. It also meant that Goodlet and Broussard—and God knows how many others—might not have been as lucky.

The police needed the information Tony Harris had given them. First, however, they would have to be convinced that Harris was someone who should be taken seriously. And the only way to do that, Virgil and Connie agreed, was to find Brian. And that house in Carmel.

TEN

The only problem, Virgil and Connie soon realized, was that pinning down any part of Tony Harris's statement about the elusive Brian was a little like standing on a melting iceberg. Every time they tried to verify a piece of information Tony had given them, it simply evaporated, giving them an ever-shrinking base from which to navigate. The first order of business was staking out the 501 Tavern that Wednesday night in case Brian kept his word and showed up for more "fun and games" with Tony.

Another investigator who worked for Virgil, Steve Rivers, dutifully parked outside the bar at about dusk that night, thinking Brian might show up early. Tony had to work, but some of his friends agreed to do what they could to help the detective. By then, Goodlet's disappearance was common knowledge among some of the regulars at most of the city's gay bars and they were eager to do whatever they could to help.

Rivers told them what Brian looked like and they kept an eye out inside the bar, while he kept watch outside.

Other than a couple of guys who tried to coax the slim, dark-haired twenty-seven-year-old Rivers into coming into the bar so they could buy him a drink, it was quiet all night.

Tony himself finally showed up sometime after midnight. But when he went in and checked out the bar, Brian was nowhere to be seen.

Tony and Steve both stayed until closing time. Brian never showed.

In the days following, Rivers checked out every gay bar in Indianapolis for someone matching Brian's description, showing up at odd times during the day and night. Virgil had warned him not to look exclusively for someone driving a car with an Ohio license plate. From what Tony had said, this guy had access to a lot of cars. But no one matching Brian's description ever turned up.

Virgil wanted Tony to set up another "date," in an effort to trap Brian. Tony paged him endlessly at the pager number Brian had given him. No matter what time he called him, night or day, he never got a response.

Despite knowing it most likely wasn't his real name, Virgil used the computer to search for all the Brian Smarts in Ohio who had vehicles registered in their name that resembled or matched either the gray Buick in which Tony had traveled with Brian or the light-blue car Roger Alan Goodlet might have gotten into.

There couldn't be that many Brian Smarts in Ohio, Virgil reasoned. Actually, there were several, but none fit the profile. There were also Brian Smarts in Indianapolis. Connie even went to a home in the northern part of the city to check on one of them. It was a wasted trip. The house was like any other in the working-class neighborhood, and the people she saw coming out didn't match Tony's description of Brian.

Virgil prodded Tony for a little more information on Brian's name. When pushed, Tony admitted that the last name Brian had given him might not have been Smart, after all, but something that sounded like it.

"It's something like Start or Stats," he said. "I had a buzz, remember?"

Yes, Virgil did remember. All too well. Another check of computer records turned up two Brian Statses, one in Ohio, another in Indianapolis. Neither had cars registered in their name that matched the ones he was looking for. Virgil called Catherine after they'd talked to Tony, filling her in the best way he knew how. He just didn't feel right giving her a lot of details about sexual strangling. Still from the old school in a number of ways, Virgil didn't think dangerous sexual practices were something you shared with a mother. Especially a distraught mother. Catherine seemed so fragile. He told her only that they had a promising lead for information about Roger but that it didn't look good.

When she insisted on talking to Tony herself, Connie hooked the two of them up. Virgil figured if Tony wanted to tell her what had happened that night, it was his business.

Connie had become something of a touchstone for Tony. After he'd arrived at the office that first time, he began calling her once a day or so, each time passing on new details about his night with Brian. As tiny as each new recollection was, he thought it might somehow help.

One of the mannequins, Tony told Connie, had been bronze-looking, "You know, like the cast-iron people they have down there at Union Station," Tony recalled. And the house, he kept insisting, "looked as if it was stopped in time."

More and more, too, Tony was seized by a feeling that Brian was "evil incarnate." He had confided to Connie that he had "bad vibes" about Brian from the start. He hadn't mentioned it during the interview with Virgil, because he was afraid Virgil would think he was nuts, he told Connie.

"I know this guy has killed people and is still killing people," Tony told Connie. He then proceeded to share more details with Connie about having sex with Brian. Yes, they masturbated, but they also had other forms of sex, he told her, without elaborating.

But Tony said it had felt almost as if he were instructing Brian in gay sex. The only thing Brian was seriously schooled in was sexual strangulation.

"I can tell you this," Tony confided. "The things that this guy is into, there's nothing sexual about it at all."

When the detectives turned their attention north in an effort to find the house to which Brian had taken Tony, they again found themselves on slippery ground.

Tony absolutely did not want to make the drive to find the house: "There's no way in hell you're getting me up there again," was what he told Connie. So Hilzley took the drive alone. A state trooper and bomb squad technician for twenty-four years, Hilzley knew the area well, having spent many a patrol shift driving back roads in both Hamilton and Boone counties, the two areas that fit geographically Tony's memory of where he'd gone with Brian that night.

Starting with a friend of his in Boone County, Sheriff Ernie Hudson, Hilzley described the property and the house. Hudson was sure it had to be in Hamilton County, not Boone.

Westfield and Carmel were in Hamilton. And Hamilton had all the horse farms. They had nothing like what Hilzley was describing in Boone.

Hilzley drove over to Hamilton next, feeling his way back into a ritzy residential area by following Tony's vague directions as best he could.

"You turn left off of 31," Tony had told him. "Then go on for a bit down the road, turn right, which would be north again, and then left, which would be west again. It's down a little lane. It's called something 'Farm.' And it's got those horse fences."

Without street names or actual distances, it was a lot like groping in the dark, but after a few loops leading nowhere, Hilzley came upon an estate in Westfield that seemed to match Tony's description.

Called Fox Hollow Farm, it was indeed set off by a split-rail fence, which was what Tony must have meant by "horse fence," Hilzley figured. A long driveway obscured the house, just as Tony Harris had described.

The problem was, not much else jibed with what Tony had told them about the house. It didn't look overgrown or abandoned. In fact, it looked quite well-tended and very much occupied.

As Hilzley wheeled his white Isuzu pickup truck down the long driveway, he ran through possible stories he could tell the property's owner, settling on his old standby of being a contractor who'd lost his way.

"If I had to recall all the times I've had to lie to get out of a tight spot . . ." Hilzley recalled later, "well, I couldn't. Been there, done that and didn't even get a T-shirt."

When he reached the end of the drive and the house came into view, he whistled. It was big, all right. Not seeing any people around, he stopped for a second, taking in as much of the house and its environs as he could. There weren't any large earth-moving machines in view, like the backhoe or tractor Tony had described as being parked on the property.

He tried to peer in the windows, looking for mannequins or any of the other strange things Tony had mentioned, but the house was a blank face. He saw nothing. No people or animals or cars. No signs of an indoor swimming pool.

Even though he wanted to get out and explore the property, he didn't dare. He was already stretching the law. He headed out the driveway. It was probably the wrong place, anyway, he told himself. Tony had described the place as overgrown, a house in the midst of being renovated. Fox Hollow looked lived-in, finished.

When he told Virgil about Fox Hollow Farm, Virgil sent another investigator to pull three aerial photos of the farm and the surrounding area from the Hamilton County assessor's office.

When they put the photos in front of Tony, however, none of them made much of an impression.

"It kind of looks like this one," Tony said, pointing at a shot of Fox Hollow, the eighteen-acre estate with the winding driveway that Hilzley had found. "But the driveway's not long enough."

Back to square one.

Hilzley decided to check with a state trooper buddy of his in Marion County, Detective Sergeant Ron Bruce. Bruce knew the Hamilton County area. He'd also worked on the Larry Eyler case.

"I don't know of anything going on up there in Hamilton with somebody strangling people," Bruce told Bill Hilzley.

"But it seems to me, there was quite a few bodies dumped in Ohio, off I-70 some years back. Most of them had been strangled. Preble County is handling that. You might want to check with them."

Virgil connected with David Lindloff, an investigator with the Preble County prosecutor's office.

"You've got two gay guys missing?" Lindloff told him. "Well, guess what? I know of twelve murders. And most of them are gay guys from Indianapolis."

Missing gay men from Indianapolis, it seemed, had been turning up dead in western Ohio and Indiana since 1980, Lindloff informed him.

None of the bodies he knew about could be Broussard or Goodlet, however. The last body in Ohio had been found in 1990. So Lindloff wasn't able to help Virgil. But Virgil's information about Tony Harris and Brian Stats could be the break he needed, Lindloff told Virgil. When Eyler had been put away and the killings in Indiana and Ohio had continued, another multijurisdictional task force had formed, like the one that had helped arrest Eyler. They'd even gotten the FBI to do a profile of the type of serial killer who might be responsible for eleven of the twelve murders. But all of their leads had fizzled. Lindloff had even interviewed Eyler in jail through his attorney, Kathleen Zellner. Zellner said Eyler told her Robert David Little, a library science professor and two other men from Indianapolis were responsible for the Ohio deaths. Only one, Little, was tried and acquitted in Vermillion County, Indiana, in 1991. And even though the FBI and Eyler said that at least two others might be involved, Eyler died before making a case against the other men.

Preble County was a pretty small shop, Lindloff explained, just two detectives in the sheriff's department and himself. The I-70 strangler case had been cold for years, he admitted. He had very few leads and even fewer places to turn.

But this Brian character sounded promising. All but two of the victims in Ohio had been strangled with some sort of ligature, possibly a rope or a necktie. It had never been determined which.

Part of the problem had been Indianapolis's gay community, which was an impenetrable wall, Lindloff said. Virgil commiserated, telling him the tough time they'd had recently getting information about Broussard and Roger Alan Goodlet.

Lindloff said he'd been helped considerably by Josh Thomas, a gay journalist who had covered the Ohio murders for *Gambit*, an Ohio magazine that was no longer published. Thomas, who had broken the story about the connected Ohio murders in 1990 and had followed them more closely than most reporters, had since moved to Indianapolis. Lindloff suggested Virgil contact him.

Thomas was a fountain of knowledge, Virgil discovered when he talked to him. The problem was that none of it was good news when it came to Roger Alan Goodlet.

Dozens of men had disappeared outside Indianapolis gay bars since 1980, Thomas told him. In fact, Indy's gay community had almost become resigned to the disappearances. Almost everybody knew or had heard of someone who had disappeared, yet they continued to believe it couldn't happen to them. Thomas was convinced that many of the disappearances were murders. And he felt the responsible parties very well could be two of Eyler's cohorts. One of the men had actually called Thomas while he had been reporting on the Eyler case, probing him in a suspicious way, he'd thought.

Was Brian Smart a friend of Eyler's? Virgil wondered.

It wouldn't surprise him, Thomas told him, although he had no evidence that was true. Eyler had named several acquaintances in open court, but Stats wasn't one of them. Still, whoever this Brian guy was, the police and the court system had been so dense about the Eyler case and about the Ohio murders, Thomas felt—releasing Eyler in 1983, never publicly announcing that a serial killer was on the loose in Ohio—he was certainly secure in continuing to go about his grisly business.

Thomas was bitter, with good reason, Virgil thought after he hung up with the journalist.

When Virgil relayed his conversations with Thomas and Lindloff to Bill Hilzley, that was all Hilzley needed to hear. They were in way over their heads, as far as he was concerned.

"Virg," he told his partner, "you've got to turn this over to IPD. This isn't about a missing persons case anymore. It's criminal. You got people talking about strangling, serial killers. We can't do what the police can do."

Connie had one last suggestion. She wanted to run the case by Wanda, a psychic from Ohio they'd used in the past with some success.

An elderly woman who lived in a small central Ohio village, Wanda had become a personal friend of Connie's after Connie used her on one of the agency's other cases. Wanda, Connie felt, might at least be able to determine whether Tony's thoughts about Brian being evil were well-targeted.

Connie knew placing faith in Wanda and her psychic "visions" was unorthodox and wouldn't sit well with everybody. But Wanda had been right about cases in the past, and Connie wanted her thoughts on this case.

Connie called Wanda and gave her an outline of what Tony had told them. The elderly woman was happy to help.

Tony was right to be frightened about both Brian and the house he had been to that night with him, Wanda told her.

Wanda said when she concentrated on that house she saw a young man "tied to a bed or handcuffed or something. He's spread-eagle. Somebody's kneeling, but I can see him kneeling like from behind with hands around his throat. His tongue is actually out and purple. His face is going blue, but I see flashcubes. But it's like he's staring at 'em as he's dying. There's pictures being—Connie, I'm losing my mind," Wanda broke off, upset. "I don't know what I'm onto."

"No, Wanda," Connie assured her. "You're not. You and I really don't know a whole lot about the seediest side of life. But think about it, if someone is into strangling or being strangled for sexual pleasure, why isn't it possible that the same kind of person would be twisted enough to take photographs of this going on? Do you understand what I'm saying?''

Wanda said she did.

''There's two people in that room with the man,'' she continued. ''It's like there's three people. I've never seen anybody strangled, but I don't think I ever want to. The tongue is swollen, quite long coming out of his mouth. And the eyes, oh.''

It was almost as if Wanda couldn't bear to see any more.

''That's a hell house,'' Wanda warned Connie. ''And the sad part of it, at one time it was a very beautiful home. Don't let Tony go back there. If he goes there again, there will be more people waiting for him. He won't walk away from it next time. I don't like this, Connie. Because we don't know what all might be going on.''

Tony's feelings about Brian being evil were real and very palpable, Wanda added.

''Connie, you run into these people and your soul shrivels,'' she said. ''That's as near as I can describe it. A blind panic fear. You've got to get away from it. It's somethin' you never lose.''

When Virgil heard of Connie's chat with Wanda, he conceded that it was probably time to call Mary Wilson, the Indianapolis police detective who was handling the Jones case. It was a last resort. He hadn't forgotten the reception Tony said he'd gotten from the police when he first called them about Brian.

The word of Virgil, a retired Marion County sheriff, apparently carried more weight than Tony's. Mary Wilson promptly returned his call. She was very interested in talking to Tony, she told him. And to Lindloff. The missing persons cases of the gay men weighed on her, too. She had, in fact, met Catherine soon after Roger went missing and had been particularly touched by her plight.

''I'll take everything you've got,'' Wilson told Virgil.

ELEVEN

A killer who took his victims from the same place month after month, year after year, had to be able to count on a number of things. He needed to be able to blend into the scenery, to be invisible. He needed to rely on the fact that society placed a marginal value on his victims. And he had to depend on the police being too uncaring or too stupid to catch him.

Nowhere in that formula was there room for Indianapolis Police Detective Mary Wilson.

If missing persons offices of large police departments are by nature sleepy closets where underperforming patrol officers are banished to push paper, then no one ever bothered to tell Wilson, a forty-three-year-old officer who throughout her career aspired to a career in missing persons work.

Wilson liked almost everything about missing persons cases. The sense of closure that came with finding people. Talking to family members and friends. Retracing someone's steps. Following every lead to its logical end, like unraveling all the threads in a piece of cloth. It was the purest kind of police work there was, as far as she was concerned. There wasn't a lot of time spent hanging around courtroom hallways waiting to testify, because missing cases usually didn't involve criminals. The majority were teenagers found within the first couple of days after they'd been reported missing. The rest, Wilson found, often turned up with a little bit of hard work on her part. Happy endings. It sounded corny, but that was one of the things she liked most about missings, that people who loved and cared about one another could be reunited.

After joining the force at the tender age of twenty-three, she'd worked patrol for several years in just about every part of the city, learning the streets and the different neighborhoods like the back of her hand. Eventually she'd been moved inside, becoming a detective in the sex crimes division. There were no happy endings there. And the victims' stories inevitably got to Wilson, whose best efforts at distancing herself emotionally from investigations always seemed to fall short. If it was possible to care too much, she was guilty. In 1980, she took a few years off to raise her own children, but work beckoned. She returned to the force in 1983, landing finally in the missing persons department, the job she'd always wanted.

Wilson quickly learned that missings weren't all hearts and flowers. In one case she worked on, a mother of two, gone less than a week, was found dead in a field, murdered by a man she'd spoken to briefly in a bar. When the woman's purse had turned up in a Dumpster a day after her disappearance, Wilson had feared the worst. She would never forget having to tell the victim's roommate. If she lived to be 110, she didn't think she could ever get used to delivering that kind of news.

Unsolved cases were also disheartening. It was devastating to hear from families year after year and not have any news for them. She prided herself on being able to let people know what had happened to their missing loved one, be it good or bad.

In September 1993, Wilson drew the case of Jeffrey Jones, the thirty-one-year-old who had last been seen July 6 outside the Salvation Army detox center in downtown Indianapolis that Vandagriff had read about in the *Word*.

Jones was gay. He also drank too much and abused drugs, a lifestyle that left him perennially on the edge, his family told police. In fact, he had a long scar on his right elbow from being beaten up by a former roommate.

Jones had promised to sign up for a detox program at the Salvation Army. But when Wilson called the Salvation Army, they had no record of his registering in the program. In fact, no one seemed to know who he was or where he might have gone. A month later, a case that smacked of similarities to the Jones case again fell into Wilson's lap.

This time the missing man was Richard Hamilton, a twenty-year-old who disappeared in late July.

Hamilton was the third of five children born to Faye Milk, a forty-nine-year-old truck driver who lived in Indianapolis. Hamilton's father, according to half sister Judy Kelley, had been out of touch with the family for more than twenty years.

According to Kelley, her brother was a "good kid" who could often be found lending neighbors a hand with tasks ranging from mowing the grass to moving.

"He tried to help everyone," she said.

At the same time, she conceded, he had a temper.

"If things didn't go his way, he'd get mad and go stomping off," she said. "But then he'd cool off and come back."

Kelley said Hamilton was a high-school dropout who supported himself doing odd jobs and working at fast-food restaurants. But she wasn't acquainted with many of his friends.

"I never met any of them," she said, "but I know he had quite a few."

It wasn't until Hamilton disappeared that Kelley learned her brother had ties to the city's gay community and that he had been arrested for prostitution. She recalled him bringing girlfriends to his mother's house on two or three different occasions. She also remembered hearing a rumor that "he had a kid somewhere." But many male prostitutes, in fact, aren't gay. Selling their bodies is simply a way to make money.

About the time of his disappearance, Hamilton had been staying on and off with both his mother and another sister. He did have a habit of picking up and leaving Indianapolis with little notice, and sometimes he'd hitchhike to California to visit friends. Other times he'd leave town with no specific destination in mind.

"Richie was a wanderer," Kelley said. "He just wanted to roam."

But, she added, "He'd tell somebody that he was going or he'd call from wherever he was to let us know he was OK. Then he would just pop back unexpectedly. You never knew when he'd show up at your front door."

One of Hamilton's friends also told Wilson that when he was in town, Hamilton kept to a regular routine. He almost always turned tricks from the same two downtown Indianapolis street corners every night: Rural and Washington, and Meridian and North. But no one had seen him at either of those places or heard from him since late July.

Wilson handled the case as she would any other, checking leads, talking to family members and friends. But she found herself operating in two separate worlds. Hamilton's family knew little about his ties to the gay community. And his hustler friends knew almost nothing of his family life.

Complicating matters even more was the fact that Hamilton's missing case was officially supposed to be closed. He hadn't shown up for a court date relating to his arrest on prostitution charges and as a result, a bench warrant had been issued for his arrest. Missing people in those situations were converted to wanteds. In the eyes of the Indianapolis Police Department they were not supposed to be missing anymore, but instead on the lam. Hamilton was still somewhere out there, his family still concerned about him. But for official purposes, Wilson was supposed to forget he'd ever existed. It was not an edict she could easily follow. Leads had dried up on Hamilton and Jones, but the cases of these two missing men stayed with Wilson, always in the back of her mind, unfinished and disturbing.

In June 1994, she had a chance to reconsider the two.

Another young gay man, Alan Broussard, was missing. Broussard, Wilson learned, drank too much. He also frequented the city's gay nightclubs. And like Jones the year before, he, too, seemed to have vanished without a trace.

By now, it was a sad, familiar song, with a refrain Wilson knew all too well.

She discussed the cases with a colleague, Richard Windish.

Windish told her he also had several cases like the ones she described. Two men, in fact, had gone missing in 1993 under similar circumstances: a twenty-one-year-old named Johnny L. Bayer, and Allen Livingstone, who was twenty-eight. Both were wanted on misdemeanor warrants, so Windish had set aside the cases. They'd been collecting dust ever since.

In talking to Bayer's friends, Windish learned that Bayer, too, had hustled downtown. His car, in fact, had been recovered not too far from the city's main library downtown, a vice spot where prostitutes routinely cruised for customers.

Livingstone also had worked as a male prostitute downtown. His mother feared the worst. "He's dead," she'd told police, adding grimly, "His body's probably in the White River," which runs through downtown Indianapolis.

Five men. All gay or with ties to the gay community. Most alcoholics or alcohol abusers. They had to be connected. There was no way around it, Wilson and Windish were convinced.

They went to their commander, Captain Richard Crenshaw, who agreed that the probability was off the charts that so many men in similar circumstances would simply up and disappear without the cases being somehow connected. They needed to find that thread. The best way to do that, Crenshaw decided, was to give the investigation a single shepherd. That person would be Wilson.

The homicide department seemed like the first logical stop for Wilson, who wanted to try mapping out some kind of game plan for finding these men or the person who was responsible for their disappearances.

Homicide didn't take a case unless there was a body. But there were still homicide investigators who remembered Larry Eyler, including Sergeant Detective Charlie Briley.

Briley was the coordinator of the multijurisdictional task force that was trying to solve the twelve unsolved murders of men that had not been credited to Eyler.

Like Eyler's victims, all twelve had ties to Indianapolis's gay community. But their bodies had been found scattered across Indiana and Ohio from 1980 to 1990. Briley had been working with David Lindloff in Preble County, Ohio, and others on those cases. Even though Eyler had been free four of the years in which the twelve were killed—1980 to 1984—Briley and the other investigators on the task force felt confident in separating the twelve from the twenty-three killings Eyler admitted to in jail because of the basic differences in the way Eyler operated and the way the other twelve were murdered.

The victims in the unsolved twelve murders had all been strangled, probably with some device such as a tie or a rope. If they had any trauma, it was usually around the head or the neck. Many had been handcuffed, their lifeless wrists still bearing the lines from handcuffs pulled tight far beyond restraint purposes. But they had not been disemboweled or stabbed repeatedly, like Eyler's victims. Nor did they bear his depraved signature of being found with their pants around their ankles.

This was entirely a separate serial killer, they felt. One with his own bizarre signature: water. There was almost always water where the bodies had been found, serving as both a practical and perhaps ritualistic method of washing away the murderer's guilt. Any small trickle of water would do—a ditch, a creek, a shallow riverbed. In almost every case, the victims had either been rolled or pushed from a bridge, their nude or partially clothed bodies coming to rest sprawled out in a shallow stream. Because the areas were remote and the season usually warm—late summer or early fall—the victims' bodies would inevitably be found bloated and maggot-infested, their faces unrecognizable because of advanced decomposition.

Few visible signs remained that they had ever been living, breathing young men who had once dreamed and loved and been held in a mother's arms. Their existences instead were reduced to a coroner's case number and an impersonal, post-mortem checklist, whose contents became all too numbingly familiar to Briley, Lindloff, and other Ohio investigators.

A typical coroner's report read like the one Montgomery County Coroner Lee Lehman prepared after the autopsy of Steven Elliott, a twenty-six-year-old whose body was found in a shallow creek on August 12, 1989, in Preble County, about a quarter mile east of the Ohio-Indiana state line:

"Regarding the autopsy I performed on the body of an unidentified white male (AC-567-89) the preliminary gross anatomic findings are:

  1. Strangulation:
      A. Contusion of skin and musculature of the neck.
      B. Fracture of the left hyoid bone.
      C. Bilateral fractures of cornea of thyroid cartilage.
      D. Pulmonary edema and generalized visceral congestion.
  2. Bilateral ligature marks on wrists.
  3. Contusions of scalp and right leg.
  4. Abrasions of lower extremities.

It is my opinion that the cause of death on the deceased is asphyxia, due to strangulation."

Briley was so intent on showing the similarities of the murders, he photographed each site the same way, standing on the bridge, looking down, the camera cocked at the same angle. The results, "scared the hell out of me," he remembered. "You could just about stack these up and they could have all been the same scene."

The FBI agreed. When Briley, Lindloff, and the other task force members met with the FBI's Behavioral Science Unit in Richmond, Indiana in June 1991, they theorized that eleven of the twelve victims probably had been murdered by the same person. Dubbed "the I-70 Strangler" in the press, this maniac had a penchant for leaving his victims off small roads not too far from I-70, a major interstate that runs from Utah to Pittsburgh, spiderwebbing through Indianapolis on its way.

Was Wilson looking for the I-70 Strangler?

Briley wasn't convinced. If she were, he had apparently taken a three-year hiatus and now had a whole new way of disposing of the bodies. Small, shallow creeks and bridges had been the I-70 Strangler's trademark. Where were the bodies of the latest victims? Without them and the bridge and water scenes that matched the I-70 Strangler's MO, it was impossible to say whether the new disappearances could be tied to the old murders, Briley felt.

Wilson also turned for advice to Sergeant Steve Garner, who had worked on the task force that had helped nail Eyler. Garner, who had worked vice for years in Indianapolis and who was a familiar face around the gay bars and bathhouses, was a wealth of information, including tips on how to mine the gay community for information. It wasn't anything magic, Garner told her. Just be there. Let them see your face. A lot.

But one of his suggestions stuck with Wilson above all others: If a survivor ever comes forward, it could be your key to cracking the case. Don't ignore anything he might say, no matter how fantastic it sounds.

Garner was thinking of a Chicago prostitute who had come forward to say he'd been drugged, hog-tied, and sodomized by Eyler. When he awoke several days later in the Indianapolis apartment of Eyler's friend Robert David Little, he asked Eyler what he'd given him. Placidyl, Eyler said. He'd put it in his beer.

That had solved a lot of investigators' questions, including how Eyler had been getting hustlers from Indianapolis and Chicago to wander so far from home when their bodies had been found without defense wounds. Eyler was knocking them out with the anti-insomnia drug, ethchlorvynol, whose brand name is Placidyl. Garner even tracked down the Indianapolis doctor who was giving Eyler the Placidyl, one of Eyler's lovers. Wilson thought she had almost as much chance of finding a survivor of the latest monster preying on Indianapolis's gay community as she did of falling headfirst into a wood chipper.

But that was before she'd heard the name Tony Harris.

TWELVE

When it came to dealing with Catherine Araujo, Wilson once again found herself bending procedure a little bit, just to be humane. Catherine lived in Marion County. Her complaint was supposed to be filed with the Marion County sheriff's office. Indianapolis police, in fact, had refused to take a report from Catherine, even after Mary had intervened, calling the district office and pleading with them to make an exception. It did no good. Catherine had been turned away.

But knowing the pattern with the other missings and the fact that this mother was not likely to get any answers soon, Wilson set aside bureaucratic protocol. She decided to take the complaint herself, in person. When she visited Catherine's house that afternoon, she was glad that she had. A visibly shaken Catherine was having difficulty bearing up under the strain of not knowing where her son was.

Mary couldn't think of any words that would soothe. She just hugged her. Hugs, again, wouldn't be found in any police manual as proper investigative protocol, but Wilson was one mother comforting another. Procedure be damned. After listening to Catherine describe Roger, how childlike he had been, and experiencing firsthand Catherine's raw emotions, she was more determined than ever to get some answers for her and for the rest of the families of the missing men.

With a dual mission, she turned to the gay community.

The men who frequented gay bars needed to know that their peers were disappearing. And some of them undoubtedly knew more about the disappearances than they had previously told police. She contacted Ted Fleischaker, publisher of the *Indiana Word*, a monthly newspaper aimed at gay readers.

He was happy to help. For too long, many in Indianapolis's gay community had been engaged in reckless, self-destructive behavior. They needed to know that they were risking their lives. Fleischaker had been ringing out that clarion call for years. Now he got back on his soapbox, writing several strongly worded editorials about the risk of leaving with strangers. The magazine also wrote about Jones's disappearance.

The response to the Jones story was minimal. Wilson got a few tips, but all of them went nowhere.

Then in mid-August, Wilson got the call from Virgil. He told her about Tony Harris and his night with Brian.

She had her survivor.

She wanted everything Vandagriff had, and more. It was difficult not to be overly hopeful. Harris not only might be the key to finding out who was snatching men off the streets of Indianapolis, he also had the possible name of the person who might be responsible: Brian Stats.

She called Harris that afternoon, talking to him for hours on the phone. Between cigarettes, he spilled the story of his night with Brian including all the details he'd confided to Connie. Harris couldn't help getting in a dig about being ignored by the police and the FBI when he'd first tried to give them the information. But he was still frightened of Brian. He might need their help now, too. He agreed to drive up to Carmel with Wilson the following day.

The very tops of the trees were just beginning to change colors when Wilson and Harris set out the next day to retrace the route Tony had taken the month before with Brian. Few would deny that autumn, especially early autumn, is the Midwest's most glorious season. But Wilson and Harris were oblivious to the weather. Harris was scared out of his wits, certain he was going to bump into Brian somehow. Wilson was thrilled at the prospect of getting a break.

They made it as far as Carmel before turning off Route 31. That much of the route Tony knew by heart. Beyond that point, however, he was at a loss. No matter how many back roads they took, he couldn't find the driveway to the estate. Nothing looked right. The house was too new or too visible from the road. The driveway wasn't gravel, as he'd remembered it. The grounds were too well-kept. He found fault with every home they drove past. Mary drove around in circles for three hours, before giving up and taking Tony back to the city.

The trip was deflating, but she still had an ace: the name Brian Stats. That had to mean something. And Brian still had Tony's telephone number. He might call. She put a trace on Tony's phone in case that happened. And she promised herself she would go back to Carmel with Tony when the leaves were off the trees. They would be able to see more then.

In the meantime, she had Tony try to draw a layout of the property and the pool area. If she ever did stumble across the right driveway, with or without Tony, she wanted to know she had the right place.

In October, she went to Ohio to meet with David Lindloff. She wanted to decide for herself whether the I-70 Strangler cases were related to her missings. Lindloff couldn't have been more helpful, taking her to all the small county roads and bridges where the bodies had been found, sharing his case file with her. She, in turn, offered to hook Lindloff up with Tony Harris. But in the end, like Briley, she wasn't convinced their cases were connected.

"It was too much of a stretch," she recalled later.

Not that Wilson thought her missings were alive. She didn't dare hope that. But the Ohio bodies had been publicly displayed, as if the killer wanted to shock, to be found out.

Her missings seemed to be nowhere. Or hidden so well they might never be found.

She turned back to the question of Stats. She found two

Brian Statses in Indianapolis and got driver's license photos of both. But Tony shook his head when he saw them. "Nope," he told her firmly. Neither was the man he spent the night with. Both were too young.

Tony's encounter, then, might have been with someone using a fake name. But why Brian Stats? She pulled all the police computer information on both of the Brian Statses, but it showed little. One had been accused of stealing a car, but the case never went anywhere. The other had no criminal record at all.

Tony and some of the other patrons of the other popular gay bars—Our Place, the 501, The Varsity Lounge—meanwhile, were now convinced that Brian Stats was actually Gary Ray Bowles, a thirty-two-year-old drifter from Chicago with a long history of violence, much of it against gay men. It wasn't difficult to trace their fascination with Bowles, who was wanted for questioning in as many as seven murders in the eastern and southern U.S., and was getting a lot of press in 1994. He was featured on the television show *America's Most Wanted* and in *Newsweek*.

But when Wilson ran down the lead, Bowles's crimes, she found, didn't fit the pattern of her missings. Bowles wasn't a one-night operator. He befriended men at gay bars and moved in with them, sometimes staying for weeks at a time, before beating them brutally, strangling them, and taking their money and credit cards.

Later, she learned Bowles had been arrested in Florida. She called the police there. Given the timelines and locations of the other crimes Bowles had committed, he couldn't have been responsible for the Indianapolis missings, police told Wilson. Bowles wasn't her man.

In late fall, she took Tony back to Carmel. More leaves were off the trees, but it was a repeat of their drive before. Mary went up and down every road, every remote lane and past every estate and home in the city of Carmel and the surrounding area, but each one had something wrong with it. They weren't the right places, Tony insisted.

Not that Tony wasn't still interested in trying to find

Brian. Exactly the opposite. He was obsessed with finding Brian. He volunteered to wear a wire, meet with him, and page him until he responded, whatever it took. He practically begged police to use him as a decoy to catch Brian.

Not too long after he made that offer, Mary got a frantic telephone call. Brian had been to visit Tony at Tony's friend's house, where he sometimes lived.

"How in the hell did he get that address?" Tony demanded. "I don't even stay there all the time. He called me on his cell phone, tells me he'll see me in a half hour. Before I know it, he's at my door. I've never had a utility or phone in my name in my life."

Mary theorized that there might be directories that cross-reference telephone numbers with addresses. But in truth she wasn't sure how Brian had tracked Tony down. Maybe he had followed him. She threw out the cross-reference idea just to help calm him down.

But Tony was far from pacified. He wanted this guy found and put away. Now. "As long as he's out there, I'm not safe and no one else is, either," Tony told her. "This guy ain't right."

After Tony caught his breath, Mary got the details of the visit, which were slender. Brian hadn't stayed long. Tony had told him his boyfriend was sleeping in the back bedroom, which was true. That seemed to have made him nervous, Tony said. He'd wanted Tony to go out with him again, but he'd left without committing to a specific date. Tony had been too upset to get the make of the car he'd been driving or his license plate number.

Brian didn't appear that night or the following day. Another miss.

Months passed without another solid lead on Stats. The holidays came and went. Wilson took Tony back to Carmel, but even in the dead of winter with no leaves on the trees, and the land starkly exposed, the trip was another frustrating repeat of the two times before.

Tony never wavered in his conviction that Brian—or whoever the man was with whom he'd spent the night—

was the man police were looking for. He couldn't seem to help Wilson take it to the next logical step, however: finding Brian so that he could be questioned. The visits to Carmel were obviously in vain. Mary didn't doubt Tony's story, but she was beginning to doubt that his information would ever lead anywhere.

Get me this guy's license plate number, she finally left it with Tony. We'll take it from there. Wilson wasn't sure Tony could come up with the number. But he and his friends had a better shot at it than she did. They were in the bars, and there was the chance that Brian might show up again there. She couldn't even verify Brian's existence.

Wilson was beginning to focus in another direction, anyway, one she hoped would be more fruitful. The man who had reported Hamilton's disappearance, Douglas Anderson, a sixty-year-old computer programmer with a history of mental illness, had been obsessed with Hamilton, she learned from talking to other male hustlers. He was also the customer of another missing hustler, a twenty-seven-year-old named Steven Hale. Anderson, in fact, had bailed Hale out of jail in April of 1994. Hale hadn't been seen since. Sadly, no one had reported him missing. But it was known on the street that Hale was among those who had disappeared.

In March of 1995, Wilson went to Hale's parents and asked them to fill out a missing persons report. Missing reports typically weren't solicited by police—and Wilson didn't relish the chore of having to deliver the news to his estranged parents. But she had no other choice. Hale, who by that time had been gone for almost a year, seemed to have no one who cared enough about him to report that he was gone. She couldn't investigate a missing without a complaint on file. His family filled out the requisite paperwork.

Wilson collected as much background as she could on Anderson, feeding it into a U.S. Department of Justice criminal analysis program known as VICAP (Violent Criminal Apprehension Program). She was assigned a caseworker in CASKU, the FBI's Child Abduction and Serial Killers Unit at the Bureau's headquarters in Quantico, Virginia.

The FBI suggested she fill out a personality assessment profile on Anderson, a lengthy questionnaire that covered everything from early upbringing to present-day marital relations. Anderson's estranged friends were happy to cooperate.

The computer programmer had been living in a house that sat on a wooded lot in northern Marion County when both Hamilton and Hale had turned up missing. The man had since moved, but Wilson arranged a search of the property, walking it with several other police officers and cadaver-sniffing dogs. They turned up nothing.

Days later, however, the search still bothered her. Would they really have known if there had been human remains on that property? Cadaver-sniffing dogs can do amazing things, ferreting out bodies that have been buried as far as twenty feet down. But in the end, she had to admit she wasn't 100 percent secure in the knowledge that between the dogs and the searchers, they had done everything necessary to find any bodies that might have been hidden on the wooded patch.

What if they had completely decomposed, leaving little or nothing for the dogs to smell? She wasn't even precisely sure what they were looking for or even if she'd know it when she saw it. This was too important a case to go off half-cocked.

For similar searches in the future, she wanted a better way of finding remains that might be obscured for some reason, be it burial or advanced decomposition. If there were victims out there in the open, chances are their bodies would have already been discovered. They'd been through a number of hunting seasons since some of the men had gone missing. Thousands of people had tromped the Indiana and Ohio woods during that time. No one had come across a thing.

Wilson consulted a pathologist she knew at Indiana University. He suggested that she contact Dr. Stephen Nawrocki, a forensic anthropologist in the University of Indianapolis's Biology Department. Nawrocki could guide the kind of search she needed to be able to do, he informed Wilson. Not only might he help her find her victims, he was often able to reconstruct the timing and manner of their deaths based in part on the placement and the condition of any bones he found.

Nawrocki's academic credentials were impeccable, Mary learned. He'd worked with state and local police departments, including IPD, for years in identifying human remains. Not only that, the forty-three-year-old anthropologist and associate professor was a nice guy who was devoted to his chosen profession. He'd turned a childhood hobby of picking up Indian artifacts in rural Pennsylvania with his architect father into a lifelong passion. One of only about forty-five board-certified forensic anthropologists nationwide, he instructed police officers and evidence technicians all over the country about how to unearth and identify human remains.

Nawrocki and his lab got about fifteen cases a year, most of them referrals from local police departments or Department of Natural Resources field agents who'd found bones. Many were animal—cows, sheep, deer, dogs. Recently he'd identified a man who'd committed suicide several months earlier from a skull a farmer had found on a riverbank. He was on call seven days a week, twenty-four hours a day, he informed Mary. If she needed him, he was at the ready.

Hamilton's and Hale's trails got cold again after the search. Every time Wilson tried to interview Anderson, he would clam up, refusing to talk. "I wish I'd never made the report," he finally grumbled to Wilson.

Still, she was happy she'd made contact with the FBI and Nawrocki. If the right suspect came along, she was ready.

THIRTEEN

Tony Harris never went more than a day without thinking about his night with Brian. From the moment they met, it was as if there were always an extra presence in his life, unseen but there and hovering, nonetheless. His attempts at banishing thoughts of the other man were sometimes successful during the day. But when he slept or daydreamed Brian's face would appear and he could hear his voice as true and clear as if he were standing right next to him.

Tony replayed his and Brian's night together so many times that he had constructed an elaborate mental catalog of all of the details of those hours. In some ways, Brian and the evening had grown clearer, as tiny bits and pieces of conversation and details of their surroundings bubbled to the surface. But in other ways, the event was becoming hopelessly obscured by Tony's fears about what might have happened to the missing men at Brian's hands, his dark thoughts blurring the edges of his own memory.

The missing men had come to play a larger role in his life, too. In vividly disturbing dreams, he had begun to see Roger Alan Goodlet, Richard Hamilton, Jeff Jones—all the names he knew from Mary and from the MISSING posters in bars, their faces distorted in pain, their arms reaching to him, beseeching him to do something, anything. Sometimes they weren't nightmares at all, but horrible visions conjured up in full daylight.

Tony described his visions to Mary and Connie and any other sympathetic ear he could find. He had become a target for "black energy," he complained to Connie. It got so bad, he was sometimes unable to sleep for days thinking about the dark powers that surrounded him. Whenever he closed his eyes, he saw Brian doing unspeakable things to the missing men.

Against her better judgment, Connie gave him Wanda's number. After talking to the psychic, Tony's fascination with visions and the paranormal went into overdrive. Wanda encouraged Tony to stop drinking, which he sometimes did to excess and which explained some of his disturbing thoughts.

But finally, Wanda's talks with Tony were too overwhelming for the elderly Ohio woman, whose health was fragile. She asked him to stop calling her.

Haunted by the families of the missing men he felt were depending on him, Tony became obsessed with finding Brian and bringing him to justice.

He talked to Catherine Araujo, to friends in the bars, to the police, to other psychics. He locked in on his visions, thinking he could will Brian to be caught. Always he felt the leaden weight of his own guilt. Although he had originally gone with Brian only to get information about Roger, Tony later admitted to himself that he was inexplicably attracted to Brian on some level. He'd had sex with him. And even then—as afraid as he was of him—he still cared about him in some strange way. How could he have feelings for somebody he suspected might be capable of doing such horrible things? Did that make him a monster, too?

Months passed, and nothing seemed to change. Brian was still out there. By the middle of summer 1995, Tony had almost given up hope of ever seeing him again.

Catherine felt equally dejected. Roger had been gone a year and she was no closer to learning what had happened to him than she had been twelve months before.

From the time Roger had begun going out to the bars, she would wait up, often into the early morning hours, anxiously anticipating the sound of him coming in the door.

"That's just what a mother does," she explained one day.

But once Roger disappeared, it wasn't just until the middle of the night that an anxious Catherine remained awake, hoping against all hope that one night she'd hear her youngest quietly letting himself in the door.

"You can't imagine how many nights I didn't sleep at all," she would later say, the accompanying exhaustion almost returning with the recollection.

Days weren't any easier.

"No matter what I did," she said, "it never left my mind."

Mary, in the meantime, was busy working another missing that somewhat resembled the pattern of the others: Michael Keirn. At forty-eight, Keirn was older than most of the other men who had gone missing. And he had a regular job. His employer, in fact, had reported Keirn gone, after a sister who lived in a small Indiana city had requested they do so. He had never gone so long without contacting his family, and they were worried about him. Wilson went to his apartment, talked to his neighbors, and found out that Keirn had ties to the gay community, but little else. Another brick wall.

The atmosphere in Indy's gay bars, meanwhile, was one of resignation. Eyler, AIDS, and now this. There was simply no end to the scourge. Tony and some of his friends—Albert Davis, Rick Rigney, Jeff Wynn—continued to mourn and miss their buddy Goodlet. But they still partied, drank, tried to forget. Sometimes they even tried to wipe out the darkness by going home with strangers.

The band played on.

On August 29, Tony, Albert, Rick, and Jeff were in the Varsity when Brian—or the man who had told Tony his name was Brian—breezed through the front door, just as calmly as if he were sailing into his own home.

Tony's heart almost flew out of his chest when he saw him.

He was as frightened as he'd ever been, but he had a few drinks in him and his closest friends were at his side. There is no way this bastard is leaving this bar tonight with some other poor, unsuspecting sucker, Tony told himself with steely resolve. He turned to Albert.

"That's him. That's the guy that killed Alan. I'm going to distract him," he whispered.

Brian had spotted Tony and had begun to walk his way.

"Get a pencil and paper from the bartender," Tony told Albert in a rush of words. "Go out in the parking lot and stay there until you see him come out. Don't leave until you see him get in a car, and you get his license plate number. Don't fuck up, Albert. Get that number no matter what."

"Hey, guys," Tony suddenly shouted out, bounding toward Brian and grabbing his hand and shaking it. "Lookee here. If it isn't Brian—or whatever his name is." Tony's voice was loud and jovial, and he had a big fake smile plastered across his face. Later, he said he felt like a "carnival barker, making a freak show out of Brian."

"Come shake the hand of the guy who's killing all these guys, strangling them," Tony sang out.

The half dozen or so patrons who heard him above the loud music couldn't tell if Tony was serious, drunk, or just acting out some macabre fantasy. But their eyes were glued to the two men.

"C'mon, Brian, old sport," Tony said, slapping Brian on the back and pulling him roughly toward the center of the bar. "Show 'em the trick you showed me, that thing where you put your hands here." Tony's large hands had encircled Brian's neck.

If Brian was nervous, he didn't show it. Instead his lips were twisted into a tight, thin smile. Some of the other patrons were not only gawking now, they'd moved in to get a better view as Tony put his hands around Brian's neck.

Brian was pulled in. He had an audience.

"No, you do it like this," he said with a shy smile, obviously enjoying the attention. He reached up to put his thumbs on Tony's neck. "You pinch it just enough to shut off the oxygen to the brain," he instructed. "It's such a rush."

Albert, meanwhile, was hiding in the darkened parking lot, waiting for Brian to come out, which he did about a half hour later. But instead of walking to a car, he headed around the block. "What the hell is this all about?" Albert thought. But he waited, heeding Tony's instructions to stay there, no matter what. And in a little while, Brian came back. He looked all around as if to see who was watching him before climbing into a large white truck.

Albert scribbled down the license plate number— 75237A—and ran back in the bar, proudly presenting the piece of paper to Tony.

It was too late to reach Mary, but Tony was so excited he could barely sleep. They'd done it. They'd found this guy. Not the police or the FBI or a private investigator. Just a bunch of gay civilians who were damn sick and tired of being preyed upon.

Both Tony and Rick Rigney called Mary the next day with the license plate number. They'd done good, she assured them. She was proud. And she meant it. She never would have gotten this far without their help. She ran the plate immediately.

It came back to a 1993 General Motors truck registered to a Herbert Baumeister at 5356 E. 72nd Street.

The name Baumeister tugged at her. Where had she seen it before?

Then she remembered. Virgil Vandagriff had mentioned the name when she first began investigating Goodlet's disappearance. When Wilson checked police files she had found a report accusing a Brian Stats of stealing a car from his employer, Herbert Baumeister.

Now it looked as if it wasn't Brian Stats at all that Tony had gone home with, but Herbert Baumeister, Mary thought. If that were the case, Baumeister had used Stats's name when he picked up Tony. Who was Herbert Baumeister anyway? And what other acts was he capable of?

FOURTEEN

Herbert Baumeister had a failing business, a failing marriage, and a criminal record, Mary soon learned. He was a man dodging a hundred different bullets all at the same time. And he seemed to be fairly adept at it. He'd been doing so for years.

Wilson's immediate supervisor Lieutenant Thomas Greene, pulled the civil court records on Baumeister, while Wilson ran a criminal check.

The Sav-A-Lot stores were teetering on the edge of bankruptcy, records showed. There were a fistful of lawsuits filed against Julie, Herb, and Sav-A-Lot's parent company Thrift Management, all from angry creditors demanding money.

Herb's marriage had also hit the skids at least once in the past. He had filed for divorce in 1991, although no one had ever followed through on the petition. Nor was Herbert a stranger to the criminal system. Mary found the 1986 conspiracy charge, noting that fact that Herb had beat the conspiracy rap after a one-day bench trial.

She tracked down Fred Hays, one of the state police officers who'd handled the conspiracy case.

How could he forget Herb Baumeister? Hays chuckled. Not only had he arrested him for insurance fraud, he'd worked practically side by side with the man for years.

Hays was commander of the Indiana State Police Vehicle Theft Section, which was in the same building as the Bureau of Motor Vehicles. Herb had made almost daily trips to Hays's section to visit a woman who worked there. The two would talk and joke for hours at a time, as if neither had anything better to do with their time. Later, when Herb was promoted to head of the audit section, Hays worked with him directly. He was one of the strangest characters he'd come across on the job, Hays told Mary.

It wasn't just the fact that most people thought Herb was gay, even back then, Hays remembered. Nor was he taken aback by Herb's effeminate mannerisms or his flashy dressing habits—both of which made him stick out like a Christmas tree in the dull, gray bureaucratic surroundings of the state motor vehicle offices.

No, it was Herb's response once the insurance scheme had come to light that stayed with him, Hays recalled. Never in his life had he met a man so cavalier about his own criminal behavior.

Hays laid out the details of the party at the lake and the story Herb had made up to save his neck. Hays said he was certain that Moe would have just "taken his licks and never concocted a story" had Herb not been in the picture.

"But Moe worshipped Herb," Hays remembered, "and he was so naive. He would have done just about anything Herb said."

Hays had built a solid case, taking months to do so, collecting the statements from almost a half-dozen coworkers, all of whom pointed the finger at Herb.

But when he had interviewed Herb, telling him point-blank what his coworkers had said, Herb had lied through his teeth without blinking, Hays said.

Herb did admit some of the obvious facts of the case, but then he had just as deftly denied that there was any scheme to collect insurance or that he was involved in any way.

"I had him cold," Hays said, recalling the interview, "but he thought he was smarter than me, and everybody else. He thought he could manipulate the system."

When Hays had pushed him, telling Herb he didn't be-lieve anything he said, "he basically told me to go jump in the lake, that I didn't know what I was talking about.

"He was a hard-core liar. He would never admit to something he'd done, even if he were sitting in an electric chair."

Get the goods on him, Hays advised Wilson. "If it's a choice between heaven and hell and all he has to do is admit his sins, he's not going to do it."

When Herb's case went to trial, his former coworkers—by then he had been fired from his job at the BMV—went "wishy-washy" on the stand, Hays said. Moe, who was granted immunity in exchange for helping police, refused to testify altogether.

"It was between me and Herb, and his allegiance was to Herb," Hays remembered. In the end, Moe took the fall for his friend. Herb walked.

Herbert Baumeister was also a man bent on keeping his family life completely separate from his personal and business existence. Herb had used the 72nd Street address for every official document in his name, from his driver's license to his telephone listing. Even his car registration came back to the 72nd Street address. On the Stats complaint, he had only given a telephone number, even though he was required to give a Social Security number, a date of birth, and a current address. Either the officer who took the complaint hadn't asked for one or Herb didn't comply. There were several other incident reports Herb had filed on shoplifting and other minor matters at the Sav-A-Lot stores, but he always put down the 72nd Street address or none at all.

Mary was beginning to think that Herbert might not have any ties to a house in Carmel like the one Tony had described, when she came across a shoplifting report from 1994 that involved the Sav-A-Lot stores. Herb hadn't filled out this one. Two of his employees had. It listed two separate telephone numbers for Herb. One was the cellular phone Tony had been using, Mary found out. And they had given an address for their boss: 1111 156th Street, Westfield.

It was smack-dab in the middle of the area Tony Harris had described. To double check, Wilson and Greene drove up to Carmel on August 24, 1995, in an unmarked detective car.

"It was a risk," Wilson said later. "We were on private property, but we wanted to be sure."

It was in the middle of warm sunny day, as the two turned in the long driveway of Fox Hollow, following it slowly around to the house. There were at least three cars parked around the house, including a white Land Rover and a van with a "Children's Bureau" logo on the side. Mary also saw several dogs, who began to bark loudly when their car pulled in.

Mary took out Tony's hand-drawn map. It was right on the money. And all the landmarks made sense. The dogs. The driveway. She had the right place, she was certain. But she quickly scribbled down the license plate numbers of the cars she saw just to double check. Just as she did so, she saw a young man watching them from an upstairs window in the house.

"Sorry, wrong address," Wilson called out with a wave, as they pulled away.

When she ran the plates, Mary found out that one of the cars came back to Herb. The other two were registered to Thrift Management.

Wilson's next stop was the Children's Bureau, the charitable organization that was getting a percentage of Sav-A-Lot's sales. She met with Ken Phelps, the bureau's executive director.

Phelps conceded that the Sav-A-Lot stores were in financial trouble. It was terribly disappointing, too, because the arrangement had begun with such promise, Phelps told her. At the beginning, the money was coming in, the stores appeared to be well-managed. And the Baumeisters seemed to have hit upon a division of labor that suited them, Herb managing the location on West Washington, Julie the location near Castleton. All around, it seemed to be a winning concept.

Things had begun to fall apart in the last year or so, he

admitted. "There are lots of problems," he confided to Mary.

Mary asked Phelps not to mention their conversation to the Baumeisters, and he was willing to comply. The bureau was bent on upholding its positive image; they would of course do everything in their power to cooperate with the police.

Mary told Steve Garner, a veteran homicide investigator, about her impressions of Herb from the interviews she'd done with Hays and Phelps. The guy sounded weird, Garner conceded. But she didn't have enough evidence to confront him.

She went back to the FBI agents she'd worked with on Douglas Anderson, the sixty-year-old man who had reported Richard Hamilton missing. They suggested she get a personality assessment profile of Herb like the one they'd done on Anderson. Unfortunately, Hays and Phelps couldn't go back as far into Herb's background as Anderson's friends had been able to. And Mary wasn't yet willing to risk going to people who might be closest to Herb, like Julie or his other family members. But Hays and Phelps filled out the lengthy forms as best they could. Mary sent them to Quantico for analysis.

Of course, the profile that the FBI returned reflected the sketchiness of what they had been sent. It was, however, helpful in that it echoed Hays's description of Herb as a know-it-all, someone who thought he was smarter than the rest of the world. Mary was more convinced than ever that she needed as much background on Herb as she could get before confronting him.

She considered the possibility of talking to Herb's family. Baumeister was not a common name. Maybe a sibling could shed some light on the man. But a check of the area turned up only Herb's mother, Elizabeth Ann. And Mary didn't see a way of approaching her without inadvertently "outing" her son. That seemed harsh, given that she still didn't have anything concrete on Herb, not even a positive ID from Tony.

She had pulled the mug shot taken of Herb after the 1986

conspiracy arrest and presented it to Tony, alongside a handful of other mug shots.

"Hmm." Tony hesitated, studying the photographs, "It could be that one," he said, pointing at Herb. "But I can't be one hundred percent sure."

Mary showed the photo of Herb to several bartenders at the gay bars. They were sure they'd seen him before. Herbert Baumeister—or Brian or Mike or Bill, the names by which they knew him—had been a regular on and off in Indy's gay bars for years, several told her with certainty.

She had one last litmus test before she talked to Herb directly. She wanted to confirm that there was an indoor pool at the 156th Street house. "I had to know," she recalled.

She telephoned the owner of the estate that bordered Fox Hollow. He wasn't home, but she left a message, and he promptly called back.

Yes, he knew the Baumeister family, but not that well, he informed Mary. He'd spoken to them only a few times. But he had been in the house once, before they had owned it. And yes, it did have an indoor pool in the basement.

Why was she asking?

FIFTEEN

Indianapolis Police Detective Mary Wilson became a Sav-A-Lot shopper. She never bought anything, but she browsed often, always with the hope of catching a glimpse of Herb.

For weeks, she popped into the West Washington Sav-A-Lot store at odd times of the day and evening, each time cruising the aisles, studying the layout of the store, her eyes peeled for a tall, thin man who looked like the mug shot she'd seen. He never appeared.

On November 1, she and Greene decided to visit the store together. She hadn't confirmed that Herb would be there, but she hoped he was. She was ready to speak to him. She brought Greene along as an extra pair of eyes.

The two detectives strolled up to the counter and asked for Herb by name. Mary couldn't see him anywhere, but a clerk went and got him from another part of the store. Mary could barely contain her nervousness when he finally appeared in front of them. He was everything Tony had said he would be. Tall and slender, he had that hard, artificial tan Tony had described. And soft pouty looks.

The thin, nervous smile Herb greeted them with grew even thinner after the two detectives introduced themselves. Mary explained that they were there on a missing persons investigation.

"I'd be happy to cooperate," he said in a small, shaky

voice. "But I'm really busy right now. Could you possibly come by later this afternoon?"

"Sure," Mary said with a warm smile. She had been afraid he would come on strong, dominating their conversation and then dismissing them as he had Hays years earlier. But she could see that Herb was far too spooked at the prospect of talking to her and Greene to get up on any high horse. His shaky voice. The frozen smile. He was practically jumping out of his skin.

The two detectives left the store and walked to a restaurant at the other end of the strip mall.

Over lunch, Greene agreed that Herb clearly had been rattled. But they still didn't know why. Still, Mary felt oddly calm when they went back to the store several hours later and Herb led them into his office at the front of the store.

"Well," he said, taking a seat behind his desk, "what can I do for you?" The frozen smile was still there, making Mary feel a little like she was speaking to a mannequin.

She explained that some men had gone missing from gay bars over the last several years and they had reason to believe he might know something about it.

He sat up straight.

"I've never been in a gay bar," he sniffed, with as much indignation as he could muster, given that his nervousness had risen another notch or two. "And I'm not gay so I don't really know why you would come to me, or how I could help you."

"Herb, we know you've been in gay bars," Mary said, her voice even and firm. She wasn't going to listen to his hollow denials. She wanted to make it perfectly clear they weren't on a fishing expedition here.

"We've got the license number from your car when it was parked outside a gay bar," Mary continued.

Herb looked down at his hands, as he nervously fingered some of the papers on his desk. Later, Greene told Wilson that the veins in Herb's neck had begun to throb so rapidly they were practically popping out of his skin when she confronted him about being in gay bars.

Herb let out a big sigh. "Okay, I've been to gay bars," he admitted. "But my wife doesn't know, and neither does anybody else. And I don't want them to."

Herb wasn't kidding. Even at the bars themselves, he kept a low profile.

"I remember seeing him here at least once," Jim Brown, owner of the Metropolitan Restaurant and Nightclub, a gay establishment that caters to upscale professionals, would eventually recall. "He had a real unusual face. He appeared to be much younger than he actually was, and he dressed slightly preppy for his age."

Herb also, as Brown remembered it, acted "kind of strange."

"Normally, people who come in here talk to everybody," he said. But Herb kept to himself.

"Some people, when they come into a gay bar, act like they're afraid of being there," Brown explained.

Herb apparently was one of them.

"He would just kind of glance around," said Brown. "He didn't seem like he was comfortable here."

A Varsity Lounge bartender echoed Brown's comments.

"He didn't seem to want to talk much," Joe Stuart told *Out* magazine. "He was always so quiet."

Yet despite his odd behavior at the bars, Herb often was able to leave unnoticed, either alone or with someone else in tow.

"No one ever notices who leaves with who," Brown said. "There's too many people and it's too dark."

After Herb conceded that he did go to gay bars, Mary wasn't quite sure what to say next, so she just came out and asked Herb if they could search the grounds of Fox Hollow. She knew it was a long shot, but it seemed the only thing to do at the time.

"I'd really like to look at your property and your home," she said.

"Well, I'd really like to cooperate, but you'd really have to talk to my attorney," Herb replied. His voice was cloying and obsequious. She didn't for a second think that he really meant what he said about cooperating. But she had to ask. Suspects had done stranger things.

He got up to lead them out. Mary shook his hand and as she did, she noticed that his shirtsleeve was rolled up and that he had hair on his arm. Perhaps Tony had exaggerated about the hair thing. But then again, it had been more than a year since the two men had spent the night together. If Herb had burned or shaved his body hair, it had had time to grow back in.

Mary told Herb they would call him about the search. Sure, he'd be happy to help, he said again. The tight smile remained frozen on his face.

Mary and Greene both shook their heads when they got back to their car. Greene's impression was the same as hers: Herbert Baumeister was one of the weirdest guys he'd ever met. And he had been nervous beyond belief.

Mary chalked it up to Herb being secretly gay. He'd obviously felt cornered. He had a wife and kids who were clueless that he cruised gay bars when he wasn't with them. He was afraid that she and Greene were going to blow his cover sky high.

Wilson called Herb the next day. He informed her that his attorney was James Voyles. She would have to speak to him about the search. Wilson recognized the name: Voyles was perhaps the most prominent criminal attorney in Indiana, and coincidentally, he was one of the men who had represented Eyler's cohort Robert David Little.

When she called Voyles, however, he said he had never heard of Herbert Baumeister. She called Herb back. He insisted that he had James Voyles on retainer.

For two weeks, they went back and forth like that. Herb telling her to call Voyles, saying he'd just sent Voyles a retainer check, Voyles saying he'd never heard of Baumeister. Finally, one day when she called Voyles, he confirmed that Herb had hired him. And no, Voyles crisply informed her, they could not search Herb's property. Herb must have finally come through with the retainer fee, Mary thought. Damn.

Julie Baumeister was still the unknown factor in the whole equation. That was in part by design. Mary didn't want to approach Julie and "out" Herb unless she had no other choice. She knew that it would create havoc in their marriage and as far as she knew, Julie wasn't tied to the missings in any way.

She talked it over with Greene. He didn't see a way around going to Julie. That had to be their next stop.

On November 30, Mary went to the Castleton area Sav-A-Lot, waiting again at the counter, as a clerk tracked down Julie, just as a store employee had gone in search of Herb several weeks earlier.

Julie looked overworked, frazzled, Mary thought. She knew she would be adding a huge weight to that burden, so she was careful in choosing her words.

"I'm a detective in the Missing Persons Unit for the Indianapolis Police Department," Mary told Julie. "I have some cases that I'm working on where some adult men are missing. I'd like to search your home and property in Carmel."

Julie's mouth hung open. She was shocked, clearly but she wasn't surprised Mary had come by. Herb had told her a short time before that he was being harassed by someone who was falsely accusing him of theft. He told her that if the police contacted her wanting to search the property, she should tell them no.

Julie would later say she had no reason to doubt Herb's word. "As far as I knew," she said, "there was no reason for the police to be searching our property."

The lawyer Herb had retained told Julie the very same thing. She called him herself, Julie said, and came away thinking that if the police truly had enough evidence to suspect Herb had committed a crime that they would be able to obtain a search warrant and wouldn't need anyone's permission to search their home.

Wilson told her she had been misinformed, at least about the theft investigation. "This is not about that at all. This involves the disappearances of several men from gay bars downtown. We talked to your husband because we know he has been in gay bars.''

Julie looked at Mary as if she'd just dropped a nuclear bomb in her lap.

When she recovered enough to speak again, she informed Mary that in any case they could not search her home. She was polite, but still stunned, almost beyond words. Mary gave Julie her card and urged her to call if she changed her mind.

Later, Julie's version of her initial conversation with Wilson would differ somewhat from the detective's.

"The police came to me and said, 'We are investigating your husband in relation to homosexual homicide.' ''

"I was so shocked," she said. "I remember saying to them, 'Can you tell me what homosexual homicide is?' ''

"I wanted to cry," Julie would later say, recalling her reaction to Wilson's revelation that Herb had been frequenting gay bars. "I was mad, too. I wanted to say, 'You're wrong. Leave me alone. No way.' ''

In fact, it didn't really matter what the police said. Julie wasn't buying it. As she once put it, "I didn't believe them at all.''

That didn't stop her, however, from questioning Herb. Stunned by the accusations, as soon as Mary left she called him at the Washington Street store.

"We'll talk about it later," he told her.

At home that evening, Julie told Herb exactly what Mary had said to her. He blamed the whole situation on a disgruntled ex-employee.

"He said that it was nothing to worry about, just someone who had an ax to grind," she would write later in *Indianapolis Monthly*. "It sounded plausible, because as a business owner, I knew the sorts of problems that can arise with employees.''

So Julie didn't press Herb any further.

"I didn't ask him for more of an explanation or an answer," she would later say, "because I knew we weren't going to sit down and resolve this by the next day.''

SIXTEEN

Over the next few weeks, life at Fox Hollow Farm swelled with tension and bizarre goings-on. One of the strangest incidents took place in November, after Wilson had approached both Herb and Julie.

John Egloff, the lawyer who had helped Herb and Julie get Thrift Management off the ground, was sitting in his office late one afternoon when he received a call from Herb.

"He said he had reached the end," Egloff would later recall. "He said there was no way the business was going to survive and that he couldn't stand to see everything he'd worked so hard for taken apart in a bankruptcy. He said that five minutes after he hung up the phone that he wouldn't be here anymore."

Egloff, at first, wasn't sure whether Herb was serious or not.

"Herb, are you talking about what I think you're talking about?" he asked him.

"I know what you're going to say," Herb insisted. "You've been a good friend and I expect you to try to talk me out of this. But my mind's made up. I've thought about this and it's best for Julie and the kids."

After hanging up, an extremely alarmed Egloff called the Hamilton County Sheriff's Department, which immediately dispatched a patrol car to Fox Hollow Farm. Julie, purely by coincidence, drove up at the exact same time. The officer told her about Egloff's call and asked if she could contact Herb on his car phone. She did, and he denied telling his attorney he was going to kill himself.

"Herb said he had talked to me but that he really didn't know where I had gotten the impression that he was going to do himself in," said Egloff. "I thought, 'Well, that's that.' But ten minutes later I got another call from Herb. He read me the riot act for calling the sheriff and for getting Julie all upset. He told me not to call anybody else and slammed down the phone."

Egloff never spoke to Herb again. But today, when he looks back at Herb's initial call, it's not his suicide threat that he most remembers, but rather the enigmatic, rambling, stream-of-consciousness monologue with which Herb ended the call.

"He said, 'There's one other thing,' " said Egloff. " 'There's this guy who's stalking me. I woke up one night and he was trying to strangle me. I hope he doesn't come after Julie and the kids.'

"I took it to mean he had gotten into a fight with somebody," Egloff would later recall. "But I didn't tell the police about it because Herb said he had another attorney helping him with that matter."

From this point on, Herb and Julie's relationship only soured. In early December, according to Julie, Herb blew up at her because he was ready before she was to leave to see one of their daughters perform in a play.

During this time, Julie took out some of her anger and frustration on Mary Wilson. She would call Wilson off and on. Most of the time she was enraged, Wilson said. How could Wilson have destroyed her life like this? How could she tell her something so shocking, so disgusting when she had absolutely no proof?

Finally, Wilson told her about Tony Harris, relating parts of his statement to her. "He's obviously been there," Wilson told her bluntly. "He described your house to a tee."

"I'm a good housekeeper," Julie insisted. "There were never cobwebs in my house," she said dismissively. Tony was trying to set Herb up, Julie maintained. He was a weirdo, a criminal bent on revenge for some strange reason. The bottom line was that the police were not coming in her house, tearing through her things, disturbing her children, all on the word of some psycho.

Another Christmas passed. It certainly couldn't have been a happy one for the Baumeisters, Wilson mused. She knew it was an especially difficult time for Catherine Araujo. Wilson had kept her promise to keep Catherine up-to-date on the progress of her investigation. That included telling her when she'd finally identified a suspect. Ironically, the name Herb Baumeister wasn't one that was totally unfamiliar to her. Years earlier, Catherine had worked for a time as a nurse's aide at Indianapolis's Methodist Hospital, the same facility where Herbert Baumeister, Sr., practiced as an anesthesiologist. Catherine was equally stunned when she learned that Herb and Julie owned the Sav-A-Lot on West Washington, which was less than five minutes away from her home on the southwest side.

"He was almost in my backyard," she thought to herself. "He could have seen Roger a million times."

The past few months had been a roller-coaster ride for Catherine. Her spirits had been momentarily lifted by the lead on Herb, and then dashed when Wilson informed her police weren't able to search the property.

Catherine, though, remained so convinced that a search of Fox Hollow would provide clues that would help the police that she actually considered taking matters into her own hands.

"I kept thinking, 'How can I get on that land?'" she said. " 'How can I look myself? Could I get on the neighbor's land and just walk over there?' Every possibility ran through my mind. But then I thought, 'No, the police have to handle it.' "

She became hopeful again when she learned that Herb and Julie were experiencing financial problems.

"They're going to lose that land," she told Wilson. "Then new people will buy it and they'll let us on it."

But more than anything, Catherine couldn't understand why Julie Baumeister was refusing to let police on the property. It could give the family members of the missing men some measure of peace. Why was she keeping them away?

Months later, Julie would offer at least a partial explanation. At the time, she said, Herb's so-called troubles with the police were the last thing on her mind. Her marriage was falling apart. That, and the couple's continuing business problems consumed her.

Not long after Herb's blowup over the play, he again moved out.

"It was a very emotional time," said Julie. "There was a lot of crying. Both of us probably needed space."

Julie's "need" led her to retain lawyer Bill Wendling and, on January 4, 1996, to file for divorce. Later, she would blame the split on the weight of the money troubles she and Herb were experiencing at the time.

Julie later claimed that she had no intention of following through with the divorce. She filed, she said, "primarily to get Herb's attention.

"I didn't want our family to fall apart, nor did I want out of the marriage . . . I wanted to make him realize that although business circumstances would probably force us to change our lifestyle, we had our family and we had love, and that would sustain us through the bad times."

Still, in court documents related to the divorce filing, Julie alleged that Herb suffered from "serious emotional instability."

Wendling would later say that claim was based on the November 1995 incident in which Herb called John Egloff threatening to commit suicide.

Julie described Thrift Management as being in "serious financial jeopardy." She also requested temporary custody of the children. Wendling said this stemmed not from concerns that Herb might be violent or from suspicions that he might be involved in the men's disappearances, as the police claimed, but from Julie's belief that if Herb didn't have to worry about taking care of the children, he could focus 100 percent on the thrift stores.

Said Wendling, "She wanted to make sure he had an unfettered ability to operate the business."

Finally, Julie asked for a restraining order that would keep Herb from "residing at, approaching, entering, or coming about" their home. According to Wendling, this request was more of a formality than anything else, designed mainly to ensure that Herb, who had already moved out of the house, "wouldn't come waltzing back in.

"There was nothing happening that said I needed to fear for Julie's safety," Wendling said.

But Julie's intentions were clear. As she told the court, the marriage was "irretrievably broken."

Yet, as had happened when Herb had filed for divorce in 1991, that turned out again not to be the case. Within weeks, Herb was back at home. And on January 31, both he and Julie agreed to postpone indefinitely a scheduled preliminary hearing on the divorce.

"They just never got to that point," Wendling would later explain. "They tried to work all that stuff out themselves."

But it didn't always work. Although Herb and Julie were living under the same roof, in certain instances they continued to look to the courts to solve some of their differences.

In February, Herb filed a petition for an emergency hearing. He claimed Thrift Management was "insolvent and in need of better financial management"; that Julie was "not being responsive to the needs of the business"; that she was limiting his access to the children; and that she had control of their bank accounts and would not release them so that he could pay the business's bills.

A judge ordered Julie to appear in court for a March 12 hearing. But according to court records, the hearing never took place. In some ways, it might have been a moot point. Thrift Management was in worse shape than ever before. On March 7, at a hearing at which neither Herb nor Julie bothered to appear, a Marion Superior Court judge ruled Thrift Management must pay the National Tea Co., which

DO YOU KNOW THIS MAN?

OR THIS ARTICLE OF CLOTHING?

If so, contact Sgt. Ken Whisman
Hamilton County Sheriff's Department
773-1872 or 776-9887

Poster distributed by Hamilton County Sheriff's Department.
(John Zich)

MISSING PERSON

HAVE YOU SEEN THIS MAN !!!!!
ROGER "ALLAN" GOODLET

HT: 5'8
WT: 150
HAIR: BROWN
EYES: BROWN

LAST SEEN ON NORTH AND
PENNSYLVANIA

IF YOU HAVE ANY INFORMATION
PLEASE CONTACT DET. WILSON WITH
THE INDPLS POLICE DEPT AT
317-327-6613

Missing poster for
Roger Goodlet.
*(Courtesy of Virgil
Vandagriff)*

Memorial stone
for Roger
Goodlet.
*(Catherine
Araujo)*

Julie Baumeister taught journalism at an Indianapolis high school after marrying Herb.
(Greg Vanzo)

Sav-A-Lot store owned by Herb and Julie Baumeister.
(Fannie Weinstein)

The 501 Tavern in Indianapolis.
(Fannie Weinstein)

The Varsity Lounge in Indianapolis.
(Fannie Weinstein)

MISSING PERSON

ALAN W. BROUSSARD

LAST SEEN
JUNE 06, 1994
820 N. ILLINOIS ST.
INDIANAPOLIS

ALAN IS 28 YEARS OF AGE,
5'8', 140 TO 150 LBS. WHEN
LAST OBSERVED HE HAD CURLY
BLACK HAIR AND A MUSTACHE.

REWARD FOR INFORMATION
CALL 317-248-9295
ALL INFORMATION CONFIDENTIAL
317-327-6613

Missing poster for
Alan Broussard.
*(Courtesy of Virgil
Vandagriff)*

Murder victim
Richard Hamilton.
*(Hamilton County
Sheriff's Department)*

Murder victim Steven Hale.
(Hamilton County Sheriff's Department)

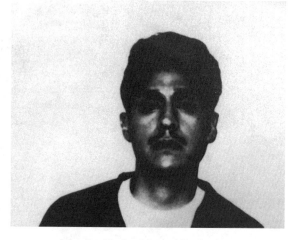

Murder victim Manuel Resendez.
(Hamilton County Sheriff's Department)

Forensic anthropologist Stephen Nawrocki and team.
(Michael S. Green)

Hamilton County Sheriff's Department detective Kenneth Whisman.
(John Zich)

Indianapolis private detective Virgil Vandagriff.
(John Zich)

sublet the West Washington store to Herb and Julie, $167,247.14. National Tea had sued Thrift Management to recover unpaid rent, late fees, real estate taxes, and attorneys' fees. Then just under three weeks later, the Indiana Secretary of State, citing Herb and Julie's failure to file annual reports for Thrift Management in either 1995 or 1996, administratively dissolved it as a corporation.

In the meantime, Wilson continued to work the case. And that same month, she thought she might have found a way around the permission-to-search issue. She had read about an infrared technology that could be used from a helicopter to sense heat changes in the soil. Disturbed soil basically reflects heat differently than undisturbed soil. She and University of Indiana forensic pathologist Stephen Nawrocki could fly over Fox Hollow and possibly get enough indication that there were human remains to be able to convince a judge to sign a search warrant.

The trip with Nawrocki was more than a tad surreal. There they were hovering several hundred feet above the Baumeisters' backyard for several minutes, their infrared sensors aimed at the woods behind the house, while the Baumeister family sat inside their house, oblivious to what was happening outside.

But the results were disappointing. The snow had thawed and the land was muddy, but the brush was so thick, the infrared beams could pick up little.

"Nothing jumps out at me," Nawrocki said, studying the scanner and the land for changes.

"With two years of leaves on the ground, even if there were shallow graves all over the property, you'd have to do a ground search," the pilot replied.

"Too bad you can't get a search warrant to go right on the land," Nawrocki added.

Mary Wilson wanted that more than anything. But it was not to be.

Not yet.

SEVENTEEN

Workers at the Sav-A-Lot on West Washington had always thought of Herb as strange—more odd, though, than dangerous. But from January 1996 on, two months after he was first approached by Wilson and just as his marriage was officially falling apart, his behavior became even weirder.

Alpha Kerl began working for Herb around that time.

"He was very fussy and particular about what he wanted me to do," said Kerl, who worked in the back of the store sorting and hanging donated clothes.

"I had been in the army, so I knew how to follow orders," she added. But other employees couldn't live up to Herb's exacting standards. In fact, said Kerl, five workers quit during her first three weeks alone.

"Either they couldn't deal with his way or they got pissed off at his way and quit," she said. And according to Kerl, Herb believed "his way was the only way to do it."

Herb was especially hard on workers in whom he detected what he considered weakness. Kerl can remember him telling one of her coworkers that she had to hang exactly eighty-five pieces of clothing an hour. Not eighty-four. Not eighty-six. But eighty-five.

"I would have said I couldn't do it," Kerl said about what she considered to be Herb's unfair demand. The woman tried to keep up, but Herb still wasn't satisfied.

"He would come back and tell her what she was doing wrong," said Kerl.

She quit after a week.

Kerl can remember another female worker Herb harassed, too. He would tell her she was fat and sloppy and make fun of the fact that she was still living at home with her mother. When he would look at her, Kerl said, "You could almost see those thoughts going through his head."

Debbie Milton, another West Washington Street employee, said she remembered Herb having little sympathy for another worker who needed to take time off because she was ill. He fired her, according to Milton, even though she returned with a written excuse from her doctor.

"I was right there," Milton said, recalling the exchange between Herb and the young girl. "He got really angry. He said he didn't have time to mess around with someone who didn't want to work."

Herb, in fact, was such a taskmaster that he wouldn't even give Kerl, one of the few employees he seemed to appreciate, time to straighten up the back work area, which Kerl described as a pit of filth.

"Everything was so dirty all the time," she said. "Everywhere you looked there were mountains of garbage bags. It was like working in a garbage heap. But he never gave us any time to throw away the trash or to clean up the work area or even the bathroom. Our job was to get as much merchandise as we could out on the floor."

Herb, himself, however, according to Kerl, was almost neurotic about the mess.

"He would never do anything that might get him dirty," she said of Herb, who usually came to work dressed in jeans with a designer polo shirt—usually Izod—tucked neatly into his pants.

"He would sort through clothes sometimes, but he would never touch any that were nasty or dirty. If he came across any, he would just pick them up daintily with his fingertips, and if he got any dirt on him, he'd go change his clothes. He wouldn't even pick up a piece of paper if he saw one on the floor. He would make someone else do it.''

Herb displayed his snobbish tendencies in other ways as well.

"He was disdainful about donations that came in from the immediate neighborhoods," said Kerl. "He didn't want people from those neighborhoods coming into the store either. He just had this kind of condescending attitude toward everybody and everything.''

But in instances where someone stood up to Herb, he usually backed down.

"If he wanted you to work on a certain day and you said, 'No, I won't,' he usually backed down," said Kerl. "And anytime there was a customer who was loud or abrasive, he made a cashier handle it. He wasn't the type to stand up to anyone stronger than him.''

By April, though, Herb wasn't around enough to act much of any way. Sometimes, on Thursdays and Fridays in particular, he'd disappear for extended periods of time in the middle of the day.

"He would say he was going to the bank to make a deposit," said Milton, "and then not come back for three or four hours.''

"As time went on, he was mostly gone," Kerl said. "He'd be in for two or three hours and then gone for five.''

By early June, Herb was stopping in only briefly once a day, then he'd disappear. He would come in, say he had to go to the Castleton store or to a business meeting, then take off and not come back. And on weekends, he wasn't showing up at all.

"He might call once, but other than that, I was on my own," said Ivy Phelps, who was asked by Herb to open the stores on Saturdays and Sundays. "I thought it was strange, but he'd just turn the keys over to me. He didn't even show me how to use the alarm system. He told me not to worry about it.''

After a while, Phelps said, Herb became such an absentee owner that "it started to feel like it was my store.''

Even when he was there, Herb would spend most of his

time in his enclosed office near the front of the store and instruct workers to tell anyone who called that he wasn't there. Many of the callers, according to Phelps, were men.

"I just figured they were bill collectors," she would later say.

Sometimes Herb stayed out of sight for great lengths of time.

"He'd be holed up in there with the door shut for hours," said Phelps. "He'd say he was doing paperwork."

Not surprisingly, rumors started flying among workers. Those who had been watching him over time were convinced he was drinking excessively.

"He'd come in the morning and sometimes you could smell alcohol on his breath," said Phelps. "He was still shaving, but he'd come in looking kind of like a bum. His clothes just didn't look as neat as they normally did."

"He started acting looser than before," said Kerl. "He wasn't as stiff."

He also started wearing a baseball cap daily. Kerl suspected it was because "he was staying out all night and wasn't getting home to wash and comb his hair properly." Too, his pupils were often dilated, and one worker told Kerl that empty and half-empty bottles of liquor were strewn about Herb's office.

Another worker, meanwhile, told the *Indianapolis Star* that Herb and a male friend would drink on Sav-A-Lot property during work hours. Herb, thinking he was safely hidden from anyone who might have been watching, even called the private drinking spot "Waco," after the notorious Branch Davidian compound in Texas.

Word also began circulating around the store that Julie had filed for divorce. Herb didn't say anything about the proceedings, but did complain more about things such as his belief that the Castleton store was getting the crème of the donations.

"That store always gets the good stuff," he would whine. "Why do I get the junk?"

Kerl met Julie only once, and it was a rather bizarre meeting, to say the least. One Saturday, Herb asked Kerl if she could come in to work for a couple of hours. She agreed. That same day, he introduced her to a woman she had never seen before.

"This is Julie from the Castleton store," he told her, speaking as if she were just another employee.

"There was nothing that would have given me the impression that they were anything more than coworkers," said Kerl. "When I found out she was his wife, I said, 'You're kidding.'"

Julie, she said, seemed cold and distant. But, said Kerl, "I just figured she was pissed off about having to work on a Saturday."

Herb's relationship with his kids, on the other hand, seemed relatively normal to Kerl and other Sav-A-Lot employees.

"He was always doting on them," Kerl said of Marne and Erich, who sometimes accompanied their father to the store. "He would let them have anything they wanted that was not already out on the floor."

And when he talked about his children, Kerl said, his tone was almost wistful.

"One day, he asked me if I enjoyed my kids more when they were little than when they were teenagers," Kerl said. "He was telling me how difficult it was to give them what they wanted and to be there with them."

"I feel like all I do is work and that I'm missing out on what my kids are doing," Herb told Kerl once.

Erich, at least, seemed to have an acute perception of what his father's work life was about.

Phelps said she can recall talking to him one day when he came by the Washington Street store.

"Are you going to take over someday?" she asked him.

"No," Erich responded. "I'm going to go to college and do something else with my life."

By May, according to Kerl, rumors were rampant that the store was going to close as a result of Herb and Julie's divorce proceedings. And Herb, by the beginning of June, had essentially become a no-show on the job. Julie, it was clear, had no idea where he was or what he was doing, either.

"She would call and say, 'Where is he?' " Kerl recalled. But no one at the store knew what to say.

"It would be two o'clock," she said, "and we wouldn't have seen him yet."

EIGHTEEN

Her helicopter trip with Nawrocki having turned up no evidence, Wilson wasn't sure what her next move was. Julie still called occasionally, but usually it was to rail at her for how she had destroyed her marriage. Sometimes Wilson thought she could hear the seeds of doubt in Julie's voice. Herb was in and out of the house, she was doing all the work. Her frustration with him seemed to have reached the breaking point. But just as quickly she fell back into a pattern of blaming all her problems on Mary.

"I got really irritated with the police," Julie would later say without apologizing. "I didn't know anything. But what really annoyed me was that they never went back to see Herb."

She did, on the other hand, explain how one day she approached Herb and asked him again about what the police were saying. He again told her he had no idea what they were talking about.

Even when Wilson got tired of listening to Julie's haranguing and was tempted to hang up on her, she always stopped herself. Everything Julie told her was new information.

"I never knew what she was going to say next," Wilson remembered.

What was predictable, though, was that with all of their personal and business troubles, Herb and Julie's reconciliation had little chance of lasting. It didn't. By the beginning of June, the situation had essentially reached a point of no return. Herb and Julie weren't even talking. They were simply coexisting under the same roof.

Meanwhile, Thrift Management was on the verge of going under, partly as a result of the Children's Bureau's decision to end its relationship with the company. From 1988 to 1994, the bureau's share of the stores' income amounted to roughly $350,000, according to Executive Director Kenneth Phelps.

"That did a lot for a lot of children," he said.

But by 1995, profits had begun to dip. Phelps attributed Thrift Management's financial difficulties at the time to what he called "bad business decisions." Concerned about the company's fiscal health, the bureau, at the end of 1995, rewrote its contract with Herb and Julie. Under the new contract, the amount of advance notice the bureau would have to provide if it wanted to sever ties with Thrift Management was reduced from six months to thirty days.

In May 1996, sensing that a turnaround was unlikely, the bureau terminated the contract altogether.

"They just weren't going to make it," said Phelps. "It was obvious they were going bankrupt."

Curiously, when Phelps informed Herb of the bureau's decision, Herb was apologetic.

"The day we said, 'It's over,' he left a five-minute message on my voice mail," Phelps recalled. "He said, 'You know, we really tried to make it work. I really thought we could pull ourselves out of this.' "

What Herb and Julie couldn't pull themselves out of was the mess they themselves were mired in.

"We avoided each other," Julie would later say, explaining the status of her and Herb's relationship at the time. Yet they still weren't ready to give up on Thrift Management completely. According to Julie, she and Herb agreed she would be responsible for the Castleton Sav-A-Lot while he would run the West Washington store. Neither, however, was able to reverse the stores' decline.

"We were working our tails off," Julie said. "But we both knew ultimately it wasn't going to work out."

That the stores had no future quickly became apparent to Sav-A-Lot workers, too. According to Alpha Kerl, the West Washington store didn't open at all on either Monday, June 17 or Tuesday, June 18. Herb told her it was because the store's air conditioning system had broken down and that the landlord was refusing to pay to have it fixed. Then, on Wednesday, the 19th, he called Kerl again. He told her she should come to the store's parking lot at 5 P.M. on Friday, the 21st, to pick up her paycheck—she was owed a total of $304—and asked her to call other employees to give them the news.

That Friday afternoon, Kerl and three or four other Sav-A-Lot workers came to the West Washington store's parking lot to meet Herb, but he never showed up. And when they went inside to find other workers' telephone numbers to bring them up to date, they found the electricity inside the store had been shut off.

Wilson, meanwhile, continued to dig, and her tenacity eventually paid off. Just when she needed it, her investigation got a shot in the arm from an entirely unexpected source: Bill Wendling, Julie's lawyer.

"I can't tell you everything right now," Wendling told her over the telephone one day in the late spring, in a call that came completely from out of the blue. "But I wouldn't give up on this lead if I were you."

Mary could hear her heart beating after she hung up with Wendling. He knew plenty, but what? Did Julie have videotapes or photographs of Herb with other men? Possibly with some of her missings?

Julie, it would turn out, had begun to question the veracity of what Herb had told her about the cops' interest in him. Their personal problems had left her wondering whether he was the person she had always believed he was. It was rapidly becoming apparent he wasn't, and if that was the case, maybe he was lying about the police, too. Did that mean she should be fearing for her and her children's safety? The thought started to cross her mind.

Julie told *People* magazine that she began asking herself, "What if the police are right and I'm wrong?"

According to Julie, the simmering situation finally exploded when Herb informed her that he intended to take the children for physical exams on June 20 and the following day would deliver them to a six-week summer program at the Culver Military Academy in Culver, Indiana.

Julie hit the roof. She immediately filed requests for an emergency hearing regarding custody of the children and for an order preventing Herb from enrolling them at Culver.

"The marital estate," she argued in court papers, "cannot support the Husband's unilateral decision to put the children in Culver." As evidence, she cited Herb's own February filing in which he claimed Thrift Management was insolvent.

Julie's filings also stated "the parties' financial matters are out of control" and asked for a preliminary hearing "to determine the method of payment of the parties' mortgage and utilities."

In fact, said Wendling, the couple's finances were in such bad shape at the time that the electricity at Fox Hollow was about to be shut off.

Then came the final blow. No longer willing to trust Herb on any level, Julie called Wendling and asked him to contact Wilson on her behalf. She was ready, she told the attorney, to let the police search the property.

On Sunday, June 23, the first day of Wilson's work week, she came in to find a message from Bill Wendling on her answering machine.

"Julie wants to talk to you," the attorney had said. "Call me."

On Monday morning, she reached Wendling at his office. She'd be happy to talk to Julie, she told him. But her boss, Tom Greene, was out of town. How was this Thursday, when he'd be back?

"You need to come up here today," Wendling said, his voice grim. "I feel I'm at liberty to tell you now. Julie found a skull on her property a couple of years ago."

NINETEEN .

All sorts of weird calls came in to the Hamilton County Sheriff's Department, so Captain Tom Anderson didn't raise an eyebrow when he got a request from the Indianapolis Police Department on Monday, June 24, 1996, to lend a hand in investigating what might be human bones on a horse farm near Westfield on the county's southwest side.

Anderson had just finished eating lunch at the jail. A department tradition for over a decade, deputies paid one dollar for a tin plateful of the same home-cooked basics that the prisoners got. Sheriff Joe Cook's mom, Nurita, did the cooking herself. The deputies figured the prisoners had no room to gripe about the quality of jailhouse food since the guys with the badges ate the same stuff themselves.

Nor could prisoners complain about their surroundings. Hamilton's state-of-the-art law-enforcement complex, built in 1993, cost more than $15 million. Equipped to hold up to 288 prisoners, the jail boasted of a lobby with skylights and attached modern offices.

County leaders were only keeping pace with area residents. Hamilton was Indiana's fastest-growing, wealthiest county, its median family income of $87,168 more than twice that of the rest of the state's. The average home went for $106,500. People from out of state had moved to Hamilton in droves in the 1990s, pushing the population to 147,719 in 1997, up 36 percent for the decade.

It was easy to understand the attraction. Just a swift twenty-five-minute highway commute north of Indianapolis, Hamilton still had a lot of what many Indianans loved about their state—green space. More than half of Hamilton's 398 square miles was farmland. The rest was dotted with picture-perfect older communities whose quaint, renovated central business districts made them postcards of suburban middle America.

Nowhere was the bucolic, upscale tone of Hamilton more apparent than in the southwestern towns of Carmel and Westfield, home to the county's wealthiest residents. Indiana-born talk show host David Letterman bought a home for his mother in that area. The late owner of the Indianapolis Colts, Bob Irsay, also made his home there. Carmel and Westfield had more one-million-dollar-plus homes than any other cities in Hamilton County, many of them the multi-acre estates of gentleman farmers.

Detective Jeff Marcum had taken the call from Wilson at 12:45 P.M. that afternoon. She had been polite but not specific, telling Marcum only that she was investigating some missing persons cases and that the search had led her to a house on 156th Street near Westfield. One of the owners of the property was willing to let them search the property.

She was calling out of professional courtesy, she informed them. It was Hamilton's jurisdiction. They could come along as backup if they chose to.

As head of investigations, it was up to Anderson, a forty-four-year-old former construction worker with forearms the size of ham steaks, to see if Wilson had found anything worth chasing. He was skeptical.

"This is probably bullshit," Anderson told Marcum, as they pulled into the McDonald's at which they'd agreed to meet Wilson, about ten miles southwest of their Noblesville headquarters. "They're probably just animal bones."

Like many of the Hamilton County sheriff's deputies over age forty, Anderson had started his career with the department as a jailer. The Indiana native could fix about anything, but he gave up construction work because he got tired of starving all winter. Not by formal education but by the sheer dint of his bullheaded personality, he had managed to climb the ladder at the department, becoming an investigator in 1988 and head of the ten-member investigative team in 1995. He was a plain-speaking sort who favored self-starters. He didn't want to do any butt-wiping or hand-holding.

Anderson's boss, Sheriff Joseph Cook, was young, handsome, and clean-cut, a Calvin Klein ad in a uniform, only he wore blue jeans much of the time. Cook, who was only thirty-nine when he took office in 1995, had practically been born to his elected post, his father having been the sheriff before him. Cook respected the guys who'd come up under his old man. Anderson was one of them.

Anderson had given Cook his skeptical assessment of the bones run before he'd left, ducking quickly into Cook's office and telling him what was up.

"This is probably nothing," he'd informed his younger superior, telling him what little he knew of the case. "We're just helping out IPD."

Over sodas, Wilson expanded on the abbreviated version of the case she'd given Marcum over the phone, including the fact that she was investigating the disappearance of at least seven men. She also told them about Tony Harris's night at Fox Hollow and Julie's sudden reversal to let them search the property. Julie now suspected that there were human remains on the property, she told them.

It was clear to the two detectives that Wilson had been through hell and high water to get this far. Anderson didn't think she was going to learn squat about a missing male prostitute by searching an estate in Westfield, but she seemed determined to push on.

What the hell, he reasoned, rolling down the window of his unmarked Crown Victoria, whose pink champagne color had made him the butt of colleagues' jokes about having a "Mary Kay" car. Unbeknownst to Anderson, several detectives had even put a sign for the cosmetics queen in his rear window once. He drove around for a week that way before he discovered the practical joke. But those jokers were trapped in the office, he told himself. He was able to enjoy the warm summer day outside. It beat the hell out of sitting behind a desk.

Wilson led the way to 156th Street, a route she'd obviously traveled before. Anderson knew the area, too, from his patrol days. There was a whole lot of nothing over there, as far as he was concerned. Most of the calls he'd responded to in that area had been for burglar alarms tripped by maids or windstorms—"bullshit" runs, to use one of Anderson's favorite words.

When Marcum saw just how impressive the exterior of the Baumeister house was, he was "blown away," he said. "It just didn't look like the kind of place where what Mary was talking about could have happened," the forty-one-year-old detective remembered.

But when Julie answered the door and led them to the back part of the house, the lofty impression Marcum had gotten from the home's exterior quickly fizzled. It was like going behind the scenes of a movie set. Nothing was as golden as it looked up there on the big screen.

The interior of Fox Hollow paled in comparison to the impressive grounds outside. In addition to a mind-numbing amount of clutter and a lack of basic, regular housekeeping, there were oddly placed items throughout the house. Two articles in particular caught Marcum's eye: A Christmas tree, fully decorated, and fake holly wrapped around the staircase's banister.

Christmas in June. Lovely, he thought.

Julie led them to the kitchen, where Bill Wendling was waiting. With handsome oak cabinets, flowered valances and copper pots hanging over a center island, the kitchen looked more warm and lived-in than the other rooms. The family obviously spent a lot of time there.

Julie launched into the story about Erich's finding the skeleton and how she was now worried that there might be more to her son's discovery than Herb had originally told her.

Anderson noted that Julie had allowed herself to dismiss the bones easily enough at Herb's behest when Erich first found them. Now she's bringing this to our attention, more than a year later? She was probably just using this as a hammer in their divorce, he told himself. He'd heard of some strange accusations between warring couples, but this had to be one of the most bizarre, he thought.

"At divorce time, all the dirty laundry comes out," Anderson would say later.

Julie went on to explain how shocked she had been to hear of Wilson's investigation, but that she now suspected it might have some foundation.

"Why call us now?" Anderson finally had to ask, his Southern-tinged mid-Indiana drawl dripping with impertinence. He couldn't help himself.

"I want to get my son back," Julie snapped. "He's with my husband." She explained that Herb had taken Erich to his mother's cottage, and that she was worried about fifteen-year-old Erich's safety.

"Why? Do you think your husband's going to hurt him?" Anderson asked.

"No," Julie admitted. "I just want him back."

That didn't make any sense to Mary Wilson unless Julie's stone wall of belief in Herb's innocence was starting to crumble.

Anderson just thought Julie was overdramatizing the situation in order to get the upper hand in a custody battle. If you've got no fear that he's in danger, why not just let him stay on vacation with his dad, lady? Anderson was thinking. But he bit his lip, and kept his mouth shut.

"What do the kids know about this?" he asked instead.

"They know a little," Julie replied.

The conversation dried up. Unspoken until then had been what they were all there for in the first place. Not one to beat around the bush, Anderson finally got the ball rolling.

"Let's get a look at these bones," he announced, slapping his knees and standing up, his signal to head outside. Julie and Bill led the way, out the back door and down the steps to the backyard, with Mary Wilson, Marcum, and Anderson following behind.

A few yards beyond the cement patio that led to the pool area in the basement, Julie pointed to a burnt spot about two yards wide. The weeds and grass that covered the rest of that area had been burned away. It looked like the remains of a small brush fire, with a charred log and other grass and debris marking its center.

"The skeleton was somewhere around here," she said, as if that summed up the entire situation.

Anderson and Marcum, however, just exchanged perplexed glances. They didn't have a clue about what she was showing them.

"I'm looking at this burn pile and I'm not seeing anything," Anderson recalled. "And I know Jeff's not seeing nothing. Then we both knelt down at the same time, and Jeff just picks up this bone."

It was about a foot long, brown from having been burned, but otherwise complete.

Julie let out a gasp. "Oh my God," she exclaimed.

It was just about the phoniest expression of surprise he'd ever heard in his life, Anderson would say later.

Kneeling and looking closely, then, Anderson's and Marcum's eyes began to focus on what they realized were several other large bones on top of many, many more tiny, charred pieces of bone, most of them no bigger than their thumbs. And there were also pieces of what looked like teeth that had shattered into little pieces.

The bones and teeth didn't end at the burn pile. After Marcum took photographs of the bones in the burned area, Wendling, who was standing just a few yards from the charred circle, looked down at his feet, leaned over, and picked up several teeth.

"I don't think I'll ever forget it," he said later. "I almost wished I hadn't gone back there." His eyes newly attuned, he was able to point out several other bones and bone fragments.

"There's some over there," he said. "And over there."

Once Anderson and Marcum realized what they were looking for, they, too, began to spot bones.

"They were all the over the place," Anderson remembered.

Marcum, in fact, spotted a bone about five inches long lying on top of the ground not too far from the burned spot.

"Look at this," he whispered to Anderson, picking it up and turning it over in his hand.

Both men's eyes widened and they exchanged glances. But neither said a word, as Marcum handed the bone over to Wilson, who slipped it into a paper shopping bag with the other bones from the burn pile.

The detectives scanned the slope for more bones, while Marcum documented as much as he could in photographs. Julie, meanwhile, did not want to dwell on the topic of the bones at that particular moment.

"It was all a blur," she would later say, looking back.

Her immediate concern was her son. She continued to press them for a promise that they would return Erich to her.

"I want Erich with me," she started up again. "When can you go get him? I want to make sure my children are going to be safe after this. Can you guarantee that?"

"Let's just see what the bones guy says about these," Anderson responded, his way of trying to pacify her. He wasn't ready to make any promises, a fact that seemed to make Julie all the more nervous.

She began stomping in and out of the house as the detectives collected the bones, intermittently shouting out questions, most of them about Erich.

"Are you bringing him back?" she demanded.

"We've got no pickup orders, no custody papers orders," Anderson finally told her flatly. "There's not really much we can do without those."

Anderson, actually, was more interested at the time in finding out exactly what kind of bones they had. He and Wilson agreed that Wilson would take the bones they'd collected to Nawrocki. Wilson would call Anderson later that evening to give them the forensic anthropologist's verdict.

Anderson laid his cards on the table for Julie. He knew Julie had stonewalled Wilson in earlier attempts to search the grounds. She was upset again now. He just hoped Julie would stay in their court long enough for them to figure out what kinds of bones these were.

"If those are human remains, we're going to have to come back out here tomorrow," he told her.

Do what you have to do, she told Anderson. She just wanted her son back. She gathered up daughters Marne, sixteen, and Emily, eleven, who had, until then, remained in another part of the house.

They were going to the store, Julie announced. They still had work to do—a burden she was shouldering alone, she reminded them. They wouldn't be home until late that night.

As he drove back to their Noblesville headquarters, Anderson and Marcum talked about the bones. How could they not? Weird calls were one thing, but this was entirely beyond the pale. Anderson was still fairly convinced that what they were looking at were animal bones. Head of investigations for less than two years, he had seen bodies in a state of advanced decomposition. Most patrol officers have had the unfortunate experience of coming upon a death in a home that has gone undiscovered for too long. But none of Anderson's training prepared him to differentiate between human and animal remains in a skeletal state, especially when most of what they had here were charred fragments.

And the idea that human bones could be found scattered around the backyard of a million-dollar mansion in central Indiana like so much grass seed—well, there was no way was he was going to buy into such a bizarre, far-fetched notion without an expert's confirmation.

Still, it bothered him that while Bill Wendling had treated the bones as if he'd already inspected the area and mentally marked significant places, Julie had noticeably distanced herself from any knowledge of what was in her backyard.

On the one hand, he couldn't blame her. It was a repugnant enough idea—that there might be human remains just yards from her patio, as if some careless cannibal had simply tossed them over his shoulder after a backyard barbecue.

But Anderson couldn't shake the feeling that Julie knew more about the presence of the bones than she was saying.

"It wasn't like I thought that Julie had anything to do with how the bones got there. But I thought she'd already seen them," Anderson said. Why hadn't she simply pointed them out in a straightforward manner?

"If any other person had found those bones," he said later, "they would have just taken us out there and pointed and said, 'Here. Here they are.' "

As convinced as Anderson was the bones were animal, Wilson, meanwhile, was certain they were human.

Like Anderson, Wilson had no special training in identifying human remains. But unlike her law-enforcement counterparts from Hamilton, she had heard the fear in Tony Harris's voice. She'd seen firsthand how nervous Herb had been and how he had done everything in his power to keep her off his land, including lying to Julie about their investigation. Now she knew why.

That morning, Wilson had asked Nawrocki to stay late at his basement laboratory at the University of Indianapolis in the event the Fox Hollow search yielded any results. Nawrocki's laboratory light was still on when she arrived that evening. He took the paper grocery sack Mary had handed him and emptied the contents on one of the rectangular black-topped tables that lined his lab.

To the trained eye, the difference between human and animal bones is rather obvious. There are a thousand or more variations between the two, all of which were second nature to Nawrocki. The flat, broad shape of a human vertebra, for example, our bowl-shaped pelvises, or our large, mobile thumbs are just a few of the human nuances that an expert like Nawrocki could spot in a flash. And if human bones are giveaways, human teeth are the forensic anthropological equivalent of first-grade math. They're simply unmistakable to the trained eye.

It took only an instant, then, for Nawrocki to verify that the bones and teeth in front of him were human. The bones they had collected, in fact, made up the components of a human arm. The large complete bone Marcum had picked up from the burn pile was a humerus, an upper arm bone. The two smaller ones were an ulna and radius. Both were broken and burned, and it was impossible to determine if they had come from the same person's arm, but there was no denying they once held human flesh.

Nawrocki looked across the table at Wilson, his blue eyes locking with hers. "They're human. They're recent. And they've been burned." The dry assessment, devoid of histrionics, was vintage Stephen Nawrocki. The young scientist wasn't short on emotion. But to him, bones were a puzzle to be deciphered. It would have been almost unbearable to work on the Baumeister case, even from the very beginning, without a certain level of detachment, he said later.

"When you stepped back and put soft tissue on these bones, you started to see people's faces—well, you just couldn't," Nawrocki said, his voice trailing off.

Wilson called the Hamilton County coroner, Joe Roberts, who by state law had to be notified of any deaths within his purview. And Anderson.

"We've made a positive identification, Captain," she told him. "They're human."

"Okay," Anderson responded in as calm a tone as he could muster given the fact his mind was racing about a million miles an hour.

"We'll be out there first thing tomorrow morning," he told Wilson. "I'll find out what we have to do on our end. You take care of yours."

Nawrocki and two of his assistants would also meet them at Fox Hollow and do a more thorough search of the property,

Wilson and Anderson agreed.

Anderson hung up, shocked. There was a graveyard in the backyard of a Westfield mansion. And there was a good chance that some of the remains were those of missing men from Indianapolis. It was too much to absorb.

He sought out Joe Cook. The young sheriff was just as astounded as Anderson when he heard the news. Not that Hamilton was immune to violent crime. Locals were still reeling, in fact, from the 1994 robbery and slaying of three teens in an affluent neighborhood in the southern end of the county. In that case, the son of a Black Panther leader, an Indiana college student with no history of violent crime, and another young man had bound, gagged, and beaten three Carmel teens and then methodically slit their throats, nearly decapitating all three. One of the victims was a thirteen-year-old girl who had just flown in that night to visit her family. It was a prototypically senseless act of violence, difficult to comprehend from any angle: five young lives snuffed out at the same time, including those of the two convicted murderers, who were both sentenced to life in jail.

But finding unidentified bones on an estate near Westfield was completely uncharted territory. There wasn't any footprint to follow in deciding what to do next in this case.

Cook and Anderson didn't sit around scratching their heads for long, though. They needed a game plan. The first order of business, they decided, was to go over Fox Hollow inside and out with a fine-tooth comb. They agreed that Anderson should take as many of the department's ten detectives as they could spare the next morning to search the estate's grounds.

The next step was to check with the prosecutor's office to find out what actions were within their legal power.

Anderson placed a call to Sonia ''Sonny'' Leerkamp, Hamilton County's prosecuting attorney. ''We've got human bones on an estate in Westfield,'' he told her. ''Lots of 'em, looks like.''

''Oh, no,'' Leerkamp groaned.

''Oh, yeah,'' Anderson shot back. He told her about the Indianapolis men, Tony Harris's night at the estate, and the Baumeisters' impending divorce. Did they need a search warrant? Julie had extended an invitation for the next day, he explained.

Julie's invitation was enough for Leerkamp. If a property co-owner allows a search, a warrant isn't necessary, she told him.

Anderson told her about Julie's desire to have Erich back, extracting a promise from the prosecutor that she would try to advise Julie about that end of the mess.

Seven of the department's detectives piled into Anderson's office for a briefing. He led them through what Mary had told them about the missing men and Tony Harris's night at Fox Hollow. The bones they found that afternoon were human, he told them. They would all need to report to Fox Hollow first thing in the morning for a more extensive search of the property. It was an all-hands-on-deck situation.

Detective Todd Uhrick, one of the department's evidence technicians, was disturbed by Anderson's news that Julie had invited them out there and they weren't going to get a search warrant. Uhrick had seen too many cases blow up in court because of paperwork snafus. He didn't want the validity of their search second-guessed because they hadn't put down the groundwork. He called Leerkamp and told her so.

"Sonny, are you sure?"

"No, the owner's consent is enough." She stood firm.

Uhrick wasn't convinced. "I operate under the philosophy that it's just better to have the blessing of a judge," he remembered saying.

Anderson called his patrol commander, David Wyler. He wanted around-the-clock surveillance of Fox Hollow. Wyler had a patrol officer seal off the entrance to the Baumeister driveway with a patrol car. No one would go in or out without their knowing about it. Even Julie and the girls would have to sign a log sheet every time they left and returned.

Before leaving for the night, Anderson went over the case in his head, mentally checking off the details. Herb was still at the lake with Erich, as far as they knew. The bottom line there was that Julie was certain he wouldn't harm the boy, although she clearly wanted Erich removed from his care, and pronto. With Sonny's help, they should be able to clear up that situation tomorrow.

Herb, himself, however, was still a big question mark. They had nothing—or next to nothing—with which to pin the deaths of the missing men on him, although he was obviously now the prime suspect in the men's disappearances. When Wilson had confronted Herb in the past, he'd "lawyered up," she had said. Anderson was convinced Herb would do the same thing in this instance. And what would they say to him anyway? "Oh, by the way, how did those bones get in your backyard?" That was pretty lame, he reasoned. Herb would refer them to his attorney, who would invariably deny that Herb had any knowledge of the bones. That, unfortunately, would be that.

No, they needed a lot more than they had now before they could confront Herb. They were days, maybe even weeks, away from being prepared to question him, as far as Anderson was concerned.

"This is a citizen of Hamilton County who's never caused us any problems," Anderson would say later about the decision not to question Herb as soon as they determined the bones were human. "I wanted to see who and what we had out there first."

In his heart of hearts, what Anderson really wanted, he would later admit, was "a billfold with identification" for each and every person whose bones were found on Fox Hollow.

What he would get, in the anxious weeks and months that lay ahead, could not have been further removed from that fervent wish.

TWENTY

Anderson threw down the Winston he was smoking and stubbed it out with his toe. It was his umpteenth cigarette of the young day. He chain-smoked when he was nervous or angry, and he was both of those things at that moment.

Anderson, nine of his detectives, and Sonia Leerkamp had been standing in the Baumeisters' driveway since about 8:30 A.M. that morning. Waiting.

When Wilson hadn't shown up at the appointed time, they'd called her. She would be late, they were informed. She was getting a search warrant from a Marion County judge.

Why hadn't they gotten the warrant? Anderson demanded of Leerkamp, more than a bit peeved. If Indianapolis thought it was necessary, it probably was. This case may have originated in Indianapolis, but they were in Hamilton County now. If a search warrant was in order, they damn well should have had one.

At about 10:30 A.M. Wilson arrived, Stephen Nawrocki and his assistants trailing behind her in a separate van. Ignoring the tension surrounding her late arrival, she handed the warrant to one of the Hamilton County sheriffs who read it aloud to Bill and Julie.

Wilson had gotten the warrant signed the night before. She had consent, but she also had plenty of cause to get a judge to sign the warrant. She didn't think it would hurt to be doubly safe. She didn't want any portion of her work thrown out of court at some future date on a technicality. Julie had balked at a search of the house in the past, demanding that they get a warrant. Reading the warrant out loud to her was an "in-your-face" move. The police are in control now, they were in effect saying. Neither you nor Herb can prevent us from getting the answers we need at Fox Hollow.

"You are hereby authorized and ordered in the name of the State of Indiana to enter into the following described residence, 1111 East 156th Street, Hamilton County, Indiana," the sheriff read, "which is a three-story stone structure with brown trim housing an indoor pool on the ground floor and an attached garage, all outbuildings on the premises, and the eighteen-and-a-half-acre wooded and grassy area surrounding the home."

The sheriff went on to tick off all the items police and evidence technicians would be allowed to seize from the estate, a grisly laundry list that illustrated just what they thought they might uncover:

"Any human remains, including but not exclusively, bone, hair, teeth, tissue, and blood; any personal effects which could be linked to any open missing persons cases, including but not exclusively, clothing, personal papers, anything else connected to said persons; any photographs or videotapes depicting a likeness of any man reported as a missing person to law enforcement."

Nawrocki, meanwhile, was unloading his vanload of tools—tarps, measuring tapes, trowels, shovels, rakes, sifters, shaker screens, brushes, and dust pans. He was helped by his two assistants, Matt Williamson and Christopher Schmidt, two part-time University of Indianapolis instructors known affectionately as the "bone twins" because of their general resemblance. Both were dark-haired, about five-foot-nine, and in their late twenties.

Each had his own specialty, however. Schmidt was the tooth expert, a focus that would prove especially valuable in the days ahead. Williamson studied the effects of trauma on bones, things like gunshot and knife wounds. The duo had worked alongside Nawrocki on other cases. And all three knew each other's field habits so well that much between them went unspoken.

Glamorized by Hollywood movies such as *Jurassic Park*, anthropology, in practice, is actually grimy, tedious, painstaking work. Days spent bent over sifter screens, swatting away bugs and filtering dirt a scoopful at a time are far more typical than "Eureka!"-type finds of bones or entire skeletons that provide crucial pieces to an anthropological puzzle.

Nawrocki spent ten minutes walking the site, trying to get some idea of the lay of the land and of how far the bones were spread out. He noted that the hill, which was covered with knee-high grass, maple trees, bushes, and poison ivy, dropped gradually down to a ditch. While Nawrocki surveyed the site, the police stayed back, waiting for his lead, a frustrating exercise for Anderson.

"I wanted to get in there and rip and tear like an Easter egg hunt," Anderson remembered. "I'm glad we did it the right way."

The "right way" involved Nawrocki and his two assistants first walking slowly across the top and sides of the slope, dropping orange flags wherever they spotted what they thought were bones.

"Within thirty minutes, they had dropped from seventy-five to one hundred little orange flags," recalled Detective Todd Uhrick, who was helping with the search.

Nawrocki said later he felt as if he had wandered into a cemetery that had accidentally been bulldozed, or a plane crash in which the wreckage had gone undiscovered for years.

"It looked like a mass disaster scene," he said.

Nawrocki and the others then began cleaning the area down to the dirt, removing all the surface brush and grass with shears and rakes. In a little over an hour, the site was stripped to bare ground, the charred area at its center. The greenery gone, it was easy to see that the bones were concentrated in the burnt area, which was selected as a central reference point. They placed a stake there, and then drew a cross with a white marker, boxing in about six square yards with string and stakes and surveyors' chaining pins. Within the boundary lines, they set up six one-meter-by-one-meter-square grids.

All of the work was being done with crime-scene reconstruction in mind. There was no road map out there, no guide as to how the bones had gotten there. Nor did they expect Herb to provide one. The only way Nawrocki could take those bones back to his laboratory and wring from them the story of that killing field was to know exactly where and how they had been found.

The day was hot, the mosquitoes were thick, but the woods were quiet. The only sound other than the buzzing insects and chirping birds was the clicking shutter of the 35-millimeter Pentax camera Uhrick was using to document every move. Uhrick noted that there was an extension cord with a socket for an overhead floodlight that ran from one of the trees on the site to the Baumeister house.

If Herb had burned the bodies, he had light to work by, if he chose to use it.

After the earth was exposed, the searchers began sifting through the topsoil of a single grid, using trowels, spoons, and picks. Bones and bone fragments found were picked up and put into paper brackets and labeled by grid. Soil, leaves, and debris were placed in five-gallon pails, and later taken to screens where they were sifted. Each fragment was handled gingerly. Burning a human bone destroys its organic components—things like protein, collagen, and hair fibers. What's left is slightly more brittle than a pretzel, and easily broken. It took gentle, patient hands to do the kind of work Nawrocki needed.

The searchers were sticky, tired, and thoroughly eaten up by bugs by the time they had finished a single grid five hours later. But between them, they had found a cluster of hand bones and a piece of a tooth. A femur and a fibula and tibia were found twenty yards west in the woods, along with hundreds of tiny bone and tooth fragments.

None of the bones had been buried. Most had been burned. There was no indication that any of those found had come from victims of stab or gunshot wounds. Many bore tooth-mark punctures from the carnivores that made their homes on Fox Hollow. Dogs, cats, foxes, squirrels, and other creatures had all simply helped themselves to what had become part of the local food chain.

Still, nothing Nawrocki's team had found that day could definitively point to any of the missing men from Indianapolis. There were no skulls. Nor did they have any complete sets of teeth, the traditional method used to identify otherwise unrecognizable human bodies.

Nawrocki said that "not burying the bodies was the nastiest trick" the murderer could have played on them. What bones the rain and other elements hadn't scattered, the animals had.

"The way they were dispersed across such a large area— well, it just didn't make any anthropological sense," a frustrated Nawrocki recalled.

It didn't make sense from any point of view, as far as the police were concerned. To let bodies rot in a backyard almost in plain view of an occupied house was the mark of either one hell of a confident killer, or someone who simply didn't give a damn whether or not he was discovered.

From the kitchen table one could look out the Baumeisters' bay window into their backyard and see the site where the bones had been burned. Julie, in fact, told the police that she saw the skull Erich had found in the fall of 1994 from that window, leaning up against a tree, according to Hamilton County Detective Cary Milligan, who helped with the search.

"It was so careless, the way he disposed of those bodies," Milligan said later. "I mean, how arrogant can you get—laying them right out there in front of God and everybody?"

By that point, any of the detectives, including Anderson, who had imagined that this nightmare would end soon realized just how sadly mistaken they had been. The daunting nature of their task was equally apparent to the five evidence technicians who had spent the day inside the Baumeister home.

That team, led by Milligan, faced the formidable job of wading through a lifetime of junk accumulated by Herb and Julie, two self-proclaimed "pack rats", in search of something—anything—that would tie Herb to either the missing men or give them a clearer picture of Herb's sexual practices.

If it was a crime scene, it was an old one, possibly more than a year old. The last man to go missing, Michael Keirn, had been seen in August 1995. Since that time, the house had been lived in by everyone in the Baumeister family. The traditional fingerprinting, diagramming, and measuring done in the aftermath of a violent crime wouldn't do police a bit of good in this case.

This was someone's home. Detectives had to wade in, sort through personal property, and separate what might be important to a homicide investigation, keeping a keen eye out for the kinds of souvenirs that would either corroborate Tony Harris's story or tie Herb to one or more of the missing men. The couple's collection of goods for the thrift stores combined with their general indifference about housekeeping made that job "a nightmare," Milligan recalled.

In fairness, Julie had been running herself ragged just to keep up with three children and a failing business, while Herb, in the months preceding, had been off being Herb—doing his disappearing act and avoiding real work as much as possible.

But the disarray inside Fox Hollow went far beyond indifferent housekeeping, police noted. It was as if Herb and Julie, exhausted from keeping up exterior appearances, had simply given up the ghost of orderly pretense inside the walls of their own home.

"Raccoons had almost destroyed that house," Milligan recalled. "They were living in the attic. There was raccoon feces and urine coming through the ceilings, so much so that the ceilings were actually collapsing in some parts. The home was totally infested with raccoons.

"The house itself was stuffed full of things you wouldn't believe. There were clothes and furniture and toys and tools. The garage was so full of crap, you could hardly move. Certain rooms were just full of boxes just laying around. The closets were stuffed full. You'd open a closet and things would just come falling out."

There was one clean room in the house—Marne's. The seventeen-year-old alone seemed to have staked out sort of a haven of tidiness amidst the clutter, Milligan said. But the calm ended at the door of her room, where a loft area was piled with boxes, trains—"all kinds of junk," he said.

The house was not only untidy, it was just plain dirty. There was a "bad animal odor" from the raccoons, Milligan said. "I've seen worse as a policeman—but I wouldn't want to live like that."

Many of the items Herb had bought from an auction of the bankrupt someday Dayton-based Lazarus chain and intended to sell someday or use as displays in the stores were being stored at Fox Hollow.

Giant maple leaves, oversize footballs, seashell displays, Styrofoam horse heads, gigantic mascara tubes—Fox Hollow had become a repository for the bizarre and the exaggerated, some of which the couple seemed to have happily incorporated into their decorating scheme.

Nowhere were these decorative touches more eye-popping than in the pool area downstairs, the backdrop for Herb's night with Tony Harris and for all of Herb's activity with the missing men, police felt.

Despite Tony Harris's frustrating hyperbole and his impression that the whole house had been covered with cobwebs, there could be no denying that his description of the Baumeisters' pool area was dead on, down to the tiniest of details.

The mannequins stood out first and foremost, including a bronze-colored male swimmer the color of the "statues at Union Station," as Tony had told Connie. There was also the foldout couch. The wet bar. Even the large-screen television parked inexplicably in front of the older console model, both unplugged, was precisely as Harris had described it to police two years before.

Milligan questioned Julie about whether Herb kept videotapes in the house. She told him Herb was a "prolific videotaper although he hardly ever watched any of them," Milligan recalled. Herb had "hundreds of videotapes" in the basement, Julie informed the detective, leading him downstairs to a storage room off the pool area.

Julie flipped on the light. "I don't get it," she told Milligan, pointing to an empty shelf. "They're usually right here."

"Do you have any idea what he did with them?" Milligan asked.

"He must have taken them with him," Julie said, with a shrug of her shoulders.

Milligan turned his focus to the pool area, but he made a mental note about the missing tapes. They would be important. They needed to find them.

In addition to looking for "souvenirs" from any of the missing men, Milligan was looking for "ligatures or anything that could be used as a ligature."

He began with the pool itself, which proved difficult. Its motorized cover, which operated on a track-and-pulley system, wasn't working properly. Milligan and his team had to fix it before they could get it pulled back to expose the pool.

That done, they took out the trap to the pool's filter. They also seized a piece of hosing roughly resembling the one Tony had told police that Herb placed around his neck.

The bar was ill-stocked: no liquor and only a few glasses. They found a cigarette in the ashtray, a man's blue vinyl windbreaker jacket, and four videotapes behind the bar.

Milligan was looking for a place where someone could

ecretly plant a camera that would point toward the area around the foldout couch. He spotted it almost immediately. A vent in the wall was directed almost exactly at that spot. And it was large enough to hold a small video camera. The vent was empty, but one of the screws was missing from its cover, another screw was loose, and the cover itself was slightly askew, as if it had been removed and hastily put back together.

In the dressing room, they found a pair of men's Speedo swimming trunks hanging up, which they took, along with a roll of duct tape from the furnace room. Milligan logged and photographed each item, tucking them away in evidence bags.

Upstairs, Julie pointed out her clothing and Herb's. The searchers went through both.

Herb's things were neatly organized, folded, stacked, and sorted. But beyond the orderliness, it was frustratingly un-informative. There was nothing hidden away in any of his drawers: no pictures or driver's licenses.

Herb's bathroom, separate from Julie's, was also a cipher. It was another indication of how disconnected the couple's lives had become, but otherwise unhelpful.

"Nothing, *nada*," was how Anderson would later de-scribe the results of the search in the house.

Milligan dutifully videotaped the entire house, but the all-day search was a "huge disappointment," he said later. Even though the outbuildings on the property—a shed and a stone storage building—were packed to the rafters with auction items, they were devoid of clues.

In all, police seized only ten items from the house, five of which were videotapes that would all later prove innoc-uous. Only one of the tapes contained pornography, and that video belonged to Erich. It was "the typical sort of thing a teenage boy would watch," Milligan said.

A frustrated Anderson turned to Detective Sergeant Ken-neth "Whiz" Whisman to run the case from there on out. It was an odd choice by some measures. Whisman, a beefy thirty-seven-year-old who'd been a sheriff since 1981, and a detective on and off since 1985, had never handled a homicide investigation before. Nor was Whisman the smoothest of communicators. The son of a railroad detective, Whisman was cut from old-guard Hoosier stock; he was a shut-up-and-take-your-medicine sort of guy.

A walking poster child for the Midwest work ethic, he'd put himself through college, working one or more jobs, doing whatever it took. Later, when police work didn't pay enough to put his own children through college, he started a police supply business to earn extra money. That meant long days and few vacations, but Whisman wasn't the type to complain. The department's Rock of Gibraltar, he, in fact, never allowed himself emotional downtimes. Not at work or at home. "My oldest daughter is absolutely petrified about what I do for a living. I don't need to burden them," is how he explained it.

Whisman had almost no capacity for small talk and could sometimes be gruff and off-putting, but his colleagues simply chalked it up to his trademark toughness and self-sufficiency.

And he was not without investigative strengths. He'd done undercover narcotics work for more than two years. He knew about long waits for small but significant payoffs. He'd spent months staking out drug dealers before moving in for the arrest. "Hours of boredom, interrupted by minutes of sheer terror," was how he described it. And he had the hide of a rhinoceros. If he got mad, he might cut your head off. But he wouldn't whine about having to do it.

Anderson described him in his inimitable fashion as a "go-get-the-sonofabitch" kind of investigator when it came to nailing suspected criminals. "He won't rest until he has the asshole," Anderson said.

Anderson smelled a case where the evidence would come in dribs and drabs over a long period of time. Whisman was their pit bull. He'd hang in there for the duration. In the spirit of balance, though, he also selected Detective William Clifford, the department's sex crime specialist, to assist Whisman. They were an Oscar-Felix mismatch. Clifford, six-foot-two, just thirty years old, was athletic and easy-going. Most people liked him. Whisman, with his clipped manner, his beefy arms, was more intimidating.

If they don't kill each other, Anderson thought to himself that first day at Fox Hollow, they might just be able to bring in a serial killer.

TWENTY-ONE

Julie was not about to let the subject of Erich rest, not until he was under her wing and away from his father. In fact, she talked about little else to police the first day they searched Fox Hollow.

Wilson and Leerkamp, the prosecuting attorney, had both suggested that Julie get an emergency petition for temporary custody of Erich, the formal court proceeding that would allow police to travel to Wawasee and remove Erich from Herb's care.

That routine worked like a charm. The bones on Fox Hollow and police suspicions about Herb were enough to convince Hamilton Superior Court Judge Steven Nation, the jurist handling Julie and Herb's divorce, that Erich needed to be with his mother. It was decided that Wilson, along with a Hamilton County sheriff, would physically secure Erich.

Herb's attorney, Frank Miroff, was notified. By law Herb had to be told the reasons for the custody change. That presented problems. Herb had never been anything but a loving father. And nothing found on Fox Hollow could yet be linked definitively to any of the missing men from Indianapolis.

But Herb was clearly headed toward some sort of cataclysm. The divorce. A failing business. The police on his tail. Herb was an intelligent man. He had to know his life was coming undone. And no one, not even Julie, could predict his response. Julie wasn't willing to risk Erich's safety in the event that Herb, for some uncharacteristic reason, sought retribution through his child. Nor were police willing to tip their hand yet about what they had found.

As a compromise, Judge Nation decided that Miroff should tell Herb about the custody order but not divulge the discovery of the bones until after Erich had been removed from his father's care. Only then was Miroff "at liberty to discuss the evidence with his client," Nation wrote in his court order. To prevent the documents from leaking to Herb or to the press, the file was also temporarily sealed, until Erich was in his mother's custody.

Erich wasn't coming directly home to Julie, however. The police also filed a petition called CHINS, an acronym for "child in need of services," in order to keep Erich in protective custody, at least overnight.

It was Julie's idea that the police keep Erich in custody, Anderson said. She was afraid Erich would try to run away from her when he found out that they were investigating his father, whom Erich worshipped, he continued. She also thought Erich would be furious about having his vacation with his dad interrupted.

Bill Clifford, it was decided, would make the 120-mile drive north with Wilson to Wawasee in Kosciusko County, Indiana, to pick up Erich. It was a logical choice. Both Wilson and Bill had extensive experience with teenagers in stressful situations.

Hamilton County wasn't carrying out the custody order just to please Julie. They wanted to question Erich about finding the skull. In addition to being able to corroborate Julie's story, there was a chance that Erich knew even more than he had shared with his mother concerning his father's activities and the bones in their backyard. They wanted to get to him first.

Clifford also had been instructed to note the license plate numbers and description of any cars in the driveway of Herb's mother's cottage. They still weren't ready to talk to

Herb, but it couldn't hurt to try to keep track of him. License numbers might help.

The trip gave Wilson a chance to tell Clifford the real side of the case, as far as she was concerned—the victims' side. She described the years of emotional hell the families and loved ones of the missing men had been put through.

Wilson found a sympathetic soul in Clifford, whose duties since joining the investigations staff had included investigating sex crimes with underage victims.

Hamilton County detectives were sketchy in their call to the Kosciusko County Sheriff's Department. It was clear that they wanted the tiny northern central Indiana department to pick up Erich. That much was spelled out in the emergency custody order they faxed to the smaller department.

But their additional request—to check out Herb—was somewhat murky. Approach Herb Baumeister with caution, the sheriffs were told. Human remains had been found on his property. They were instructed to look for any items Herb might have with him that could help in a criminal case—things like videotapes and photographs. But nothing was said about missing men or the possibility that Herb was a serial killer with a penchant for sexual strangulation.

"I would have liked to have known a lot more," remembered Kosciusko Detective Tom Brindle, who, along with his partner, Tom Kitch, drew the assignment.

Kitch and Brindle didn't cross paths often with suspected murderers in Lake Wawasee, a seasonal playground for some of Indiana's wealthiest citizens. Homes facing Kosciusko's Lake Wawasee, the state's largest freshwater lake, went for $100,000 and up. In recent years, residents had begun paying $175,000 or more for lakefront cottages, only to tear down the older structures and replace them with multimillion-dollar showcase homes, some of which were used just two or three months a year during the summer. Crime in the recreational region ran mostly to break-ins during the quiet winter months. The county often went several years without a murder.

Brindle and Kitch were understandably nervous, then, when they drove to the lake that afternoon and spotted the Land Rover parked outside Herb's mother's white-frame condominium, a modern structure on the east side of the lake. The detectives called in the license plate number. It came back registered to Herb. They had the right place.

They had no idea what to expect, but their primary goal was to get Erich away from his father without incident.

Herb answered the door, wearing long pants and a summer shirt. He looked rested, and not at all surprised to see two local sheriffs at his door. Erich stood behind him, listening, as Brindle explained why they were there—to carry out the emergency custody order. The two men said nothing about the bones or Herb being investigated.

"Before you do anything, let me just get my attorney on the phone," Herb asked the officers politely, inviting them in while he made the call. That was fine, Brindle said. But they wanted Erich to wait in the car. Erich began to cry. Herb put his arms around him, saying he was sure it was a misunderstanding. He would take care of it as soon as he could, he promised Erich.

Kitch led the teenager to his patrol car, while Brindle went inside with Herb. "Just let me go back inside and get my stuff," Erich pleaded with the officer. But Kitch didn't want him back in the house. Hamilton County had been adamant about keeping Erich separate from his father. That accomplished, they weren't about to risk a reversal of the situation.

Herb was unable to get Frank Miroff, his divorce attorney, on the phone, but he raised one of Miroff's associates. The custody order change was a fact, she informed him. He had to turn Erich over to the sheriffs. There was nothing else he could do at the moment.

Brindle used the time Herb was on the phone to give the condo a once-over. He noted that their luggage still stood in the lower level. It didn't appear that they had even had the chance to unpack. He saw clothing and personal effects, but not much else. The condo itself was neat, well taken care of. Nothing appeared out of order. If there was something Brindle was supposed to be seeing, he certainly hadn't spotted it.

Herb was surprisingly calm, even in the face of Erich's distress. He brought Erich's things out to the car and said good-bye to his son. This was all a mistake, he kept telling him, as Erich gulped back sobs. He would take care of it right away.

"Don't be mad at the police, Erich. They're just doing their job. I love you," he said, hugging him good-bye once more.

Erich was even more difficult to console once he'd left his father. Herb was the best dad, he kept telling the police. He wanted to stay with his father. He was old enough to know what he wanted; they should respect his wishes.

Brindle and Kitch exchanged raised-eyebrow looks that said, "Yeah, other than this little bone problem, your dad is Ward Cleaver." But they said nothing to Erich. The kid was innocent. They were bound by the law, was all they told him.

"We don't take sides," said Brindle, afraid to say much more. Still, his heart went out to Erich. He was obviously in for some bigger bumps ahead.

Erich was sulking in a small administrative office in the sheriff's headquarters when Mary Wilson and Bill Clifford arrived.

Clifford started out the interview gently, explaining that they were investigating his father and that they had to ask him some questions as well. Erich's replies were mostly monosyllabic, mumbled yeses and nos. Clifford finally asked pointedly: "Did you know your father was gay?"

No, Erich said, he didn't.

"Do you remember finding a skeleton behind your house, Erich?"

He denied it ever happened.

Wilson and Clifford decided that the best thing would be to get him back to Hamilton County. Erich kept making requests to go outside—he needed a cigarette, he just wanted to go get a drink of water, he wanted some fresh air.

Wilson was so concerned about Erich running, she voiced her fears aloud, hoping that would defuse the situation somewhat.

"Bill, I've got the distinct feeling that Erich doesn't want to leave and when we walk out of here, he's going to try to run away."

Erich didn't reply, but a wary Clifford kept his hand on Erich's shoulder as he led him to the backseat of the unmarked Camaro. "We're going to get you back to your mom," Clifford assured him.

Erich said next to nothing in the two-hour drive home. But he went ballistic when he found out that he would be kept overnight at the Hamilton County juvenile facility.

"I didn't do anything," he yelled, half screaming and crying at Wilson and Clifford as they turned him over to juvenile authorities.

When Julie and the girls tried to visit Erich the next day, there was another scene. It wasn't visiting day. They wouldn't be allowed in. Julie was livid. The girls were also upset. Whisman smoothed things over, getting permission for them to visit.

When Clifford and Whisman interviewed Erich after Julie left, the boy continued to insist that the skeleton incident never happened. "I want out of here," he whined. "I didn't do anything."

Later, Clifford was able to reach Kevin Dennison, the friend who had been with Erich when the two had found the skeleton. The fourteen-year-old former neighbor of Erich's had since moved to Colorado. He remembered the skeleton incident quite clearly, he told Clifford.

He and Erich had been playing outside in December 1994. The time of year stuck in his mind because winter was just about the only season Erich was allowed to run freely in the woods, due to bad allergies.

They'd found the skeleton in the wooded area just beyond the walk-out patio that led to their basement. They'd taken the skull and put it on a long stick and paraded past one of the windows in the house, hoping to scare Marne. They tired of the game and put it back. Later, Erich had told him what his father had said, that the skeleton had been part of his grandfather's medical practice and that raccoons had dragged it out from the garage.

He remembered being bothered by that explanation because he had seen fillings in the teeth of the skull and he didn't think that medical skulls were real and that they had fillings. Erich never brought up the incident again.

TWENTY-TWO

Julie also talked to police on June 26, two days after they'd found human bones in her backyard. But her interview was far more illuminating than her son's. In fact, it was a bombshell.

Whisman and Clifford purposely chose the ''family room'' in the Hamilton County jail to conduct the interview session with Julie and Wendling. Like the other interview rooms in the jail, it was fitted with a video camera and a recorder, but it was decorated in muted, soothing tones and was larger and more comfortable than some of the other rooms.

Even with Bill Wendling glued to her side for support, Julie looked strained, shell-shocked. The search at Fox Hollow and the entire unraveling of her outwardly preppy, suburban existence in such a macabre fashion had obviously taken a toll. Wendling announced they would have about two hours with his client and that was about it. He had a schedule conflict later that afternoon.

Whisman wanted a complete picture of Julie and Herb's life together, but he didn't want to have to elicit every answer with a series of specific questions. He planned to throw out some open-ended statements and just let her ramble.

It was clear from the time Julie sat down that in addition to being tired and overwhelmed, she was angry. Barely suppressed rage, was how Whisman would describe it later. But rage was good. She might just be pissed enough at Herb to tell them the truth.

Whisman started out with gentle questions about how they met, what their early married life was like. He asked how she would describe her relationship with Herb over the years they were married.

Julie took a deep breath. "I'm not sure there is a real easy answer to that," she began, choosing each word carefully. "I've done a lot of soul-searching. Ultimately, my world was being pretty much controlled by Herb. He is a very mean man who could do very mean things to people. Our life together has always been based on my world being pretty much controlled by Herb. I had no family, no place to go, and Herb would get his way by making my life so miserable, by playing head games, that I would do what he wanted."

"What do you mean 'He's so mean'?" Whisman gently prodded.

"He liked to play mind games," Julie responded.

Soon after they were married, she explained, he got mad at her and moved to an upstairs apartment in their house. He wouldn't speak to her for a year, Julie remembered. It was typical of Herb to hold grudges against relatives and friends for minor infractions, and then cut off all contact with the offender by way of punishment.

"He didn't talk to his mother for four years when she did something that he didn't like. He didn't let her see the grandkids or let me talk to her."

Herb's depression and admission to the hospital had been frightening, she admitted. Well-adjusted people didn't have mental breakdowns over car repairs, she acknowledged.

"He was driving home from Bloomington and three or four cars hit him. They didn't bend the frame, but the car was totaled. He wanted to keep it. He never got rid of anything," Julie continued, her voice bathed in barely disguised disgust. "He would keep used toilet paper. He just never cleaned up."

When his car got wrecked, Herb was so depressed he sat

"for several days on our apartment floor crying" until his father had him committed, Julie remembered.

On the subject of Herb's father, Julie softened a little bit. He, above all Herb's family members, had welcomed her into the Baumeister clan and she felt very close to him because of that warm reception.

"Herb's dad loved me like a daughter and I loved him like a father," she said.

When Herb's father was dying, Julie said, she had walked into the room and he greeted her and began to cry. She sat down on the bed and they both cried for about twenty minutes. All during that time, Herb's father kept repeating: "I'm so sorry, I'm so sorry."

"He never said what he was sorry about," Julie mused. "But that always stuck in the back of my mind. Why would you say you're sorry? Did Herb's dad know something about Herb, I wonder?"

After his father's death, Herb used his father's prescription pads to forge prescriptions for drugs, she told them. Most of the prescriptions he wrote were for diet pills. He was adamant about staying thin. And he did lose weight from the pills, Julie said.

Julie related no fond memories of Herb's mother, however.

"Is his mother still living?" asked Clifford gently.

"Yes," Julie snorted derisively, "she hovers at—" and went on to list Elizabeth Ann Baumeister's address.

Julie took her shots where she could, Whisman noted. There was obviously no love lost between her and her mother-in-law.

"During the course of your marriage, how was your love life?" Whisman asked. The stiff query was his way of finding about the couple's sex life, he said later. "I was trying to be delicate," he remembered.

"Shit," Julie spat out. The gloves were off now. All the guards Julie had kept up over the years, all the Herculean efforts it must have taken to depict Herb as the model husband and theirs as the ideal marriage—all came tumbling down in an instant.

"This is coming from what I know today," Julie explained. "But I'll be happy to discuss that with anyone. On our wedding night we did not have sex. He took a magazine to read and we didn't have sex. By the time we got to the hotel—"

Clifford's leg hit the table, interrupting Julie's train of thought. Damn, thought Whisman, she was on a tear, too. This is stuff she must have waited years to tell somebody. But the bump had given Julie a chance to collect herself. She dropped the yarn of their disastrous honeymoon night, and the two detectives didn't take her back.

She seemed relieved to be getting these things off her chest. And it was a vindication, of sorts. After years of wondering to herself, she finally had an audience with whom she could voice her doubts about her husband's behavior. She had never had that before, she told them.

"I had no friends to talk to, no mother to go to and ask: 'How often do you have sex?' " Julie informed them.

"Let me tell you about our sex history," she continued, clearly warming to the topic. "We can do this in five minutes—and maybe there's something wrong with me, I don't even care—we did not have sex often. It was always strange. Herb was never open. I have never seen him nude."

"Never?" Whisman asked, his eyebrows raised, his tone incredulous. He couldn't help himself. This was totally outside the bounds of any normal married existence he knew of. "No, my kids have," she snapped, "but I haven't. If he has a birthmark, I don't know."

"What?" a stunned Wendling asked, turning to Julie. But she didn't respond.

Instead, Clifford prodded Julie about the few times she had had sex with Herb.

"Was there anything unusual about activities that he would request or want you to perform?" Clifford asked.

"No," Julie answered quietly.

"Did you use a different variety of sexual positions or strictly missionary?"

Clifford then elaborated, in the event she didn't know what the missionary position was. "On top of each other?" he queried.

Yes, that was the only position they had used during sex, she responded.

"He is weird as hell," Julie finally blurted out. "Everybody that knows him will tell you that he's weird as hell."

Aware, perhaps, that her indictment of Herb also spoke volumes about her own existence, Julie quickly reversed herself, tossing out an explanation for what attracted her to him in the first place and why she stayed with him for so many years.

"I always thought he was unique, not strange," she said, defending her choice of Herb as a mate. "He made life fun. He was a fun person to be with. He could make an everyday activity fun. He was very, very creative. He could do very fun things."

And Herb put his family first, she felt.

"There were not many nights in our life he wasn't home," she explained. "He was a good father. We would have dinner together. We had dinner as a family—old Ward Cleaver here . . ." she said with a wry smile, her attempt at gallows humor.

Still, Herb's sunny side didn't always dominate, she conceded.

He could also be unreliable, flighty. And he wasn't always around. Especially in the summer months. When he did have unexplained absences, he lied about his whereabouts, hatching some implausible story that she found too insulting to even consider.

When his lies affected his kids, however, she drew the line. Herb could step on her. But the kids were another matter. They didn't deserve his duplicity, she seethed.

Herb's lies to the children were most unbearable when she and the kids spent time at the condo in Wawasee during the summer, she said.

"I went up there as much as I could," she explained. "Herb never spent a week there with us. He would come up on the weekends. I used to get real mad—just like the fact that he would call on Friday night and say, 'I'm leaving.' That would be six P.M. My son would fall asleep on the couch waiting for his dad to get there, and dawn would come.

"No Herb. Instead his dad would walk in looking like hell warmed over at two o'clock Saturday afternoon."

Herb's excuses for being late were always so lame, so pathetic, it sickened her just to hear them.

"I would hear such bullshit," she hissed. " 'I took a wrong turn.' 'I got tired and pulled off to the side of the road.' 'I didn't get away until late.' It always made me angry. Not that I cared whether he was there or not. I had a better time when he wasn't there. But his son wanted him there. The kids would wait up until one o'clock in the morning for him to arrive."

In her book, people "did what they said. Herb never did what he said," she complained bitterly.

The summer weeks at Wawasee weren't the only times Herb went off by himself, Julie admitted.

Early in their marriage, there was an entertainer he made excuses to see by himself, "Dr. Bop," Julie told them. Dr. Bop was a regional entertainer who played seventies music—Herb's favorite—often doing shows at the Vogue, a movie theater that had been renovated into a nightclub and bar in a gentrified area of downtown Indianapolis, "the preppy section of town," Whisman called it.

Even in that simple activity, Herb found a way to squeeze her out of the picture, Julie complained.

"Dr. Bop would come on Thursday or Friday. On Friday night at eight-thirty, he'd come in and say, 'Let's go.' When we couldn't get a baby-sitter, he would go without me. When Saturday night rolled around and he still couldn't find a baby-sitter that met with his approval, I'd be home with the baby again."

Later, when the kids were older, he'd simply take them

out by himself and leave her home alone, she said.

To smooth things over, there was always money and the things it would buy.

When the Sav-A-Lot stores started doing well, they gorged themselves on pricey luxuries, largely at Herb's insistence.

They had three phone lines, one for her and Herb, one for Erich, and another for the girls. Everyone in the family had a cellular phone. There were go-carts. Boats. Cars.

Of course, they were raking in the dough at the time. The stores were humming. Their personal income topped out at $225,000 a year, she said. But even that couldn't keep pace with Herb's profligate spending, Julie said.

Around that time, she made the mistake of asking for a jet-ski for her 45th birthday.

"I asked for one, I got two," she said, shaking her head. "And then I had to figure out how I was going to pay for them. His classic comment at the time—and I really think this is how it all started—was, 'It's so easy.' Here we are, so on top of the world. We were making a good income, and then all of a sudden he just started spending, spending, spending."

They wanted to find out why there were human bones in her backyard and Julie wanted to take a bitter stroll down the memory lane of her marriage. The interview broke off. Wendling had to go. Whisman asked Julie for all of the telephone and credit card records she could produce and she promised to try to dig out what she could.

After she left, Whisman and Clifford met with Anderson. Anderson shook his head when he heard what Julie had told them. "She never saw him naked? She's gotta be shittin' me," he said. Whisman said he doubted she was lying. As bizarre as everything Julie had told them had been, it all had a ring of truth to it.

"Well, she doesn't keep very good track of her husband," Anderson retorted.

He and Whisman agreed that even though the entire interview had been staggering—their infrequent sex, her never seeing him nude, his access to his father's prescription pads—Julie's comments about Wawasee were perhaps the most revealing. Coming a day or so late to the lake looking like "hell warmed over" gave Herb plenty of time to do whatever he wanted.

Plenty of time to meet strangers in gay bars.

Plenty of time to kill.

TWENTY-THREE

Whisman and Clifford also re-interviewed Tony Harris. Wilson did the best she could to prepare Tony for the sterile, good ol' boy atmosphere of the Hamilton County Sheriff's Department when she drove him from Indianapolis to Noblesville. But Tony was petrified nonetheless. Mary could tell how frightened he was as they settled into the family interview room at the Hamilton County sheriff's headquarters with Whisman and Clifford sitting across from him, Whisman videotaping the conversation for posterity.

Wilson got the ball rolling by explaining to Clifford and Whisman how she and Tony had met. No matter how Tony appeared to them today, two years after he'd spent the night with Herb, she wanted them to know he had once been genuinely afraid of Herb.

"He felt he easily could have been killed, and he was afraid that was what happened to the two Alans in the summer of '94," she said, referring to Goodlet and Broussard.

With the passage of so much time since Tony had actually spent the night with Herb, however, Tony had scrambled some of the details in his mind. He couldn't remember dates, months, seasons. His memory lapses were exacerbated by his conversational habit of skipping from topic to topic.

The result was that he came off as spacey, unsure of himself. It was a far cry from the frightened but thorough accounting he had given to Virgil Vandagriff two years earlier, a week after the incident happened.

"You say that you first met this man in '94; is that correct?" Whisman asked.

"I—vaguely, yeah, I mean this has been a long time ago. Um, I'll tell you what I will do. You can ask me whatever you want to ask me. If I—I'm not going to guess, okay?"

Whisman took a deep breath, reminding himself that patience was the order of the day.

"Okay, well, I don't want you to guess."

"Okay, um—'94 could have been when I met him, ya know. It could have been before that."

Tony related the story in much the same way as he had told it to Virgil, Connie, and Wilson. Herb had said his name was Brian. He asked him to come for a swim and a cocktail at a mansion in Carmel. But now Herb's car was a black Buick instead of a gray one. And their actual sexual encounter involved Herb in the pool masturbating while Tony strangled him.

"We're down at one end. There are hoses running in the pool, like vacuum, all that. I'm—he comes up behind me on the concrete surface, reaches down with the hose and from behind and puts it around my neck, okay. Now this is before anything ever happened at all, and this is what got into the strangulation asphyxiation business. Um—he did try that, he backed off immediately, and when he—he was a little scared of me, he was very leery of me. Um—I think that he knew then by the quickness of my reflex, that I hadn't, that ya know, I'm not drunk, I'm not out of my mind, ya know. I've got my sense to me. And at that point, he did back off. I initiated several different—I was digging actually, I'm going on the assumption, and asking questions, making out like I'm into this, into that, that kind of thing. Then he starts talking to me, um—boy, this is just back and forth like a Ping-Pong ball, isn't it? Um, but he—"

Tony took a deep breath. These guys were so serious, so straight. It was so difficult to explain this kind of stuff to them. He was struggling, but he stumbled on as best he could.

"There were several different attempts there with, like I said, with a tie, a belt. He had a fascination with strangulation. Obviously. I-I-I do believe that if I had been severely under the influence that he probably would have went further with me. There is one other thing. We were talking about people that night. Talking about—he's out of it, he's gone, he's on his way to la-la-land, okay—and he's just mumbling this and talking about accidents that can happen. And doing the strangulation routine, that you can lose consciousness, you can drown in the pool, different things like that.

"Then he starts talking like he has some experience, accidents   I had the neck hold on him in the pool, standing in water. His eyes are bugging out, his lips are turning purple, the whole nine yards. He's into it. I mean, this guy is into it. He told me he lost consciousness, but he went limp in my hands, he fell underneath the water, very briefly, came right back up, spitting and choking and stuff like that. Told me that I almost killed him, for letting him go underneath the water and that I had to hold him above the water when he loses consciousness."

Tony took another deep breath. "And then that's what brought on the conversation about accidents that can happen and different things like that. My personal opinion about it all, is that this guy's not going to fight with someone to kill them. I mean, I don't even know if he's a murderer. My assumption is that he is. But this is going to be something that is going to be a participant involved. Not somebody that's forced. Okay."

Tony had obviously thought about what had happened with Herb a lot in the two years since it had happened.

"And this type of person that's into narcotics, alcohol, and they're going to enjoy this," Tony added. "I mean, this is something that they are going to fight against."

Clifford asked if he thought Herb planned these evenings

with the intention of killing someone or if they were truly accidents.

Tony took another deep breath. This was so hard. He really hardly knew the man. There was just that one night.

"I have thought about it, I have thought that it would be an accident. That was the assumption that I got, that instinct, that it would be accidental, ya know."

Then Tony thought back. He really didn't know, he realized. How could he know? Herb had been so in control, so ready for him.

"It was set up for an encounter that night. I mean, he had everything ready, ya know. All of it ready. He was planning on bringing somebody back to the house that night. If it hadn't been me, it would have been somebody else."

Whisman asked about the neck hold Herb had showed him. "Is it any different than me putting my hands around my own neck?"

Tony explained patiently that it was done with the "jugular vein"—actually the carotid artery. "You can breathe," he explained. "I know this, because I have done it. And you can get a high off of it. This, this—it's very real. Anybody that's into drugs or alcohol and stuff like that would do this because it is a unique buzz, ya know."

Whisman asked Tony to demonstrate on him. "But don't knock me out," he added.

This was way past strange for Tony. "How about I do it to myself?" he suggested.

Tony put his hands on either side of his neck, pinching both his carotid arteries between his thumbs and forefingers.

"It would be between the jugular and the gland," he explained. "You just pinch a little stronger and stronger, until you finally have it. Discoloration of the lips would be your indicator. 'Cause discoloration of the lips is to let you know if you got the jugular or not."

Tony knew so much about sexual asphyxiation, Clifford had a difficult time believing that his night with Herb had been his only brush with that form of sexual orientation. "Had you done this before that night?" he quizzed him.

Tony snorted derisively. "Not with anybody but this character, I'll tell ya."

Tony told them how he had drawn Herb into a demonstration of sexual strangling the night Herb surfaced at the Varsity Lounge in August 1995. "I brought people over there just to embarrass the hell out of him, run him out of there, basically," he said.

"That's when you got the plate number for me," Mary interjected.

"Yeah, I sent Albert out to get the plate number," Tony remembered.

Mary jogged Tony's memory about some of the nuances of the night he spent with Herb, including the fact that Herb had been frustrated when he first pulled up into the driveway of Fox Hollow.

"Yeah," Tony remembered. "It was like somebody was supposed to be there, but wasn't there. And then again in the morning, I have a chance to go look through the house. And then when he comes back . . . he seems frustrated again."

He also recounted how Herb had gotten upset when Tony pretended to be unconscious during their sexual interlude on the foldout couch in the basement.

"That's when the conversation of accidents came up again, ya know. 'You can die doing this,'" Tony remembered Herb saying. "He was real concerned."

Whisman, who wanted to test Tony to be certain that he was telling the truth about having visited Fox Hollow, led him through a description of the house, focusing on the pool area.

"You said the pool area was all set up?"

"Well, what I meant by that was that he was ready for company. There was lubrication there for intercourse."

Tony talked about the sliding doors that led outside to the patio, the big screen TV, the couch, and the kitchenette. He was more in his element now, having calmed down considerably now that the conversation had veered from sex. And he practically pounced on the subject of mannequins. That was something he would never forget as long as he lived.

"They were all posed. One woman in a dress reaching up into the cabinet in the kitchenette down there. One was a lifeguard. Several others were just posed round as if they were enjoying the day, or whatever."

His memory was a little fuzzier about the upstairs. There were cobwebs, he was certain of that. And a bedroom that had contained the closet with the photography equipment.

He remembered being surprised when Herb had left him alone in the morning.

"It seemed like forever," he said.

In his absence, he had sneaked a peak at a list in the kitchen that had "names and amounts that looked like somebody was going door-to-door or something, charity or maybe business."

The telephone number Herb had given him was that of a landscaping company in Ohio, he later learned. But he told them how Herb had kept in touch, showing up out of the blue the one time.

"Describe him to me," Whisman demanded, testing again.

"Which time?" Tony shot back. "Because each time he was different."

Tony remembered Herb as tall and slim. Sometimes he looked old, other times he appeared to be a younger man, Tony said. That was vague, he knew. But it was true, as far as Tony was concerned. Herb had that baby-faced quality that made him look young, but his artificially darkened skin, tough from tanning, aged him as well.

That Herb had shaved or burned his body hair was something Tony did not equivocate about.

"Arms, legs—all shaved," Tony recalled. "His whole body seemed like it had razor stubble from a recent shaving." When Tony had asked him about it, Herb had said he'd scorched himself "burning leaves or something," Tony remembered.

The night in the Varsity, after Albert had gone outside,

Herb—who was still trying to pass as Brian—had confronted Tony about calling the police.

"Why don't you ever call me?" Tony had asked coyly, knowing at the time that whoever he was, Brian was playing a cat-and-mouse game. "You gave the police my phone number," Herb had responded.

Herb, of course, had no way of knowing of Mary Wilson's efforts to track him down. And of course, in his mind, he was too smart to be traced in any simple way. Tony must have ratted him out, he'd probably figured.

"Did you have any other sexual encounter with him after that night?" Clifford wondered.

"One night. That was it. Just that one night."

Herb was someone who ducked in and out of the gay scene, flitting from bar to bar, never staying too long, Tony said he'd come to realize. "This guy is in and out. He doesn't hang around one place very long."

Clifford asked if there was anything important that Tony had left out, perhaps something they'd forgotten to ask. It was a pretty standard interviewer's trick, one that sometimes yielded bonus information, but just as often turned up a big fat zero.

Tony saw it as his cue to get in his two cents on what kind of person Herb was and why he'd ever gotten involved with him in the first place. He didn't know if it would do any good, but he wanted to leave these people with the impression that he wasn't just some flighty gay guy who didn't know what he was talking about.

"I went into this on a wing," he explained, "just instinct alone. And instinct was telling me from day one that this guy's a wacko. I mean, he's nuts. He's a crazy man. I was very fearful of him and that's not something that I usually am with people. I'm not very leery. And this guy here, I know for a fact he's nuts. There is no doubt in my mind about it, he's done it. That's the impression I got from him the second we walked into that house."

Tony remembered Herb telling him that he did cocaine and that he could drive from one coast to another without stopping. "That's how he got places fast. He told me he had just got back from Florida, and I believed him. He was tan, saddle-faced actually."

Wilson knew Tony's alcohol consumption that night would be brought up eventually, possibly eclipsing Tony's credibility as an informant. So she broached the subject first, quizzing Tony about how drunk he might have been before he left the bar with Herb.

"I was with it," Tony insisted. But then he added that he had been high on marijuana, actually quite high.

"Are you kidding me?" He laughed. "I was smoking dope like you wouldn't believe. I smoked marijuana at the time. That's my kick, more so than alcohol. So, yeah, I was probably stoned," he conceded.

Tony wanted to know what was going to happen to Herb. He certainly didn't feel very safe knowing Herb was out there somewhere, and he was in here, blabbing to the police.

"Are you going to arrest this guy?"

"We're certainly going to work on it," Whisman told him, somewhat obliquely.

"Because there is definitely something there," Tony said. "I'm telling you, if there is a bent human being, that's it. That's one right there."

Clifford leveled with him. He felt like at least the police owed Harris that much.

"We're going to do everything we can. If we were to tell you that we were going to make an arrest, we'd be lying to you, because we don't know for sure."

Then Clifford made a plea to Tony. Hamilton wanted the help of the gay community. They had been shut down in past investigations by Indianapolis gays, and they wanted relations to be more open in this case. "Will some of your friends be cooperative if we need to talk to them?"

Tony froze. It was one thing for him to foist himself into this ugliness, but he couldn't drag any of his friends into this. These guys were so straight, so serious. Some of the people he knew would just freak if they had to talk to them.

"I don't have friends by name," he said in a rush. "Just

faces. And they don't call me at home because they don't know where I live. I mean, I don't know anybody well enough to tell you whether they would cooperate or not."

Clifford led Tony out of the room, leaving Wilson and Whisman to compare notes. Tony had been far too nervous to suit Whisman. Why had he survived a night with Herbert Baumeister when others might not have? And why had he changed significant details of his story, things like the color of the car Herb had been driving? Still, his information about Fox Hollow was too detailed to have been concocted. He had to have been there. That meant they not only had the bones; they had a witness—albeit a nervous and "flaky" one, as Whisman later described Tony—who could put Herb in his own home engaged in dangerous sexual activity and talking about "accidents" in which people had died. It was something. It wasn't enough to lock Herb up, but it was a beginning. Whisman intended to dig for the rest.

"I don't care about anybody—" Whisman started to say.

"You want Baumeister," Wilson finished for him.

"Yeah, just Baumeister."

TWENTY-FOUR

When the dig at Fox Hollow continued on Wednesday, Nawrocki and the searchers moved on to the next grid, expanding the area they were covering to include more of the hill. The heat and the bugs were still unbearable, but the searchers had gotten into a kind of quiet rhythm. They layered themselves with insect repellant and set about their grim business, methodically digging, sifting, washing, and bagging.

Every hour turned up dozens more bones and bone fragments, each piece, no matter how small, a source of accomplishment. With enough pieces, there would come answers.

Significantly, they found two fractured hyoid bones. The hyoid, a tiny bone that sits above the voice box, is often broken when someone has been strangled to death. They didn't know who they had out there yet, but the fractured hyoids gave them at least some idea what the victims might have succumbed to: strangulation. That fit with Tony Harris's account of Herb's penchant for sexual asphyxiation.

Nothing at the site was overlooked. Small roots were growing through some of the bones, indicating that they had been there at least a season or two—helpful later in dating when the bones got there. The shotgun shells were likely those of hunters; none of the bones showed any signs of gun or knife trauma, but the organic material could prove more informative, Nawrocki hoped.

Just as there are anthropologists who date and identify human remains, forensic botanists and entomologists can date plant and insect life in the same way. A Purdue University forestry professor took a tree-core sample to find out approximately when it had been burned.

The discovery of human bones on a million-dollar suburban estate was a blockbuster news story waiting to explode. And explode it did, the second day searchers were out at Fox Hollow. Unfortunately, the reverberations would drive a sharp wedge between the two police agencies investigating the case.

By Wednesday night, June 26—with Herb's whereabouts still unknown—the quiet lane that led to Fox Hollow had became a three-ring media circus, with satellite-outfitted television trucks broadcasting live from the front of the estate, TV anchors doing stand-ups, and print people clamoring for police and family interviews outside the yellow crime-scene tape. Eventually, everyone from *Hard Copy* to the *New York Times* would weigh in on the story.

Managing the media deluge turned into a full-time job, one Whisman termed "a royal pain in the ass. They always wanted more than we were willing to give them."

Early on in the investigation, Whisman said he relayed a request to IPD from his boss, Hamilton County Sheriff Joseph Cook, about handling media for the case: If any information went to the press, it was to come through Hamilton County. Cook wanted the two agencies to speak with one voice, and he wanted that voice to be the Hamilton County Sheriff's Department's.

IPD officers remember it differently. No one was to speak to the media until they had a clearer understanding of what they had at Fox Hollow, the two agencies had decided jointly at the outset of the case. But Hamilton County, looking to hog the glory, jumped the gun and announced a press conference without consulting IPD. Angered, one of Wilson's superiors leaked some of the details of the story that

Hamilton wasn't ready to release to a local television reporter.

Whisman later said that was a "crock of shit," that someone—not Mary—at IPD was simply leaking information just to make themselves look good. "I told that person twice to keep his mouth shut, but he didn't."

In any case, Cook held a press conference several days after the bones were found, at which Cook managed to say as little as possible. Nothing was brought up about Wilson or her two-year investigation of missing gay men in Indianapolis, or about Tony Harris. The reporter who had been clued in finally asked point-blank: Did any other agency have anything to do with this case? Cook denied it, but he and Whisman exchanged a nervous glance.

After the press conference, the television reporter pulled Cook aside. She knew for a fact that police had gotten information from another agency and that that agency had an informant who tied Herb to the gay community and to sexual asphyxiation, she told him right out. She was careful not to mention IPD because she didn't want to give away her source, but she said later she was galled that Hamilton County officials would stand up at a press conference and lie to her about IPD's involvement in the case.

Cook tried to cut a deal with her. If she would hold the story until they had Herb in custody, she could have an exclusive on the entire case and all of its tangled subplots. She agreed to sit on it, but only for a while.

Whisman, an easily irritated, prickly sort of person to begin with, was furious about the leaks.

"We wanted to use the media to bring Herb in," Whisman said. He reasoned that if Herb felt enough heat from a carefully calculated media campaign, he would either come to them or trip up somehow. That meant micro-managing every tiny piece of information that went out. The fact that he had neither the time nor the patience to oversee such a media strategy was beside the point, Whisman felt. They were all cops. And in Hamilton, that meant they stuck together. If IPD didn't understand that, then they would damn well be cut out of the loop.

Even Sonia Leerkamp became the subject of Anderson and Whisman's ire after she did a television interview reporting that there might be as many as three skeletons on Fox Hollow, when numbers were still speculative because of the lack of skulls and comprehensive dental reconstruction. Leerkamp remembered it being late when she was roped into the interview just outside the gates of Fox Hollow. She was tired, and perhaps more candid than her colleagues would have liked.

"We're cops," Anderson said in defense of their close-to-the-vest policy. "We don't want to tell 'em nothin'."

Hamilton's cursory, no-news press conference, however, only further fanned the flames of interest. Reporters could smell a good story under the subterfuge and they were not about to be managed. Naturally they turned to the IPD.

The IPD had the history of the case and a fuller understanding of both the missings and Herb's background. Wilson had been working it for two years. Whisman had it for two days. Reporters being reporters, they went where they thought they could get the best information.

As more leaked out about Herb and Tony Harris, however, the simmering feud between the Hamilton County Sheriff's Department and the IPD turned into a full-blown war.

Part of the problem was that there were no easy answers to a lot of reporters' questions. No positive identifications had been made on any of the bones. A body count at that stage was highly speculative, at best. They had bones. Hundreds of them. It would take weeks, possibly months, before they could be reconstructed and identified. Tony Harris was the only definitive tie to Herb and the victims, and that was a tenuous connection. Besides, Hamilton County sheriffs weren't ready to play that card yet.

To ease some of the media pressure, Whisman did allow cameras to come to the edge of the dig site at Fox Hollow on Thursday to film searchers' efforts.

Wilson, meanwhile, did her best to distance herself from the whole imbroglio, reporting every day to Hamilton County's headquarters in the first few weeks after the bones were found and sharing everything she had with Whisman, while trying to play down any tension that existed between the two departments. But the damage had been done. Whisman never felt completely comfortable sharing information with IPD again. The two agencies, in effect, went their own ways.

With the investigative efforts aimed at him now split in half, the only threat against Herb Baumeister was the one he himself posed.

TWENTY-FIVE

As wily as Herb was, he had to have done and said things that at least hinted at the character Tony Harris had described picking up that night in the bar, Whisman felt. Somebody had to have seen that side of Herb besides Tony.

In going over Herb's arrest record again, he found a charge Wilson had missed. Herb had been arrested for drunk driving in 1994 in Rochester, Indiana, a small northern town near Herb's mother's condo at Wawasee. Herb had been driving the Land Rover, towing a boat on a trailer without rear lights or a license plate at three A.M., the Saturday before a long Fourth of July weekend. A police officer pulling out of a McDonald's spotted him, pulled him over, and noted that Herb smelled from liquor. His eyes were also bloodshot and his speech was slurred, all the classic signs of a drunk driver. The portable Breathalyzer test confirmed it. Herb tested .12 percent, .02 percent over the Indiana limit for being legally drunk. When they towed his car and hauled him back to headquarters, however, Herb conveniently "forgot" how to take a Breathalyzer, twice fumbling with the tube when police asked him to blow into it.

"I'm doing the best I can," he whined, when they informed him he wasn't blowing into it properly. Frustrated, they took him to a local hospital for a blood test, which confirmed what the portable Breathalyzer had indicated a little over an hour earlier. Herb was drunk. His blood alcohol content was .15 percent.

Unlike the insurance fraud case, Herb didn't beat the drunk driving rap. Convicted, he was fined $150, given a three-day jail sentence, and a year's probation. He never told Julie about the arrest. She found out almost a year later when she went to add Marne to the family's car insurance policy and their rates had skyrocketed. Herb did everything he could to hide the arrest from Julie, again using the 72nd Street address on all the arrest paperwork and listing his brother Brad as his closest relative.

When Whisman called the tiny Fulton Superior Courthouse, he was stunned to discover the existence of an extraordinary letter that Herb had written to the judge who had handled the drunk driving case, pleading for leniency. He wrote:

Dear Judge Higgins-Burke,
I am writing this letter to you and the court after personally speaking with Prosecutor Richard Kehoe yesterday, June 28, 1995. I am asking if you would possibly consider a hearing or modification of what I believe to be the last remaining portion of the legal and monetary requirements set forth by your court last fall— this being, the July 10th initiation of a 36-hour incarceration within the Fulton County jail. Due to my work misunderstanding, you were kind enough to defer the incarceration date from June until July 10, due to my vacation date. Prior to and during this time, I have attempted to make arrangements for the care of my 3 children (Marne, 13, Erich, 12 and Emily 8). Being a single parent since last September 11th, I feel I have done quite well at adjusting to being both a father and mother, head-of-household & home-maker, cook & story-reader, and the like. I have tried my best to live under my adjusted income (approx. $18,900 in 1994, vs. $27,300—due to no longer having transportation as a result of my July 2, 1994 charges.) . . . To supplement

my salary from the business I share with my brother-in-law and brother, I have been able to add extra income on the week-ends as a framing carpenter on jobs near my home. At just over $14 per hour, this really helps offset the roughly $12,000 yearly income my wife was able to earn as a permanent middle school substitute before passing away. . . . I am fortunate in that the vast majority of my work is performed at home with files, records, phone, etc. This will continue through the future, which allows me to be here when the children get on their busses and return home from school. I have pretty well overcome their earlier fears that I 'am not going to die too.' They are happy yet very clinging— and I have absolutely wonderful friends and neighbors who constantly try to overly help us in any way they can.

I am more than willing to appear before your court immediately and to additionally furnish you with any other additional information you may require or request (employer's statements, income statements/forms, and the like) . . . I personally have contempt for those criminals you have to have paraded through your court with reason-this and reason-that why they feel they should receive a ''break'' in their sentencing. I have no argument with any portion of your original sentencing and did my best to comply in an honorable manner . . . Would you please consider my request and not hesitate to contact me at the letterhead address or telephone number at any time. Again, my brother Brad is able to drive me to our court on a moment's notice if you wish. Thank you so much in advance for taking the time to consider this request.

Sincerely,
Herbert Baumeister

Pretending his wife was dead to get out of a drunk driving jam? It was clear to Whisman just what elaborate and bizarre lengths Herb would go to in order to manipulate the system and keep his legal and personal troubles hidden from his family. This wasn't a short note, dashed off in a hurry. It was a carefully planned, two-page handwritten letter, in which Herb played every sympathy angle he could think of, from the aggrieved, penniless widower to the single father whose kids were worried that he was "not going to die too."

In case all of that didn't push him over the top in the judge's mind, Herb wanted her to know that he was also a tough-on-crime guy who had "contempt" for those criminals who paraded through the court asking for sentence breaks. Apparently the judge was to believe from Herb's letter that he wasn't part of that group. On what she would base that belief was unclear. Perhaps she was to intuit from his statement that he was a hardworking single father who had made a "senseless mistake."

Herb's probation officer apparently had been swayed by that same story. In a note to the judge accompanying Herb's letter he wrote: "If you remember Mr. Baumeister, his wife recently passed away and he was traveling back to Indianapolis from Rochester to pick up a boat when he was arrested." State Police Commander Fred Hays had been right, Whisman thought. Herb's arrogance about being able to manipulate the system was breathtaking. It knew no bounds.

Herb's letter also provided a chilling glimpse into his subconscious. How telling that he had conjured up a world in which he was single, Julie-free, and surrounded by loving neighbors and friends. Could there be any doubt that this was Herb's secret fantasy?

But in the end, Judge Rosemary Higgins-Burke didn't buy it. Herb had to serve thirty-six hours in the Fulton County Jail almost a year to the day after his arrest. Again, Julie never knew, she told Whisman.

Closer to home, the police decided to search the Baumeisters' 72nd Street house. Focusing on the couple's first home made sense for a lot of reasons. Whenever Herb and Julie fought, Herb would retreat to the smaller house in town. The fact that they held on to the house after they moved to Hamilton County made no sense to Whisman. Money was tight and yet they kept a second house which they didn't always rent? It must have been a cover for Herb's in-town activities, he felt.

Neighbors also had found this strange. "Nobody just abandons a house," one longtime resident noted recently.

The house's deteriorating condition became a concern to the neighborhood's loosely organized residential association, too.

"It became a disaster. It started disintegrating," one local said, recalling how at one point the gutter started coming down. "People complained, but there really wasn't anything that could be done about it."

It was after eleven P.M. when Whisman, Clifford, and several other detectives, armed with a warrant, got to the older, two-story brick structure on the north side of the city. Because it was dark and Herb's whereabouts were unknown, they were a little bit wary going into the house. They found the door unlocked. Clifford went in first, gun drawn. "Hello," he called inside. Nothing. He walked around a corner into the kitchen, where he made out the shape of a person.

"Oh my God," he gasped, raising his Glock .40-caliber pistol. One of the other detectives behind him flicked on a light. Clifford saw that he had almost shot the head off of one of Herb's mannequins. He put his gun down and leaned up against a wall, waiting for his heart to stop pounding.

That would be the only excitement at the 72nd Street house that night. Like Fox Hollow, it was messy and chock-full of Herb's bizarre collectibles, including more mannequins and wholesale clothing, obviously spillover merchandise for the stores. But a search turned up no evidence that would tie Herb to the missing men. They seized only some shotgun shells and a length of rope.

When Wilson told Whisman the background on Brian Stats and the fact that Herb had used his name when cruising the bars, the three detectives set out to find Stats and any other men who might have spent time with Herb. They started with Herb's employees, including a college student who had done some tree-cutting work at the house.

Yes, he knew Herb was gay, the muscular young man told them. Herb had invited him in for a swim one day when he had been working at the house and no one else was there. It was a hot day and Herb kept pushing beers on him, the young man remembered. Finally, Herb had stripped down to his underwear and begged the young man to do the same. He'd refused. "I'm not going to get in the water with you," he had spat at Herb. "What are you, some kind of fag?" Afraid, Herb had backed off. The young man had hightailed it out of there.

The detectives also tracked down Stats, who was working on a striping crew at a local baseball field. Like the tree-cutter, Stats was handsome and well built.

Stats told them that he had worked at the Sav-A-Lot store for a short while several years back. Herb often went out drinking with him and some of the other young men who worked there, he told police. He didn't know that Herb had been using his name at bars, but it didn't surprise him. But it was he—not Herb—who was the victim in the car incident, he told them. Herb sold him the car and then reported it missing.

Stats denied that Herb had made a pass at him. But "he wouldn't have told us if he had," Clifford said later.

Herb, it was increasingly clear, went out of his way to hire attractive young men who were at his beck and call— or who he at least hoped he could bend to his will, Clifford said.

"You could see the pattern," Clifford said. "He surrounded himself with all these good-looking guys who he paid seven or eight dollars an hour. Half the time they wouldn't even work, they'd just go out drinking."

Whisman also got the names of the missing men from Wilson, which he entered into the Marion County sheriffs' computers. It was just as Wilson had said. Most had substance abuse problems. Many had been arrested for prostitution. Herb, or whoever (and Whisman was increasingly convinced it had to be Herb) had targeted the weakest victims he could find.

TWENTY-SIX

In the first two-and-a-half days at Fox Hollow, the team led by Nawrocki painstakingly uncovered more than 5,500 bones, teeth, and bone fragments. Most were no wider than small puzzle pieces, and just about as thin. Despite the number of bones, Nawrocki estimated at the time that the remains of at least four men lay in the Baumeisters' backyard.

Not one entire skull was found among the remains. And the skull pieces that were discovered weren't large enough to allow the anthropologists to reconstruct an entire skull. Someone had either taken the skulls or burned them, destroying them beyond recognition. There was no way to tell which. Nawrocki, ironically, had published one of the only papers ever written on the transportation of skulls by water, which noted that skulls roll almost like beach balls when a body is left to decompose aboveground. In that way, a skull can be borne by air or water to a spot miles away from the rest of a skeleton that has not been buried.

Hamilton County evidence technician Melissa Butterworth, one of the police agency workers assisting Nawrocki, said she was haunted by the idea that the searchers would somehow find the skulls.

"Every time we uncovered a new area with bones, I'd think to myself, 'This is where all the skulls are buried. We're going to find them.' "

But it was not to be. The closest the searchers came to an entire skull was finding three mandibles, or lower jaw-bones, all containing teeth. One of the mandibles was discovered by Milligan, who, once he was finished with the house at Fox Hollow, joined Nawrocki's team and the other evidence technicians outside. Walking through the property while talking on his cellular telephone, Milligan spotted the jawbone simply lying on the ground in front of him, still containing teeth in its sockets.

In the few rare minutes when Nawrocki was able to catch his breath back at his university laboratory and regroup with Matt Williamson and Christopher Schmidt, they talked about what they had and what they would do the next day. And the telephone constantly rang off the hook with calls from the media asking for comments, answers, anything. Nawrocki politely referred them to Whisman or the Hamilton County coroner. He knew they wouldn't get any hard and fast answers there, either, and he felt bad about it, because they were only doing their jobs. But it was not his place to be the mouthpiece for the investigation.

Occasionally, a moment of gallows humor would lighten the tedious excavation work at Fox Hollow. As detectives and evidence technicians became more familiar with the parts of the human skeleton under the tutelage of Nawrocki, they began calling out to the scientist when they came upon different bones they recognized. Uhrick motioned to Nawrocki after one such find. "Doc, look," he said, proudly holding up a dark, round, fossilized object. "A vertebra!"

"Nope, walnut," Nawrocki said, tossing the nut over his shoulder.

As a way of combing the entire eighteen acres behind Fox Hollow, beyond just the small area around the burn pile on which they had been concentrating, Whisman got together a group of about sixty men and women, most of them police and fire department volunteers. On Friday, June 28, they met at a local fire station. Nawrocki gave them a short briefing.

"Look for depressions, mounds—any suspicious disturbances of the soil or piles of debris,'' he instructed the group. They were then transported by school bus to Fox Hollow, where they stood abreast of each other, arms' length apart at the northernmost boundary, forming a line about a quarter-mile long. Like an infantry marching into battle, they swept south to the property's edge, scanning the ground and woods directly in front of them for human remains.

They found mostly non-bone items, a lot of garbage from hunters, things like shotgun shells and casings, pieces of rope, a black-and-blue flip-flop with a piece of duct tape on it, and an arrow. To document the location where each item was found—information that might later prove useful—Milligan, a sailor, used a global positioning satellite, a box-shaped device he kept on his boat for plotting courses by latitude and longitude.

By late afternoon Friday, Nawrocki and the team felt pretty good about what they had been able to accomplish that week. They'd cleared all the grids, done a thorough search of the woods with the help of the volunteers, and had uncovered thousands of bones and teeth. Tired and overwhelmed, Nawrocki looked forward to sitting down with all the bones in his laboratory and starting to make sense of them, possibly giving closure to some of the victims' families. The excavation stage was, in effect, over. It was time for reconstruction and identification.

Anderson, who had been out at the site every day, was equally pleased. The two men, in fact, were discussing their next steps now that the excavation was through, when several young men came walking up through the woods from behind the search site.

They were mowing at the farm next door, they informed him. They noticed all the commotion on Fox Hollow, and had heard about the case on the news. If you want bones, follow us, they told Anderson and the others. The two young men headed west through the woods to a large compost pile that sat on the western edge of Fox Hollow. Just below it and to the south, sticking up from the muck on the sides and bottom of a small drainage ditch, were dozens more human bones—ribs, vertebrae, mandibles, spines—all of them much larger and more complete than any they had found to date.

"Jesus Christ, they're everywhere," Milligan groaned as he started down the creekbed, gingerly stepping around the bones. The other searchers were dazed. Nawrocki was too shocked and sickened even to speak.

"How many people died at Herbert Baumeister's hands?" he wondered to himself in amazement. He could see now that their work at Fox Hollow, far from being over, had just entered another phase. Apparently, burning was just one way Herbert Baumeister disposed of bodies. He had also simply tossed bones into a pile and then covered them with mulch, where they were allowed to decompose. Erosion and the elements later washed the bones south, into the small creek.

Nawrocki and his assistants. Matt and Chris, stood side by side, leaning on the fence that separated Fox Hollow from the horse farm next door, staring in disbelief at the bones sticking up from the creek.

"It's like a bomb went off in a people factory," Nawrocki remarked dryly.

The searchers decided to regroup Monday to concentrate on the new area. Uncertain now just how much carnage Fox Hollow held, Nawrocki suggested taking down all the brush and tall grass around the ditch and digging out the compost pile with a backhoe. He didn't want any more latent discoveries like the bones in the ditch. They were going to get every last shred of evidence at Fox Hollow or grow old trying.

On Monday morning, July 1, a Carmel Parks Department crew mowed the grass. Again more non-bone items were found. One find, in particular, was unsettling. There were three beer cans, one full and two empties. One of the empty cans was a Miller Genuine Draft, Herb's favorite beer. The cans had been too exposed to the elements to allow for fingerprinting, Whisman said later. And though they might have belonged to hunters or kids out drinking in the woods, Whisman and the others couldn't help imagining Herb taking the beers back to the spot to share a sick, sadistic toast to his "buddies" who were no longer among the living.

The backhoe brought in the next day was used to clear the compost pile and other debris from the ditch area, now officially labeled "Area Three." Area One was the burn spot, just twenty-five yards from the back of the house. The second site, labeled after a tibia, fibula, and foot bone were found there, was about twenty yards west of the burn site.

But it was Area Three, the compost pile and creekbed, that would yield the most significant finds.

Since the bottom of the creekbed was filled with up to a foot of muck and debris in places, the searchers had to shovel it out before they could remove many of the large bones they'd spotted in the ditch the previous Friday. Uncovered, they were in markedly different shape from the bones unearthed at the burn site. Few were broken and none were burned. And, again, even though there were no skulls, there were plenty of other major bones. In addition to three complete mandibles, they found an entire spinal column, several rib cages, and dozens of arm bones.

With the bones so complete, the workers had an increasingly difficult time separating themselves from the sad reality of the task in which they were engaged. When burnt and tiny, the bones were easily enough viewed from a safe scientific distance. But fully articulated human feet and entire human hands were another matter altogether. It was the most fascinating forensic material she had ever encountered in her life, thirty-one-year-old evidence technician Melissa Butterworth later acknowledged. But as evidence of Herb's knowledge of the bones mounted, filtering back to Butterworth and the others on Nawrocki's team—things like Herb's routine of carting debris to that compost pile and the fact that neighbors often saw him burning leaves in the area where the bones were found—the animosity for Herb and for the horror he had wrought became overwhelming.

"I could picture the bodies lying there," Butterworth remembered. "It was so easy to put the whole scene together. He'd just tossed them into that compost pile like sacks of potatoes. No remorse. No feeling. It was so haphazard, so uncaring. I really felt compassion for the families of the victims."

Once the debris was removed from the banks of the stream, searchers made yet another startling discovery: handcuffs. Rusted, hinged handcuffs, which had been manufactured by a company named Peerless. Upon investigation, Whisman discovered that that particular make and model had been available in April 1993.

Unlike chain handcuffs that allow some wrist movement, someone wearing hinged cuffs cannot move his hands at all. Police sometimes use the hinged cuffs for greater control of a prisoner. They are available to the public, "although I don't know why anyone would need them," mused Milligan.

Nawrocki, who was also there when the handcuffs were found, held them up so that Matt and Chris, who were working downstream, could see them. It was a significant find and Nawrocki was smiling, a gesture he will forever regret. Still parked in front of the estate, with their telephoto lenses aimed at the site, were the press, one of whom caught the moment on film. That night, the picture of a grinning Nawrocki, holding the cuffs high in the air, flashed across the news, a picture that crystallized the bizarre case for many of the state's residents.

To the outside world, his reaction must have looked uncaring, Nawrocki said later, as if he had been irreverent or glib about a possible instrument of death or torture. The opposite was true, but the scientist knew right then and there he wasn't cut out for the limelight.

"It bugged me that it was being filmed without me knowing it," he remembered.

In all, the ditch held another 140 bones, which, when taken together, upped the body count to seven. The remains of at least seven men—and Nawrocki could tell they were all men by the shape and size of their bones—had been found in Herb Baumeister's backyard. But who were they? How had they been killed? And when had their lifeless bodies been placed there? With the excavation complete, reconstruction could begin, a laborious process they hoped would answer those questions and others.

TWENTY-SEVEN

If Julie didn't know what was going on with her husband's personal life, perhaps her children had been more observant, Whisman reasoned.

On July 2, Julie came into Hamilton County Sheriff's Department headquarters with daughters Marne and Emily, Bill Wendling in tow, for a follow-up interview. Whisman first met with Julie, Wendling, and Clifford. Again, he asked about finding the skull.

It wasn't just a skull, Julie informed them this time. It was an entire skeleton "that looked as if someone had hit their head and just laid down and died." In general, the second interview with Julie proved far less informative than the first. She was shell-shocked by the growing press fury surrounding the case. And life at Fox Hollow had become almost unbearable. That morning, in fact, she had awakened to discover more than a dozen police cars in her driveway, along with a huge piece of construction equipment parked on the estate, a backhoe that searchers had borrowed from the city of Carmel to more quickly unearth any remains that might lie beneath the area Nawrocki's team had been able to excavate by hand. Beyond that, the media had staked out the entrance of the estate, their TV trucks and satellite dishes clogging the tiny lane that led to the house. In reality, Julie and the kids could have left Fox Hollow. The police, in fact, wanted them to leave while they conducted their search. But Julie decided it would be best if they remained. She would later say staying behind seemed the safest possible option, considering she didn't know where Herb was or what his state of mind might have been. "I was like this mother huddling all her puppies together," she said. Julie also found herself attempting to no avail to answer the children's questions about exactly what was going on, as she would write in *Indianapolis Monthly*, even though her main source of information was the television reports being broadcast from the scene.

"I really had little knowledge. The mere fact that [the search] went on for so long made all of our imaginations leap."

Because she didn't have any real answers for her children, Julie wrote she "tried to laugh as much as possible and keep the situation low-key, but they obviously knew that their dad wasn't home and that the situation was serious."

So where was Herb? The Hamilton County Sheriff's Department had taken a stab at tracking him. The same day Bill Clifford and Mary Wilson went to get Erich, they also sent several detectives up to Wawasee to stake out the lakeside condo. But by later that night, when it was clear that Erich wouldn't talk and they didn't have enough evidence to get a search warrant for the condo, they pulled off and returned to Noblesville. Kosciusko Detective Tom Brindle stopped by the condo again the next day, but Herb's Range Rover was gone. He had vanished.

Wilson quietly fumed about Hamilton County's choice not to question Herb that day. "I think we need to try to talk to Baumeister," she told Whisman and Anderson before she and Clifford left for Wawasee.

Nope, that wasn't going to happen, they crisply informed her. It was their case and their call. They would talk to Erich and watch Herb. If Erich gave them enough for an arrest, then they would move in. If not, they would just have to wait until they felt they had enough evidence to hold or to question him.

Whisman, too, had had it with Wilson's second-guessing them. "A lot of people, including Mary Wilson, wondered why we didn't arrest Herb as soon as the bones were discovered. This is typical of a person who has never worked or prosecuted a criminal case."

If Herb died, though, questions about the missing men and their fates would go unanswered. So why wasn't Herb taken into custody and questioned immediately after the bones were discovered?

Whisman maintained that even after the gruesome discovery, police didn't have enough evidence to charge Herb with any crime.

"We still didn't know who the victims were, we didn't know what the cause of their death was, and we didn't know whether he was the one who had caused their deaths," he would later explain. "There were all kinds of variables that had yet to be answered."

Whisman also doubted that Herb would have voluntarily agreed to be questioned by Hamilton County investigators.

"He had already told the Indianapolis Police Department that he had retained counsel and that he wasn't going to tell them anything or cooperate in any way," he said. "That quashed everything from that point on."

Wilson vehemently disagreed, but she wasn't the type of person to stomp her feet and demand to get her way. It was their case, after all. Her hands were tied. Later, however, she conceded that even if they had confronted Herb, the outcome would have been doubtful. "He was just too slick," she said. Still, if there were ever a time that his defenses might have been down, it was after the police picked up Erich.

"He was at the most vulnerable he'd been in his whole life," she said. "I just wanted to do something, anything, while we still had the opportunity."

Emily and Marne, meanwhile, were very composed, very serious when they met with Clifford and Whisman. They seemed more willing than Erich to help with the investigation, and politely answered every question put to them as best they could.

They knew there was tension between their mother and father, they told the detectives. But it rarely carried over to their relationship with their father, they said. They loved their dad. If anything had been amiss with him personally in the last several years, he didn't show it in how he behaved toward them. He was always fun, always caring.

The two young women remembered the skull incident quite clearly. But they had been satisfied with their father's explanation, they said. He saved everything. So it really wasn't odd for him to have kept some medical relic of his father's. They really hadn't given it much thought.

Still, they had made a discovery in the pool area several years earlier that struck them as even odder. They found a blue windbreaker jacket behind the bar that they didn't recognize. Fishing through the pockets they discovered condoms and a pack of Kool cigarettes. When they took the jacket and its contents to their dad, he'd told them it must be Uncle Brad's. That struck them as strange, because they didn't know when their uncle might have left it down there and they had never seen Brad wearing such a coat.

Clifford asked them gently if they'd talked to their father recently. Yes, in fact, they had, Marne told them. He had called them at the Castleton store the day before, and had taken turns talking to each of the kids. He'd made a point of telling each one of them how much he loved them, and of saying good-bye. They were worried about him.

Whisman and Clifford exchanged a glance.

After Julie and the girls left, Whisman and Clifford held a quick powwow with Anderson in the conference room.

"He's going to kill himself," Whisman said with absolute certainty. He told Anderson about the call Herb had made to the kids. Whisman knew in his considerably sized gut right then and there that Herb had made a choice to end his life. He didn't know when or how, but he was certain that they would never get the opportunity to question Herbert Baumeister. Fox Hollow would be the only key that unlocked his secrets.

TWENTY-EIGHT

On July 3, Herb's lifeless body was found by campers near a beach area in Pinery Provincial Park in Sarnia, Ontario, about sixty miles northeast of Detroit. He had taken his own life, firing a single shot from a .357 Magnum revolver into his forehead.

At about eleven P.M., Herb had parked his 1989 gray Buick Century near the beach and then walked across the sand to a quiet spot near the water's edge. Sitting facing the lake, he took out the gun, pressed its barrel to a spot between his eyes, and pulled the trigger, setting off a blast that ripped through his forehead and exited the back of his head.

A perfectionist to the end, he was dressed impeccably for the occasion, in gray slacks, a white, button-down dress shirt, and red-and-blue-striped tie, all of which were relatively blood-free—a surprising fact given that the exit wound in the back of his head was about the size of a tennis ball. When another park-goer found him less than an hour later, Herb's eyes were open, fixed in a horrible crossed position that would have been aimed directly at the barrel of the gun he used to take his own life.

Along with Herb, Canadian police found a rambling, three-page suicide note, written in ink on yellow, lined notebook paper. It was in an envelope that said "Attention Canadian Authorities."

In the note, Herb wrote he was sorry about the breakup

of his twenty-five-year marriage. He expressed regret about spoiling the scenic beauty of the site where he killed himself. He apologized for leaving Thrift Management in financial ruin. He did not, however, make any mention of the bones or refer to any of the missing men.

Just where had Herb been from the time the bones were found until his body was discovered?

Herb's brother Brad provided the first clues to Herb's whereabouts. Whisman had talked to Brad after he interviewed Julie and Tony. Herb, Whisman knew, often turned to Brad—or rather used him—in times of trouble, obviously thinking that his unmarried younger brother provided the perfect cover for his screwups.

Shocked at Herb's latest scandal, Brad was happy to help the police in any way he could. But he couldn't be of much help to them in delving into Herb's secret life, he informed them. He hadn't known or even suspected that Herb might have been gay.

"You could have knocked him over with a feather," Whisman said, recalling Brad's reaction after being told about the missing men and Herb's double life. Still, Brad loved his brother and he was genuinely worried about him, Whisman could tell.

With good reason. After Herb left Wawasee, he headed north, stopping briefly on June 28 in the small southwestern Michigan town of Fennville, about 170 miles west of Detroit. He called Brad from there, telling him he was traveling on business and that he needed money. Brad wired $125 to Herb at a grocery store in the tiny town (population 800), which was home to a fruit cannery and some of the state's seasonal farm workers.

Herb couldn't have spent the night in a motel in Fennville, because it doesn't have a motel. But a bar and hotel that has long been a favorite with the gay community was less than ten minutes away, near the lakeside town of Saugatuck. The hotel doesn't release records about its guests, so it's impossible to say whether Herb actually stayed there. But there was probably a good chance that having traveled extensively throughout the Great Lakes region, Herb knew of the hotel's existence.

In any case, by June 29, Herb had migrated east across Michigan, to Port Huron, a shipping center in the "thumb area" of the mitten-shaped state on the shores of Lake Huron. He called Brad asking for more money. Brad dutifully complied, wiring another $280 to a Western Union office in a Kroger supermarket.

"Tell him to call us the next time you hear from him," Whisman urged Brad after he heard about the calls for money. He knew it was probably futile, but he had to try.

Ontario Provincial Police told the *Indianapolis Star* they believed Herb arrived in Sarnia on June 30, spending several days there before driving east along the Lake Huron shoreline to Grand Bend, Ontario, where he paid seven Canadian dollars for a day pass to the park where he ultimately killed himself.

Canadian authorities said that besides Herb's apologies, his suicide note was relatively unremarkable and included such minutiae as a daily travel log and notes about whether he had enough gas to go from one place to the next. At one point, Herb described a bridge he had crossed going from Port Huron to Sarnia.

"He talked about how high it was and that he was afraid of heights," a Canadian detective told the *Star*. Pinery Park's security supervisor, meanwhile, told the newspaper that Herb had also noted that he had planned to kill himself earlier, but that he had decided to drive on after noticing children near the site he had chosen.

Herbert Baumeister ended the note by writing that he was going to eat a peanut butter sandwich, as he had done every day at five P.M. while he was growing up, and then "go to sleep."

It was shortly before sunrise on July 4th that Julie learned of Herb's suicide.

"We aren't morning people," she wrote in *Indianapolis Monthly*, "but I had awakened and was on my way to the kitchen to plug in the coffee when someone knocked on the door. As I went to answer it, I looked up and saw that my two girls were also awake and standing at the head of the stairs. The person at the door was Bill Wendling, my attorney and friend. He had come to tell us that Herb had been found dead.

"Everything fell apart. Everything we'd worked for was gone. But at least, at that moment, the kids and I were together. That was important. During the previous days, it was as though our house were being destroyed by a tornado, and there was nowhere to hide and no way to control our fear of the unknown. From that point on at least, the kids could take part in what was happening and mourn the loss of their dad."

Aside from these comments, Julie has said little publicly about Herb's suicide. The comments she has made, though, have focused on its impact on their children. She wrote, for instance, that she didn't hold any kind of service because she was afraid it would turn into a circus.

"We didn't have funeral services for Herb because we were afraid the media wouldn't let us," she wrote in *Indianapolis Monthly*. "So my kids didn't have closure. They couldn't go to the mortuary and let their friends come and give them a hug because the press would have come to watch them hug. They robbed my children of that."

Even so, Julie would later say, "There is nothing on the face of this earth that can take away the love these kids had for their dad. Their love for him was real."

Others, however, did weigh in on Herb's being linked to the missing men's disappearances and his suicide, offering varying opinions.

John Egloff, Herb and Julie's business lawyer, was among those caught off guard by the allegations.

"Herb never lost his temper or threatened anyone in my presence," he said. "He wasn't someone I thought would do such terrible things."

But Garry Donna, who knew Herb when he worked as a copy boy at the *Indianapolis Star*, said that when he first heard news reports that hundreds of bones had been found on an estate belonging to someone named Baumeister—and this was prior to Herb's being named as a suspect in the missing persons cases—he almost immediately concluded it was his onetime coworker.

"I just knew it was him," he said. "I didn't think, 'Oh, maybe that's Herb's cousin.' I thought, 'Well, that's Herb.' "

As the story unfolded and Herb was linked to the men's disappearances, Donna said he wasn't at all shocked when he learned that Herb had been leading a double life.

"The nature of it all was unbelievable," he said. "But there was always a little mystery surrounding him."

Herb's suicide didn't baffle Donna either.

"That was in character with the person I had known twenty years ago," he said. "Herb was so self-conscious about what people thought of him and the image he projected that it didn't surprise me when he took that way out. How could a person like that have faced what he would have had to face, the condemnation and so forth? He never could have accepted the shame."

Alpha Kerl, who worked for Herb at the West Washington Sav-A-Lot, said that despite what she and fellow store employees referred to as the "weirdness of Herb," that she was taken aback when she learned of his suicide.

"I still have a hard time believing he shot himself," she said. "He was a coward, yes. But I just can't picture him splattering his brains all over himself. I would think he'd be more concerned about what a mess he'd make."

Relatives of victims expressed a mixture of regret and relief.

"I kind of had a feeling he might kill himself," said Catherine Araujo, Roger Alan Goodlet's mother. But as a result, she added, "there are so many things we'll never know."

Still, she said, "I don't know if I could have stood a long, drawn-out trial. I've already suffered so much."

Yet others expressed little sympathy for the man they believe responsible for their loved ones' deaths.

Judy Kelley, Richard Hamilton's half sister, said she considers Herb's suicide the equivalent of an admission of his involvement in the deaths of her brother and others.

"If he wasn't guilty and didn't have anything to hide, then why did he kill himself?" she asked. "When he committed suicide, he convicted himself."

TWENTY-NINE

Whisman, like Julie, also learned of Herb's suicide in the early morning hours of July 4.

At four A.M., Brad Baumeister paged him. He had gotten a call from the Ontario police the night before, he told the detective in an obviously agitated voice. Herb had killed himself in a provincial park in Canada, a Canadian authority told him.

"I think it's some kind of sick joke," Brad told Whisman. "But can you check it out? I'm really worried."

Whisman pulled on his clothes and made a pot of coffee. He called the number for the Ontario Provincial Police that Brad had given him. It was no joke, he was informed by the Canadian officer who answered the telephone.

Whisman called Brad. It was true, he told him grimly. He and Clifford would be traveling to Ontario. A suicide note had been found and they were hoping against hope that it made mention of the bones and the missing men.

Whisman had another detective rouse Clifford from sleep. The detectives and a prosecutor from Leerkamp's office set out at about seven A.M. for the seven-hour drive to Ontario.

At the Canadian border in Port Huron, where the Blue Water Bridge connects the U.S. to Sarnia, Ontario, they were pulled over to the side by border authorities. There was a problem. They would not be allowed to take their guns into Canada, the border guard informed them. But they were police investigating a murder, the two detectives protested.

It didn't matter, she informed them. The guns couldn't go across the border. Nor would they be doing any investigating on Canadian soil, she told them tartly. They would leave that to Ontario police. It was all Whisman could do to contain himself. But he bit his tongue.

"Okay," Clifford told her, flashing her his best Boy Scout smile. "No investigating. No guns." They filled out the necessary paperwork to leave the guns with her and retrieve them on their way home. Out of earshot, Whisman blew up. No guns. No investigating. Who the hell did she think she was? They would damn well do whatever they needed to do to get some answers.

The Ontario Provincial Police proved much more cooperative. They took the two detectives to the Pinery, pointing out the spot where Herb had ended his life. They also took them to the morgue, where they allowed Clifford to take pictures of Herb. There was no mistaking the tall, slender man the detectives knew from his arrest photos. Half of the top of his head was missing and his eyes were still open in a glassy, cross-eyed stare. It was Herb, all right.

The Ontario police handed over Herb's suicide note to Whisman, who quickly unfolded it. Two pages long, it was handwritten on lined paper in Herb's careful script. And though every word was legible, its contents were horribly disappointing but inevitably predictable. Rambling, unfocused, Herb had used his last opportunity to communicate with the world to deliver a whining diatribe that made no mention of the victims or the investigation or his double life. In the end, it was all about Herb and no one else.

"My whole life is falling apart," he wrote of his decision to kill himself. But he was being noble about it, he informed them. He had only "one bullet in the chamber, so that some unsuspecting child wouldn't find the gun and accidentally harm themselves."

The drive across the Blue Water Bridge had been pretty, he wrote in a bizarre aside that seemed apropos of nothing.

He had been thinking about his children when he'd crossed the bridge, he told them. He intimated that Julie was to blame for many of his problems. And he instructed that it be his attorney, not his wife, who told his children about his death. Pretentious to the end, he signed it, "The Herb Baumeister."

How like Herb even in death to try to pull everybody's strings as he had in life, Whisman thought. How typical, too, that he would take the coward's way out, blaming his suicide on someone else and leaving his victims without any answers. It was sickening.

Herb's suicide wasn't the only brush he'd had with law enforcement while he was in Canada, the OPP informed Whisman and Clifford.

The night before he killed himself, on July 2 at about four A.M., a female officer from the Point Edward Police Department, the city nearest the bridge, spotted Herb's 1989 gray Buick parked underneath the bridge. She noticed a man in a fetal position, sleeping in the front seat.

She had tapped the window with her flashlight and Herb woke up. His eyes were glassy and bloodshot, his hair was unkempt. But he didn't smell of alcohol, she noted later in a report.

He apologized for parking under the bridge, but said he had been traveling in Ontario for the last two days. He was going to meet his family the next morning to celebrate the Fourth of July, he told the officer, and he was just catching a little nap before their scheduled rendezvous.

She shined the flashlight in the backseat, revealing an overnight bag, roadmaps, envelopes, newspapers, and piles of other paper and items she couldn't make out. He was "calm and friendly," she also noted in her report, so she moved him on and basically forgot about the incident, until she heard about the suicide the next day and matched the car with the one she'd seen the night before.

When Ontario police led them to Herb's car, however, it was completely empty. No maps, no garbage. Most important, no videotapes. Although some of the videotapes Herb had taken from the house had been found, Whisman and Clifford both felt that Herb had taken the videotapes with the damning evidence on them. They had hoped to find them in Herb's car. But of course Herb was too smart for that. The only things Whisman and Clifford were able to pull from the largely immaculate car were one small piece of a breadlike substance, a piece of fingernail, and a strand of hair. Canadian police said they hadn't touched the car. Herb had to have cleaned house before he checked out.

The two detectives spent the rest of the day combing through Dumpsters in the Ontario parks where Herb had been, starting with the area near the bridge and ending at the Pinery. They found nothing.

Herb's autopsy the next day was also singularly uneventful. The British doctor who performed it began with the usual Y-shaped incision. A look at Herb's internal organs showed no abnormalities. An X ray of Herb's skull revealed that he had two screws in his jaw, the result of jaw surgery. The doctor then peeled back Herb's skullcap, showing the path of the massive bullet wound that caused his death. The detectives were told they would get an autopsy report, but it would take "about a year." An HIV test had been included as part of the autopsy. Herbert Baumeister did not have the virus which causes AIDS, they were informed.

The two men were given Herb's blood samples and fingerprints. They were also, oddly enough, given the .357 Magnum Herb had used to kill himself, an ironic turn of events considering they were not allowed to bring guns into Canada, but they would have no trouble taking a firearm back to the U.S.

When the Ontario police responded to questions about the suicide letter to Indiana journalists on July 4, the information made its way into print and on television. Julie saw and read the reports and was livid. She wanted the suicide note, she informed Whisman. He faxed her a copy when he got back to his Noblesville office. The original went into the three-ring binder that was now bulging with documents on the case.

Herbert Baumeister might have been dead, but the investigation would live on.

THIRTY

For years, David Lindloff had been working and waiting quietly. He had been down dozens of blind alleys, had his hopes dashed a hundred times or more, and each time he came up fighting. Now all the trips to Indianapolis, the calls and letters to the FBI and the Indiana state task force, the interviews with Larry Eyler's lawyer and mother—all the years of painstaking, plodding work were finally going to pan out, he felt. He had his strongest lead yet on the man who might have been the I-70 Strangler: Herbert Baumeister.

For while Whisman was conducting his investigation, Lindloff, a silver-haired, burly, fourth-generation mortician who gravitated to police work first as a part-time job and then later as a full-time investigator in the Preble County, Ohio, prosecutor's office, was pushing forward with his own inquiry into Herb's possible ties to the Ohio murders. And he'd found out plenty, all of which made Herbert Baumeister the strongest and best suspect he'd ever had.

Herb had been to Ohio dozens of times in the late 1980s and early 1990s, Julie told him. From antique hunting and having attended auctions in the state, Herb knew many of Ohio's back roads. The fact that there had been no I-70 Strangler cases after 1990 fit with Herb's purchase of Fox Hollow Farm in 1992. Herb, forty-seven at the time of his death, would have been thirty-three in 1980 when the first I-70 Strangler case was found, a plausible age for a serial killer to begin taking other people's lives, according to the FBI profile of the suspected I-70 killer.

The fractured hyoid bones and the handcuffs found on Fox Hollow were perhaps Lindloff's strongest link between Herb and the bodies found in Ohio. Autopsy reports showed that most of the I-70 victims, otherwise healthy men, had succumbed to strangulation. Almost always, their hyoid bones had been fractured. Too, many were found with handcuff marks on their wrists.

In the eleven years that Lindloff had been working the case, there had been more setbacks than moves forward, however. Glitch after glitch had threatened the case, some of them heartbreaking. One crucial mistake in particular set his teeth on edge. It might have cost him the case.

Eric Roettger, a seventeen-year-old whose body was found in May 1985 resting in a shallow stream in Preble County, had been strangled to death, an Ohio coroner ruled.

Roettger, who appeared otherwise healthy, had a fractured hyoid bone and bruises around his neck. Sperm was found in Roettger's throat, which was saved for future testing. Two weeks before Lindloff planned to meet with the FBI in Richmond, Indiana, in 1991, he went to the Preble County Sheriff's office to collect the sperm sample found in Roettger. He would have it analyzed, he reasoned, and distribute the results to all of the other departments working on the I-70 case. But when he asked for the sample, it had disappeared. Different sheriffs pointed fingers at each other, and it was never discovered exactly what had happened. In any case, the sperm sample was gone. And with it went the one and only piece of physical evidence that police had that might have led them to the I-70 Strangler.

Lindloff had just one other ace up his sleeve. A palm print. When the body of Clay Boatman was found in Preble County in 1990, it had been thrown from a small wooden bridge. From the wood at the edge of the bridge, at precisely the place someone would have had to rest his hand if they were leaning over to roll Boatman's body from the bridge, police were able to lift one clear palm print. Lindloff had been hanging on to that print as if it were gold, waiting for someone precisely like Herb Baumeister to come along.

When he heard Herb had committed suicide, he called Whisman immediately. Can you get his palm print?

They were happy to oblige. Hamilton County sent a technician to the funeral home where Herb's body had been delivered.

Lindloff drove down that day to pick up the print and deliver it personally to the Miami Valley crime laboratory, the lab that handles all the state and most of the local police analysis work in Ohio. The next day he got bad news. The print didn't take; it wasn't clear enough. He needed to get another.

He called Mary Wilson and told her what had happened.

"I need someone to try again," he told her.

"I'd be happy to, Dave, but Herb's been cremated. It's too late."

How many times would he get kicked in the teeth over this case? Lindloff wondered. The next day he got a page from Wilson. Herb hadn't been cremated. The information she'd gotten was wrong. He could try again.

This time they sent a technician from IPD. Again, Lindloff traveled from Ohio to Indianapolis, personally picking up the print and delivering it to the Miami Valley laboratory. Again, the news was bad. It still wasn't clear. Lindloff was ready to go back a third time and personally take Herb's palm print if he had to, but by then it really was too late. Herb's body had been cremated.

The last shred of physical evidence that might have linked Herb Baumeister to the I-70 killings was toast.

THIRTY-ONE

With Herb dead and the work on Fox Hollow suspended for the time being, a good deal of the focus of the case shifted back to Stephen Nawrocki's forensics laboratory at the University of Indianapolis.

How easy it would have been if Nawrocki and his assistants could have simply assigned the more than 6,000 bones and bone fragments they had found to seven separate piles, and set about rebuilding the skeletons of seven men. But that wasn't possible. The bones were in such a jumble and the skeletons so incomplete, they would never be able to match a significant number of bones to the same person.

Instead, they had to separate and reconstruct the bones by identifiable body parts, including clusters of teeth.

Mary Wilson thought that at least ten missing Indianapolis-area men fit the profiles of the cases that could be tied to Fox Hollow. She had tracked down dental and medical records for six of those individuals, including Roger Alan Goodlet, no small feat given some of the victims' transient lifestyles.

Nawrocki, meanwhile, could say for certain that the remains of at least seven men had been found behind Fox Hollow. He knew that much because seven left thumbs had been discovered—the largest number of any single identifying skeletal element that would be unearthed.

Dental records, however, are the fastest, easiest way to identify otherwise unidentifiable human remains. And tooth expert Christopher Schmidt worked doggedly to assemble and reconstruct as many sets of teeth as possible, a tedious process that involved mounting teeth in clay, mouth-shaped "arches" and using wear patterns and tooth color to match bottom teeth to top.

Schmidt soon discovered that although there were at least seven men's remains found on the property, he could only re-create teeth sets for six individuals.

The complete mandibles obviously provided a big boost. Preparing the mandibles so that they could be used to identify a victim involved largely matching teeth roots to sockets, which tend to fit like hand and glove.

The loose teeth that didn't fit into the mandibles had to be consigned to one of three other teeth clusters that Schmidt had identified. By the end of July, Schmidt had assembled at least three complete sets of teeth. But police decided to wait until he had exhausted his efforts. They wanted to notify as many victims' families as they could as part of one effort and not drag the process out over a long period of time.

While Nawrocki and his team labored to sort out the evidence that had been laid before them, Julie Baumeister began working to restore order to her and her children's lives.

Not long after investigators finished digging at Fox Hollow, ownership of the estate reverted back to the Kentucky man who had sold it to Herb and Julie on contract back in 1991, and Julie and the kids moved back to the house on 72nd Street; the house where Herb and Julie had lived as newlyweds and that they had held on to over the course of their marriage. But because it had been uninhabited for so long, it was in need of some major repairs. It didn't even have a furnace.

At the same time, Julie had to cope with the financial mess that Thrift Management had become.

In August, the company filed for bankruptcy.

According to U.S. Bankruptcy Court records, Thrift Management's assets totaled $156,500.00. Its total liabilities: $1,089,929.55.

By September, Christopher Schmidt had sent all six teeth sets off to a forensic dentist, who made matches to four individuals from their dental records: Roger Alan Goodlet was among them. Steven Hale, 26; Richard Hamilton, 20; and Manuel Resendez, 31 were the others.

The victims who couldn't be identified by their teeth, it was decided then, would have to be matched to family members through DNA testing done on bones. That would mean taking blood from all the possible victims' families and using the identified men as a control group. Although DNA testing was a lengthy and expensive process, there was no other way.

Catherine Araujo, who had been getting regular updates from Wilson, had asked to be notified as soon as the identifications were made. The night before Wilson and Whisman had planned to go door-to-door to the victims' families to deliver the horrible news, Wilson called Catherine. Before she could say anything, Catherine demanded, "Is it Roger?"

Wilson and Whisman had agreed to wait and tell all the families at the same time, but Wilson couldn't lie to Catherine. She'd been through so much.

"Yes," she told her. "Roger was one of them."

Whisman, Clifford, and Wilson went the next day to visit the relatives of all four of the victims who had been identified. Whisman said it was the worst day he'd spent on the case.

"It was bad," Whisman said later, with his characteristic lack of loquaciousness. "I just remember everything about it being bad."

Catherine, like the other victims' families, had a lot of questions, and Wilson was happy Whisman was there to provide the answers. "It was real important that she meet Ken," Wilson said. Because at that point she didn't know where the case would go next. That wasn't her decision.

Nawrocki and his team's work provided closure for another family as well: Herb's.

In the fall, the anthropologist got an unexpected call from Whisman. Julie and the kids wanted to see the bones. Nawrocki thought it was an odd request. How could they possibly want to see the destruction that their husband and father had in all likelihood caused?

But Whisman assured him it was okay. Julie wanted this for the children, she had told him. During the dig at Fox Hollow, they'd been kept away from the site. Afterward, much information had filtered back to them from the media and from what Julie had shared with them. And without tangible evidence that there actually had been bones in their backyard, it all seemed unreal. They needed to see the bones to believe that it had happened and to somehow start to heal, Julie had told Whisman.

Nawrocki was a little nervous, but he welcomed them into the laboratory just the same. They arrived as a group one afternoon: Whisman, Julie, Erich, Marne, and Emily. Nawrocki's lab is a captivating place for young people, full of lively posters and large animal bones, so on that level the three found it interesting. But, clearly, their focus, Nawrocki said later, was on the remains found at Fox Hollow, which were spread out across more than a half-dozen laboratory tables. They walked around the lab tables staring at the bones, mesmerized. Had these really come from their backyard?

As soon as they got their bearings, they were polite and curious, asking many of the same questions the police and the media had: How and when did they get there? How many people's bones were there? How could they tell the gender? Nawrocki answered as best he could, careful to use the word "assailant" rather than "Herb" in describing how the bones had gotten there, even though the police by that time had decided that Herb was definitely responsible for the deaths, even if they had only circumstantial evidence to prove it.

Nawrocki got a chance to ask some questions of his own. He quizzed Erich and Julie about the discovery of the skull. The timing of that find was important because it provided information that could possibly help them to distinguish victims among those at the burn site, which was more recent, from those whose bones were found in the creek.

Julie was certain it was 1995. Erich, who had recovered from his trauma with the police, now said he believed it was the winter before, in 1994. Nawrocki leaned toward Erich's memory of events, which more closely matched the sequence of events beginning to emerge from his reconstruction of the bones.

In the end, Nawrocki was glad Julie and the children had come, he said. He now understood why Julie wanted to bring them there. "The kids handled themselves very well," he said. "It was a draining experience for everyone, but I came away from it with a positive feeling. And I think they got a sense of closure. It made it real in their minds. They understood more about what had happened out there."

Nawrocki, himself, was beginning to see more clearly "what had happened out there."

Trying to cover his tracks after the skull was found, Herb started burying the bodies rather than laying them on the surface, Nawrocki felt. There were clearly two distinct deposition sites, the burnt area being the more recent, the ditch and compost pile being the older one.

Some bodies had been burned "fresh." Others had been allowed to decay. "There was evidence of both," Nawrocki said. "He might have decided he had too many bodies piling up and it was time to burn them." Some things were clear: there was no attempt at burial. None of the victims had succumbed to trauma. There were no gunshot or knife wounds.

"The fractured hyoids were the only real physical evidence we had to explain cause of death," Nawrocki said.

Tony Harris's night with Herbert Baumeister was the tightest thread police had to tie Herb to the victims whose bodies were found on his estate, but it would not be the only one.

THIRTY-TWO

Herb's life on the gay scene remained something of a mystery to police. Whisman was surprised that more people from the gay community hadn't come forward when news had broken about Herb.

But if Mohammed wouldn't come to the mountain, Whisman decided later that fall that he and his colleagues would go out into the gay community.

What was meant to be an information sweep had the aura of a fraternity field trip. Indy's gay bars were not usual stomping grounds for the belly-bumping, chest-thumping types who largely made up the Hamilton County Sheriff's investigative team. But the detectives were polite and focused as they split up in pairs, taking in all the gay hotspots one night in the fall, including the Varsity, the 501, the Unicorn, and Our Place.

Herb—or Mike or Brian as everybody in the bars knew him—had been a pretty common fixture at most of the bars, according to the dozens of bartenders and patrons they interviewed that night. Most described Herb as someone who came in and out, always drank Miller Genuine Draft, usually kept to himself.

Besides getting lots of giggles from the sex films that play on a continuous loop in most of the bars, the detectives did turn up several promising leads: Herb had left a bar with a bartender at one of the bars and had oral sex in a car in the

parking lot, the man told them. Herb had asked about strangulation, and when the man had replied, "I'm not into that
shit," Herb had backed off.

Over the winter, Whisman continued to get every document related to Herb that he could lay his hands on. He
called experts and read everything he could find on sexual
asphyxiation. He subpoenaed all of Herb's cellular telephone records, and put the hundreds of numbers Herb had
called in the two years before his death on index cards. The
only thing that showed in the end was that he had definitely
called Tony Harris. Some of what Harris said had to be true.

He tried to track down the dental records for several victims, with no success. Frustratingly, one of the mandibles
not identified contained extensive dental work, including ce-
ramic crowns. With the right records, it would have been
easy to match it to a victim. Whisman ran ads about the
dental work in national dental magazines and sent out a
nationwide bulletin picturing the teeth in question through
the American Dental Association. He got no response.

In February of 1997, the local news stations got a ratings
boost from a story by a man who bought a station wagon
at an auction of the Baumeisters' possessions the summer
before and claimed that the car contained a leather strap with
blood on it, "bootie beads," K-Y jelly, human hair, and
used condoms.

When Whisman confronted him, he admitted it was a
hoax. He had called the media hoping they would give him
money for the story. Incensed, Whisman was itching to
prosecute him for fabricating evidence, but he inevitably
begged off. It wasn't worth wasting his time on, he decided.

All spring, Whisman continued to work steadily on the
case, but with few results. Nawrocki had planned to issue a
report later in the year, but no new identifications had been
made. Harris's statement was still troublesome for a lot of
reasons. For one, he kept changing it. He began sharing his
"visions" with the police, a bizarre jumble of ruminations
he labeled as "psychic intuitions" in which everyone from

Julie to a group of unidentifiable men were involved in the killings.

Harris also told Indianapolis television reporter Adam Shapiro on a local Fox news magazine show that Herb had intimated to him during their night together that he had killed "fifty or sixty people."

Whisman had no evidence that that number was even in the realm of possibility, but Harris had tossed it out there, like throwing mud against the wall, and in some of the national media it stuck.

Also, Harris admitted he had lied to Mary Wilson about seeing a "blue car with Ohio license plates" at Herb's the night he was there. He had just wanted to get their attention, he told her apologetically. He also told Connie Pierce, whom he continued to call fairly regularly, that he had known all along how to return to Fox Hollow, but he was afraid that if he took Mary or another police officer there, they would try to pin the killings on him.

Whisman was furious with Harris, and the dislike was mutual.

Tony called Connie in late January to complain about Whisman asking him to come in again for another round of questioning. Tony said instead of making the trip to Noblesville, he'd downed some tequila and psychically cued in on what their plans were for him once he agreed to an interview.

"The only reason why they wanted me to come up there was to try to trick me or to polygraph me. And so I just didn't call him or nothing. I just didn't show up. . . . I know that the record that I gave the police department and the hand-drawn maps that I drew and the information that I wrote down and put there in my file with IP Missing Persons is complete and very accurate. There's enough evidence in that file to shut 'em down."

If he talked to Whisman again, Tony Harris told Connie, "They'll bring that file out and I'll be asked questions like 'If you knew so much, then why didn't you take the police up to the house? Why did you lead them on a wild goose chase?' ''

"Well, you truly couldn't remember how to get there, right?" Connie asked.

"I knew how to get there."

"You little shit," Connie chided him.

"Connie, listen to me, you can't take the police up there, directly to the house and point down and say, 'This is where it happened, and there's a pile of dead bodies.' They are going to lock you up and the only time you see the sky is when they're walking you across the parking lot to the damn gas chamber or electric chair. Emotionally, I feel very responsible for a lot of the deaths up there. Because I was afraid to show 'em where the house was."

"You're not responsible for any of that stuff," Connie assured him.

Tony admitted he was proud of the maps he'd drawn for Mary. He was trying his best to lead her to the house without having to go directly there, he said. Tony then went on about his visions, his lover's drinking problems.

Connie being Connie, she just listened. Later, she said she understood why the police were frustrated with Tony Harris, but through it all she believed him. The changing stories, the paranoia, the wild visions—"That's just him," was how she would sum it up. People were people to Connie. They made mistakes, they had problems. None of those things made them less human.

Still, with Harris's statement and actions so tangled, Whisman wanted a backup witness, before he could feel even remotely comfortable definitively declaring Herb the killer.

In May 1997, he got one.

THIRTY-THREE

"I need to talk. I can't sleep. I've been having nightmares. I need to tell you something. Something important."

Those were the first words uttered by a nervous informant who called Detective Kenneth Whisman in May 1997.

The man had been to Fox Hollow with Herb and another man, be told Whisman, and he had never seen the other man alive again.

Whisman immediately set up a meeting with the surprise informant. Sometime in 1994, he told the detective, he had been picked up by Herb in downtown Indianapolis. Herb didn't offer his name, but from media accounts of the case, the man recognized him now as Herb Baumeister, he told Whisman. A younger man was sitting in the backseat of the car Herb was driving. The informant said he knew him only as "Steve," someone he'd seen hanging around Indy's gay bars.

When Whisman showed him Steven Hale's photo, the man immediately identified him as the same man who had been with Herb. The three of them had gone to a house north of Indianapolis. Herb and Hale had sex. The informant told Whisman that because he was unsure of his own sexuality, he preferred to just watch the two. While he did, he downed a drink that Herb had given him. Within a short period of time he lost all of his motor skills, he said. He felt as if he had been drugged. When Herb took him back to

Indianapolis later that evening, Hale was still sleeping on the floor of the house, he told Whisman. He never saw Hale around the bars again.

If there were any doubts in Whisman's mind that Herb had killed the men whose remains were found on Fox Hollow, this second informant erased them. This man had no reason for coming forward. Unlike Tony, he had insisted on a low profile. Steady, believable, he had all the qualities in an informant that Tony had lacked.

Julie helped provide another important link. She called Whisman in the summer of 1997 to tell him she had found some belongings in the garage at the 72nd Street house that she didn't recognize. One was an Indiana man's driver's license, the second item was a time sheet with a different man's name on it. Julie didn't recognize either of the men's names. But Whisman found out after quizzing Tony that both men had been friends with Hale and Goodlet.

Then there were the hang-ups.

On at least a half-dozen occasions, according to Whisman, people have called the sheriff's department claiming to have information about Herb.

"But before I can get to the phone," he says with an obvious sense of frustration, "they'd hang up."

Bruce Ceyburt, who publishes *Outlines*, a monthly magazine aired at Indiana's gay community, said these calls likely came from members of Indianapolis's gay community.

"A lot of people who may have information are hesitant to provide it because they're not out to everyone in their lives," he says. "They aren't willing to risk being inadvertently outed as a result of their cooperating with a police investigation."

Whisman has no way of knowing whether these calls were legitimate. But, he says, "I've got nothing to say they aren't."

Whisman shies away from speculating why some people might be reluctant to come forward with pertinent information. But part of the problem, he says, is that Herb's suicide left people with the mistaken impression that the police are no longer investigating him or the crimes he's suspected of having committed.

As Whisman put it, "A lot of people assume the case is closed."

THIRTY-FOUR

That spring Nawrocki was busy as well. He and a team of searchers went back out to Fox Hollow. Julie and the kids had moved out nine months earlier and the previous owners, who were working hard to shed the estate's legacy—renovating the home's interior, cleaning the grounds—were reluctant to allow the police back on the property. But in the end they complied. They had one request, however: Don't bring Julie. Burned under the land contract's terms, they had lost thousands of dollars because of the Baumeisters, not to mention the fact that the house needed significant work when they repossessed it. They were understandably bitter. They didn't want Julie anywhere near Fox Hollow.

Julie hit the roof when she found out. Relations between her and Whisman, already strained, broke off completely when he told her she would not be accompanying Nawrocki and other evidence technicians on the second search of her former home.

In any case, the spring of 1997 search turned up a little over 150 more bones, most of them in the creekbed, visible after the spring thaw. Evidence technician Melissa Butterworth, still obsessed with the idea that the skulls had to be somewhere, followed the small drainage ditch for two-and-one-half miles downstream looking for more bones. Even though the drainage ditch was clogged by fence lines, bridges, and debris, no skulls or bones had been caught in any of the traps that held back everything else in most places.

"We walked all the way to where it ended at a railroad, and we didn't find anything," Butterworth recalled. If the skulls had washed downstream, she—or someone—would have found them, Butterworth said. "It was so frustrating."

Ironically, when police canvassed the subdivision that abutted the rear of Fox Hollow Farm to ask about the bones that spring, they learned that local children had a nickname for the small drainage ditch, which none of them could explain: Skull Creek.

After the second search, Nawrocki upped the number of remains to nine from the seven he had suspected the year before. He could only definitively prove seven, again, because he had the seven left thumbs. But because of the way the bones were distributed, he was certain there were four bodies in the burn site. After the second search, it was determined that the ditch held a total of five first left ribs. There was a remote chance that some of those rib bones could have been from the four people whose remains were discovered in the burn site, but Nawrocki thought not. The bones had not been commingled, as far as he could tell. "I can prove seven," he said. "But my gut tells me we have nine."

THIRTY-FIVE

David Lindloff isn't the kind of investigator who gives up. Ever.

The fact that Herb was cremated before Lindloff could get a valid palm print might have persuaded a less tenacious investigator to close the book on the I-70 Strangler case, but Lindloff merely redoubled his efforts.

He found an ally in Julie Baumeister. When Julie broke off discussions with Whisman, she turned to Wilson and Lindloff for answers, cooperating fully with them in an effort to learn all that she could about her husband.

Julie told Lindloff that Herb had made hundreds of trips to Ohio in the 1980s. But Lindloff wanted telephone records and credit card receipts, anything Julie could find that could definitively tie Herb to Ohio during the time the I-70 Strangler was killing young men from Indianapolis and dumping their bodies in Ohio.

Julie also offered to let Lindloff tow and process the car that Herb had driven to Canada, a 1989 gray Buick Century that Herb had bought new. Canadian authorities had returned the car to Julie, and it had been sitting in front of the 72nd Street house. In May 1997, Lindloff had it towed to the Miami Valley crime lab in Dayton, Ohio. When technicians opened the trunk, they found that all of the carpet had been pulled out. But upon close inspection, in the center, they found one drop of blood, no bigger than a dime, flaked onto the metal.

The technicians were able to remove the flakes and have the blood tested, but the results were inconclusive. Roughly six months later, though, investigators finally got a break.

It was back in June 1983 that two young boys on bicycles found the body of a partially-clothed young man in a stream on a rural road in Hancock County, Indiana, about 10 miles east of Indianapolis. Clothed only from the waist down, the dead man had been either pushed or rolled from a tiny bridge into the stream that ran under the road. The cause of death was ligature strangulation, an autopsy revealed.

In the course of investigating the man's death, Hancock County Sheriff James Bradbury contacted the Indianapolis Police Department. It turned out the IPD recently had received a report on a missing man whose physical description matched that of the man found in the stream. After checking with the missing man's relatives, police were able to make a positive ID. The dead man was Michael Riley, a 22-year-old laborer who had disappeared from the Vogue Theater, an Indianapolis nightclub, on May 29, 1993.

A friend of Riley's informed police he had seen him leave the Vogue that night with a man he described as tall and slim and as having worn a long-sleeved, buttondown shirt. Sometime past midnight, an exhausted Riley, who had tickets to the Indianapolis 500 the next day, told his friend he was getting a ride home from the genial stranger he had just met. Conveniently, he lived in the same area south of Indianapolis that Riley did.

After Riley disappeared, police artists drew a number of composite drawings of the man he had gone home with, based on Riley's friend's description. But with no other solid leads to follow, Bradbury eventually relegated the case to his unsolved file.

Then, in June 1997, as details of the case against Herbert Baumeister rocketed around the state, Bradbury thought of Riley and the other unsolved I-70 cases: the nine gay white men who had been found strangled and dumped into shallow streams in Indiana and Ohio. Bradbury dug out the composites from the Riley case and compared them to a police photograph of Herb. The similarities were stunning. Both Herb and the man Riley's friend had seen him leave with had the same slim build and the same haircut.

It wasn't until late 1997, however, that Bradbury had the opportunity to show the photograph of Herb to Riley's friend. Initially, the man was of little help. "I can't identify him as the same guy," he told Bradbury. Undaunted, the police veteran tracked down another photo of Herb, this one taken in April 1993, just weeks before Riley disappeared. He then showed this one to Riley's friend. The man immediately identified Herb as the man who had left with Riley.

"The watch," Riley's friend exclaimed excitedly. "He's wearing the watch I told you about." Indeed, when Bradbury pulled the man's 14-year-old statement, the one detail he had been most specific about was the watch the stranger had been wearing: one with a flex band and a dial with a stainless steel outline.

Finally, Bradbury thought, the families and friends of Michael Riley and the other I-70 victims might finally learn what had happened to their loved ones. But that would take almost another six months, thanks to a request by Julie Baumeister.

In late December 1997 Bradbury called Julie with the news about the link between Herb and Riley. Julie's main concern, according to the sheriff, was the impact the new development would have on her children. Pointing out that Christmas was only days away, Julie begged Bradbury to wait to go public. He agreed. "It had been more than ten years," he said. "What was a couple more months?"

Finally, on a cloudy day in late April 1998, Bradbury, Ken Whisman, and several other sheriffs from around Ohio and Indiana gathered on the steps of the Hancock County Courthouse for a press conference. Herbert Baumeister, they said, could now be linked definitively to at least 16 deaths: the estimated seven to ten men whose remains were found on Fox Hollow Farm, and the nine men whose bodies had been found in Indiana between 1980 and 1990.

"There are too many things pointing to Herb," Bradbury said. "The watch. The shirts he wore. The fact that he went to the Vogue Theater during that time."

Some members of Indianapolis's gay community dismissed the announcement as a shameless political ploy on the parts of Bradbury and the other sheriffs to help them gain re-election. But Bradbury pointed out that he had already served the maximum two terms allowed in Hancock County and that there was no political gain he could realize from the move.

"Herb is the strongest and only suspect for all these murders," he maintained. "These cases are closed until someone comes forward with some new information."

THIRTY-SIX

Catherine Araujo's struggle to cope with the gruesome aftermath of Herb's spree likely will never end.

It was because of Catherine's vigilant record-keeping that Roger was one of the first victims to be identified.

"I had all these dental records going back to the time he was a little boy," she once said wistfully. "And I had just taken him the spring before he disappeared to have a wisdom tooth pulled so I had a brand-new, full set of X rays."

"But that's not him anymore," she has told herself over and over again about the fact that the only trace of Roger police discovered at Fox Hollow was a few teeth.

"Those teeth—that's not him. He's gone."

It was only after police confirmed Roger's remains were among those discovered at Fox Hollow Farm that Catherine Araujo purchased a burial plot for her son at Maple Hill Cemetery in nearby Plainfield. But because Roger's remains are still considered evidence in a police investigation that remains open, and because it could be years before authorities identify the as-yet-unidentified remains also found on the estate, it could be some time before Catherine can truly lay her son to rest.

For Judy Kelley, meanwhile, the identification of Richard Hamilton, her younger brother, as one of Fox Hollow's victims did provide some consolation for her and other family members.

Hamilton, a wanderer who often took off on cross-country jaunts without telling his family, disappeared in the summer of 1993. But when he failed to return home for Thanksgiving or Christmas, Kelley knew something was wrong.

"It wasn't like him not to come home at all or even call," explained Kelley, a mother of two who works as a cashier. "I didn't know if he was dead or alive."

In the end, she'd learn it was the former.

Catherine did find some solace in a memorial service held for Roger on June 7, 1997.

"I didn't think I could do it until I had something to put in his grave," she said afterwards. "But it turned out to be the best thing I could have done. I sleep better and now I don't cry as much."

More than 200 people attended the service which was held at Indianapolis's Lakeview Christian Center, the same church where a young Roger had attended Sunday school. Mary Wilson was there. So were Virgil Vandagriff and Connie Pierce and the families of some of the missing men whose remains are suspected of being among those found at Fox Hollow. "They're going through a hard time," Catherine said following the service. "Believe me, I know."

Among the service's high points was a moving solo rendition of "(There's Got to Be) A Morning After," the haunting theme song from *The Poseidon Adventure*, Roger's all-time favorite movie.

A childhood friend, meanwhile, recited the following poem:

> Do not stand at my grave and weep,
> I am not there, I do not sleep,
> I am a thousand winds that blow;
> I am the diamond glints on snow.
> I am the sunlight on ripened grain;
> I am the gentle autumn's rain.
> When you awaken in the morning hush,

I am the swift uplifting rush
Of quiet birds in circled flight.
I am the soft star that shines at night.
Do not stand at my grave and cry.
I am not there; I did not die.

Even if police do ultimately learn more about the circumstances surrounding Roger's death, Catherine is not sure she
wants to know the grisly details.

"At this point, I don't know if I want to know how he
died," she has admitted.

Instead, she'd rather hold out hope that his fate wasn't as
cruel as she imagines it might have been.

"I just keep thinking, 'Well, maybe he didn't realize what
was going on,' " she has said. "Maybe he didn't suffer."

THIRTY-SEVEN

It's not uncommon for individuals who commit heinous crimes to live what appear to be, on the surface at least, perfectly normal lives.

"Many persons who ultimately are discovered to have committed outrageous acts are individuals who in most other areas of their lives function in what most people would say is a normal and customary way," says Dr. James Cavanaugh, Jr., a professor of psychiatry and director of the Section on Psychiatry and Law at Rush-Presbyterian-St. Luke's Medical Center in Chicago told an interviewer several months after Herb's death.

Cavanaugh, a nationally renowned expert in the area of forensic psychiatry, also noted that criminal types who successfully manage to juggle distinct and separate lives generally are intelligent, boast refined social skills, and often have achieved a degree of wealth.

The majority of persons found to have committed serial murders with a sexual component, too, are alike in many ways.

"They're very obsessive, compulsive people," Cavanaugh said. They also tend, he added, to be detail-oriented planners, in part out of a desire to remain in a position of control.

Herb Baumeister, to a great degree, demonstrated all of these characteristics. He was born into wealth and remained a social climber throughout his life. Those who knew and worked with him use terms such as "meticulous" and "perfectionist" to describe his personality. Moreover, Herb, like many sexual serial murderers, apparently was smart enough to keep, in Cavanaugh's word, his "malignant" life secret and "to hoodwink those closest to him."

"Their ability to move relatively easily between their two worlds allows them to prevent those who know them in their normal world from learning about their disordered criminal world," Cavanaugh has said of some serial murderers.

This was true, for instance, in the case of John Wayne Gacy, who was convicted in 1980 of the murders of thirty-three young male hustlers, drifters, and runaways.

When Gacy's crimes came to light, Cavanaugh pointed out, his wife was "one of the people most surprised."

Julie Baumeister, too, has pleaded ignorance from the start.

Like Cavanaugh, Dr. Fred Berlin, a professor in the Department of Psychiatry and Behavioral Science at The Johns Hopkins University School of Medicine, has said it's not unusual for those closest to someone who's leading a double life to be completely in the dark.

In some cases, he has suggested, it's a simple case of denial, "in the sense of, 'Gee, there's things going on here that I really don't want to think very much about.' "

But there are instances according to Berlin, who is also director of the National Institute for the Study, Prevention and Treatment of Sexual Trauma, where the duped spouse or family member is truly unaware. In other words, as Berlin has put it, rather than being a conscious attempt at avoidance, "it's more that lots of things we see day in and day out don't seem all that significant until we stop to dwell on them."

Still, Berlin has said, it's not unusual for the person closest to the perpetrator—the person who is most likely to be aware of his or her activities—to be blamed by outsiders for not having realized what was going on. He, however, has found some fault with this argument.

Say, for example, a wife did notice that her husband was anxious to see her leave town, Berlins has suggested.

"The last thing that's going to be on her mind is that he wants her out of town because he's waiting to go out and engage in sadistic homosexual acts that may end up in death," Berlin argued. "That's so far beyond the pale of what any of us would ever imagine."

As for Herb's never having exhibited obviously violent tendencies in his so-called "normal" life, Cavanaugh suggested this can be attributed in part to the likelihood that it was over time that Herb became increasingly violent.

Herb's interest in erotic asphyxiation—strangling or suffocation during sex—indicates he was someone with what Cavanaugh characterized as "extremely disordered sexual impulses."

Often, he added, "these feelings become linked with very aggressive, hostile kinds of emotions." This could explain, Cavanaugh noted, why Herb, over time, may have become increasingly violent.

Berlin, meanwhile, has suggested that both these impulses and the feelings that accompany them may also lead someone to keep the part of their life in which they act on them hidden.

"If one is having recurrent cravings to engage in sadistic sexual acts, that might be something they wouldn't want others to know about," he has said. But the pressure that comes with keeping this type of behavior secret and apart from one's everyday life can result in the kind of stress and strain from which Herb seemed to have suffered.

"Having to cover one's own path creates a whole host of problems." According to Berlin, "How do you explain to others where you've been? How do you continue on in your everyday life knowing there are things out there that might begin to catch up with you?"

Then there's stress that often accompanies any taboo behavior.

"There are people who may, because of the unacceptable sexual cravings they have, do things that are very dangerous and unacceptable," Berlin has explained. "Then, because they're afraid of the consequences, they'll try to hide what they've done.''

However, the stress that results from keeping this behavior secret could lead one to repeat the very same behavior he or she is attempting to hide.

''It can become a vicious cycle,'' Berlin has said. ''It's similar in many ways to alcoholism. People give in to their cravings for alcohol, but they don't want others to know so they try to hide it. But the more they do it and the more they hide it, the more pressure they feel. And because of that increased pressure, the more they might want to drink.''

Individuals like Herb who engage in sadistic sexual behavior might also find themselves feeling similarly.

''It's the very same sort of phenomenon,'' Berlin has explained. ''Just as pressure could be a trigger that would make the alcoholic want more to drink, pressure could be a trigger that would make the sexual sadist want to engage in more sadistic acts.''

THIRTY-EIGHT

Some of the detectives involved in the Herbert Baumeister case have said they are convinced Herb qualifies as Indiana's most prolific serial killer. Others, including Whisman, are more cautious. But one sentiment they all share is anger about Herb's cowardly insistence on taking his secrets to the grave.

"He liked it too much," said Hamilton County Sheriff's Detective Cary Milligan of his belief that Herb killed a dozen or more men. "Herb was really into it. He enjoyed it. I'm sure of it. By the time Julie found that skull by the tree, he'd been doing this for a long time. Think about it. He could get up, have his morning coffee, look out the window and know that he smoked somebody and they were still laying right there in the backyard."

Mary Wilson, too, had few doubts about Herb's guilt. And she is enraged that there are still families who don't have answers because police were never able to question Herb. "This isn't over," Wilson has vowed. "Four of my missing cases were identified, but that still leaves six others. There are things that we can do and that we are doing to see that this case doesn't end until every family knows."

One thing Wilson did to keep the case alive was send cadaver-sniffing dogs to the 72nd Street house on August 6, 1997, to see if there were any bodies buried in the backyard there. Nothing was found, but Wilson said she'll continue to search for evidence. A feud, meanwhile, has broken out between the Indianapolis Police Department and the Hamilton County Sheriff's office over the handling of the case. Wilson even went to Noblesville to pick up all her files. The two forces now are proceeding independently.

Hamilton County Prosecutor Sonia Leerkamp, for her part, said, "Common sense tells us Herb had to be involved somehow. He might have been just a pickup person who scouted out these men for someone else, but I doubt it. Herb was a loner. He did everything by himself." Leerkamp, however, has not ruled out the possibility that others may have been involved. Tony's statement to police, that Herb appeared to have been waiting for someone the morning after Tony had spent the night there, certainly left open the question of accomplice.

Leerkamp admitted that if Herb had survived to be charged with multiple murders that his case would have been a difficult one to prosecute. The fact that so much time had passed since most of the killings, the lack of physical evidence tying Herb directly to the murders, and the likelihood that Herb would not have confessed would have made her job difficult, Leerkamp says.

Still, she would have liked to have had her day in court, for the victims' families at the very least . . .

"It makes me angry that Herb didn't have the guts to admit in his suicide letter what he'd done," Leerkamp said, shaking her head. "Instead, he used his suicide note as his one last chance to try to manipulate the system. It doesn't surprise me. It just makes me very sad."

Leerkamp, too, vowed that the case is not over. She met with some of the victims' families in the summer of 1997 to discuss how they might achieve some closure since the case might never be officially solved.

Those involved in the investigation also had thoughts about Julie's role in the entire ordeal.

Few dispute her innocence in terms of the killings, but most have not suspended their disbelief long enough to ac-

cept that she knew as little about Herb's secret life as she
has said.

Hamilton County Sheriff's Captain Tom Anderson has
said he thinks Julie "knew a lot more than she let on. I
don't think she had anything to do with the murders, but
she knew for a long time that something was not right. She
was protecting herself and her cozy little world. She's just
a strange woman. I couldn't believe it when I watched her
on *Oprah*. I thought, 'There's Julie, still playing naive.'"

Leerkamp, who spent the early part of her career prosecuting child abusers, has likened Julie to the wife of a child
molester who refuses to believe that her son or daughter is
being violated right under her nose.

"I was never displeased with Julie's level of cooperation," Leerkamp said. "My perception is that she wasn't in
any way involved, but that she was in denial for a long time.
It was a coping mechanism for dealing with the fact that
she might have been married to a serial killer."

As the case wore on, Leerkamp recalled hearing Julie say
things like, " 'Maybe I had seen something before.' She just
never stopped to analyze it. Not everybody wants to get to
the bottom of things. Some people just want their lives to
be a fairy tale."

Mary Wilson also has said she has seen moments of reck-
oning in Julie, who still calls the Missing Persons detective
once a month or so.

"I don't think she blames me anymore," Wilson said.

Whisman, who no longer speaks to Julie at all, has said
he doesn't second-guess anyone's coping strategies or involvement in the case. For him, Herb was probably the
killer, and that was the issue he most wanted to resolve. He
bristles at the suggestion that Hamilton County mishandled
the case in any way, especially when it comes from the
Indianapolis Police Department.

He was especially incensed by Wilson's questioning of
his refusal to take Herb into custody after the bones were
found, as seen in *The Secret Life of a Serial Killer*, an Arts
& Entertainment cable network documentary on the case.
"They [IPD] fucked up the investigation by showboating,"

Whisman said. "And they continue to act as if they are innocent."

Even though the trunk of Herb's car has yet to provide David Lindloff with any answers, the Preble County, Ohio investigator has said he is about "80 percent certain" Herb is the I-70 Strangler.

"He had plenty of time to have a normal life," Lindloff said. "Since 1980, he killed about once a year. And before he acquired Fox Hollow, he left them along the sides of roads."

One of the I-70 Strangler's victims' family members, in particular, has haunted Lindloff: Eric Roettger's father, who has quietly and patiently waited for answers for more than a decade. "He called me once and said, 'If you ever hear anything, please sit down with me and let me know,' " Lindloff said.

The willingness of the man to accept so little when so much has been hanging in the balance for so long tugged at Lindloff's heart, which at times has grown heavy since the I-70 case began.

"I want to have something to tell him," he said. "To tell all of the families."

THIRTY-NINE

The first national story on the case appeared in the *New York Times* in October 1996. Julie declined through attorney Bill Wendling to talk to the *Times*'s reporter. But eventually she did break her silence, first to the *Indianapolis Star*, then to *People* magazine, then to *Out* magazine, and then to the film crew that shot the Arts & Entertainment documentary. She also co-authored a first-person piece that ran in the December 1996 issue of *Indianapolis Monthly* and on March 19, she appeared on *The Oprah Winfrey Show*.

It was on *Oprah* that Julie conceded for the first time that after telling Herb she had been approached by Mary Wilson, he confessed he had been going to gay bars.

"He said he had been going to gay bars, but he told me he had never hurt anyone," she told the talk-show host. When Winfrey asked her if Herb's admission had rattled her, Julie said it had.

"I certainly felt betrayed," she said. But not betrayed enough, skeptics would later note, to question whether Herb had misled her about other things, too, like the skeleton she saw in back of Fox Hollow after Erich discovered the now infamous skull. It also should have dawned on her, they said, that the bones of a classroom skeleton would be strung together with wire. That was not the case with the one she had stumbled upon.

Julie would go on to say she never suspected at any time

in their marriage that Herb was gay or even bisexual. There were occasions when he would come home late, and a few times when it turned out he wasn't where he said he was, she said. But she never saw any of the classic signs: lipstick on a collar, a match cover in a pocket. In other words, she really had nothing to go on.

As Julie put it, "I didn't imagine I was married to someone who was being unfaithful in any way. I felt very much loved, supported."

She also noted that Herb never displayed any violent tendencies.

"I knew Herb better than anyone on the face of the earth," she said. "I will never know anyone as well as I know him. I never saw one single thing in his character that was violent, that was physically violent. He never hit me. He never spanked the kids. He wouldn't even kill a bug."

For these reasons, and "for the kids," Julie said she was willing to continue trying to save her marriage.

"I wanted to work through it," Julie said. "I wasn't just going to say, 'OK, well, we'll go on the same way.' "

Julie's appearance on *Oprah* seemed to be an attempt on her part to elicit sympathy from the public, a population that seemed to find it hard to believe that she was as in the dark as she claimed to be. But the effort backfired. She came across as chilly and distant.

Julie didn't do herself any favors either by granting an interview to *Out* magazine. The comments she made that ended up making the piece were, to say the least, stereotypical. They also could be perceived as homophobic.

"The things that I'm finding out about the gay community are things that are going to take gay rights back thirty years," she said in a story that appeared in the publication's March 1997 issue. "Things like one-night stands. Conceitedness. Lack of humanity-ness. Bestiality. Disrespectful, hurtful, immoral—anything bad, you name it!"

She even went as far as to express disdain for Herb's apparent victims.

"Of course I am hostile toward them—this lifestyle happened in my home!'' she said angrily. ''What makes pure lust more important than mankind? Can you tell me that? Is sex going to rule the world?''

Julie also told *Out* she and Herb had never discussed his visits to gay bars, a direct contradiction of what she would tell Oprah several weeks after the magazine story hit newsstands.

''He never expressed this to me,'' she said of Herb's cruising habit. ''Did I see him buying a pink shirt ever? No. He didn't even own a pink shirt. None of his guests ever left me a note or mailed me a hostess gift. I simply had no idea.''

Julie has admitted that as a mother, she can understand the pain that Catherine Araujo and other victims' relatives are forced to live with day in and day out. But she has argued at the same time that her children are victims, too. In the *Indianapolis Monthly* piece, for example, she described how Emily, at the age of twelve, came home from school one day saying that ''everyone in the world thinks Dad did this.''

According to Julie, it wasn't always this way. ''. . . Before this happened, their friends used to tell my kids they had really neat parents. Herb was involved in the kids' lives. He did lots of things that made them proud that he was their dad. One day he went to Emily's second-grade class on Valentine's Day . . . and . . . brought carnations for everyone in Emily's class. . . . Emily went home thinking, 'Wow, I'm glad he's my dad.' ''

Julie also has spoken openly about the financial hit she and the children have suffered. In January 1997, she was forced to file for personal bankruptcy, claiming $152,450.00 in assets and $908,310.45 in liabilities.

Catherine Araujo, also the mother of three, has said she does feel bad for Marne, Erich, and Emily Baumeister.

''I do feel sorry for the children,'' she says. ''My heart goes out to them.''

Julie is another story entirely.

''I can't understand her,'' Araujo said after Roger's remains were identified as being among those found at Fox Hollow. "I can't understand why she would protect him if she knew he was doing it."

Julie has maintained from the start that she was totally unaware of Herb's activities. But not everyone buys her story.

"There's not a person in this city who [believes] she didn't know something was going on," former Sav-A-Lot employee Alpha Kerl has said.

An ex-neighbor, citing Julie's voracious appetite for gardening, also has doubt.

"She's a yard person," the woman says. "She's always got her hands in the dirt."

Because of this, the neighbor says she finds it hard to believe that Julie wouldn't have noticed any of the thousands of bones found only a matter of yards from the house.

But it's Judy Kelley, the older half sister of Richard Hamilton, who has been Julie's most ardent critic.

"Nobody can be that dumb," she says, questioning Julie's claim that she was totally unaware that Herb was leading a double life. "And if she didn't know anything and didn't have anything to hide, why didn't she let the police on their property?"

Kelley is especially angry that Julie waited so long before telling police about the skull Erich found back in the fall of 1994.

"If one of my kids brought a skull home, how fast do you think I would call the police?" she asks rhetorically.

"She wants everybody to feel sorry for her and her kids. She says she's looking for some kind of closure for them. Well, what does she think we're looking for?"

FORTY

Exactly how many dead or missing persons may have crossed paths with Herb Baumeister may never be known. But according to Indianapolis journalist Ted Fleischaker, the gruesome find at Fox Hollow has led some gay men to think twice before leaving a bar with a total stranger.

"There was alarm in the gay community when this all hit," said Fleischaker, publisher of *The Indiana Word*, an Indianapolis-based gay and lesbian monthly newspaper. "It made people aware that they, too, could be killed. I know one person who was tied up after going home with someone he didn't know and who was afraid he was going to be killed. He even told me that while he was tied up, he thought of those people who never came back."

But other gay men, particularly those who engage in professional escorting or prostitution—three of the four Fox Hollow victims whose remains have been identified had been arrested for solicitation—have to continued to go about their business as usual. During the first six months following the discovery of the bones, for instance, the number of ads for escort services that appeared in *The Word* doubled.

In most cases, said the forty-seven-year-old Fleischaker, it's a question of economics.

"Most of them are in it for the money," he explained. "It's high-risk, but it's high-risk, high-pay. I don't know of any other job that's going to pay you $100 or $150 an hour tax-free other than drug sales. And at least half the ones who are in the business here are college kids who do it because they need money for tuition."

Then there are those men who, as Fleischaker has said, simply refuse to acknowledge the risk they're putting themselves at. Simply put, he said, "People always figure it's not going to happen to them."

Jim Brown, owner of the popular gay hangout, the Metropolitan, has echoed Fleischaker.

"It's especially true with the younger guys," the forty-nine-year-old Brown, who has lived in Indianapolis for more than fifteen years, said one day. "They think they're infallible."

Others, Brown has said, are simply "looking for the high that goes along with meeting someone."

Fleischaker conceded following Herb's death that in some corners of Indianapolis's gay community there was little sympathy for the missing men, especially those considered to be "fast-movers," like escorts and prostitutes.

"The gay community tends to reject these people," he explained. In fact, he said, "a good chunk of the gay community feels they got what they deserved."

But longtime gay activist and journalist Josh Thomas has said this marginalization is not necessarily a conscious decision.

"People can't form a tight-knit community when they're surrounded by discrimination from nearly every social institution around them and that's the case in Indianapolis," said the forty-seven-year-old Thomas who, with little attempt to hide his disdain, characterized Indianapolis as a "paint-by-numbers" city.

Still, Fleischaker has said the deaths at Fox Hollow sounded an alarm to Indianapolis's gay community. A sector of the gay population, he said, has finally acknowledged that in some ways the city's gay scene is not all that different from those in other major metropolitan areas. It may not, they've been forced to admit, be the relatively safe haven they've long perceived it to be.

"People are waking up and saying, 'It can happen here,' " he said.

Yet at the same time, a significant percentage of the gay population apparently seems content to put what happened at Fox Hollow Farm out of their heads.

"A lot of people have forgotten all about it," Jim Brown said a year or so after Herb's death. "They just don't want to give it a second thought."

For these men, Fleischaker has one simple message:

"There will always be a Jeffrey Dahmer out there. There will always be a John Wayne Gacy. There will always be a Herb Baumeister."

HE STOLE THEIR HEARTS—THEN TOOK THEIR LIVES...

SMOOTH OPERATOR

THE TRUE STORY OF SEDUCTIVE SERIAL KILLER GLEN ROGERS

Clifford L. Linedecker

Strikingly handsome Glen Rogers used his dangerous charms to lure women into the night—and on a cruel date with destiny. For when he got them alone, Rogers would turn from a sweet-talking Romeo into a psychopathic killer, murdering four innocent women during a six-week killing spree that would land him on the FBI's "Ten Most Wanted" list. Finally, after a twenty-mile high speed police chase, authorities caught the man now known as one of history's most notorious serial killers.